DEADLIER THAN THE MALE

DEADLIER THAN THE MALE

Why Are Respectable English Women So Good at Murder?

MACMILLAN PUBLISHING CO., INC.

NEW YORK

Copyright © 1981 by Jessica Mann

All rights reserved. No part of this book may be reproduced or
transmitted in any form or by any means, electronic or mechanical,
including photocopying, recording, or by any information storage and
retrieval system, without permission in writing from the Publisher.

Macmillan Publishing Co., Inc.
866 Third Avenue, New York, N.Y. 10022
Collier Macmillan Canada, Ltd.

Library of Congress Cataloging in Publication Data
Mann, Jessica.
Deadlier than the male.
Includes bibliographies and index.
1. Detective and mystery stories, English—
History and criticism.   2. English fiction—Women
authors—History and criticism.   3. English fiction
—20th century—History and criticism.   I. Title.
PR830.D4M3   823′.0872′099287   81-3760
ISBN 0-02-579460-4   AACR2

10   9   8   7   6   5   4   3   2   1

Printed in the United States of America

Contents

Preface 7
Introduction 9

PART I
1 Development 17
2 A Kind of Vice? 39
3 Detective Heroes 61
4 Heroines 92

PART II
Introduction 117
5 Agatha Christie 121
6 Dorothy L. Sayers 154
7 Margery Allingham 189
8 Josephine Tey 210
9 Ngaio Marsh 218
10 Conclusion 234

Bibliography of Non-fiction 245
Bibliography of Fiction Cited 249
Index 253

76946

Preface

The published sources from which I have derived information are listed in the bibliography. But I have also received much other help and advice for this book. Miss Catherine Aird (Kinn Hamilton Macintosh), the crime novelist, is now working on a biography of Josephine Tey, using unpublished papers, including a journal. Miss Aird has been most generous in providing factual information about this enigmatic woman. Miss Joyce Allingham has kindly co-operated in my research into her sister's life. Mr James Brabazon has discussed the life of Dorothy L. Sayers with me, in advance of the publication of his authorised biography, and allowed me to read its manuscript. Miss Patricia Cork, of Hughes Massie Ltd, gave me information about Dame Ngaio Marsh. I thank them all most warmly. I am also grateful for their counsel and comments to The Lord Hardinge of Penshurst; Mr H. R. F. Keating; Mr Eric Quayle; Mrs Leina Schiffrin; Mr Julian Symons; Miss Elizabeth Walter; my husband, Professor Charles Thomas; and my mother, Mrs Eleonore Mann, to whom I dedicate this book.

Introduction

'The rise of the feminine author in the field of detective fiction may well serve some future scholar as the subject of a learned thesis,' wrote Howard Haycraft in his pioneer study of crime novels.

This volume is not the learned thesis he envisaged, but an attempt to answer, at a less exalted level, the question, 'Why is it that respectable English women are so good at murder?' In an article about Dorothy L. Sayers, P. D. James, herself a respectable English woman who is extremely good at murder, said that this enquiry is one to which any female writer of mysteries is accustomed, particularly from American readers. The ambiguous wording of the question refers not to practitioners of real-life murder, but to those writers collectively described by authorities on the crime novel as 'Grandes Dames of Detective Fiction', or as a 'Quartet of Muses', or else as 'The Big Four': Agatha Christie, Dorothy L. Sayers, Margery Allingham and Ngaio Marsh; to these, most readers would add the excellent, though less prolific, Josephine Tey.

It is remarkable that the novels of these writers should have survived as popular reading, some for half a century, when the work of so few of their contemporaries has done so. In 1938, Cyril Connolly wrote: 'I have one ambition—to write a book which will hold good for ten years afterwards . . . contemporary books do not keep. The quality in them which makes for their success is the first to go. They turn overnight.'

Connolly then described English literature a decade earlier, in 1928. He listed Lawrence, Huxley, Moore, Joyce and Yeats, Virginia Woolf and Lytton Strachey. 'If clever,' he said, 'we would add Eliot, Wyndham Lewis, Firbank, Norman

Douglas, and if solid, Maugham, Bennett, Shaw, Wells, Galsworthy, Kipling.' By 1938, Connolly could say that the reputation of most of these writers had declined. Of the eminent writers of ten years before, 'only the fame of Eliot, Yeats, Maugham and Forster has increased'.

Half a century on, literate people will admire a few of the authors on Connolly's list, will have read the works of several, and probably heard of all. Some of the writers have become cult figures, others quarries for an academic's excavation. Most of their works will be available in libraries, or in editions published as 'modern classics' or as students' texts.

Connolly left out books which have remained popular with non-specialists. Authorities on literature will take his omissions for granted, but to a general reader it must be noticeable that none of the popular authors whose work has been continuously available in print, in hard and soft covers, in general and specialist bookshops and on the shelves of current fiction in the public libraries, is included. Survival in commercial terms seems to be something of which 'genre' fiction is especially capable. Comedies, such as the works of P. G. Wodehouse and Nancy Mitford, adventure thrillers with their continuously rejuvenated heroes, romantic novels, so unchanging in form and outlook that they can be reprinted word for word except for updated details of clothing, and historical novels, like those by Georgette Heyer and C. S. Forester, can be very long lived. All share with the conventional detective novel a lack of serious purpose; most show a class consciousness which has rendered light fiction odious to many commentators. In each category, a few writers found a style that still entertains readers of a later generation.

The period between World Wars I and II is sometimes called 'The Golden Age of Detective Fiction' and vast numbers of mystery novels were published during those years. A type of book at one time regarded as a deplorable aberration, they are now the object of collectors' attention and the subject of scholarship. But today few of the names of their writers are familiar to any but an educated enthusiast. In 1939 Dorothy L. Sayers published an article in *Illustrated Magazine* called 'Other People's Great Detectives'. She concluded it:

Dr. Priestley, Dr. Gideon Fell, Bobby Owen, Asey Mayo, Philo Vance, Roger Sheringham, Max Carrados, Hanaud, Charlie Chan, Mr. Pinkerton, Inspector Poole, Sir George Bull, Albert Campion, Colonel Gore, Sir Clinton Driffield, Superintendent Wilson, Miles Bredon, Sir Henry Merrivale, Dr. Eustace Hailey, Drury Lane . . . which, if any, would you back for the immortality stakes—fifty years on the level, with a fair field and no favour?

I do not think that Dorothy L. Sayers herself or any of her readers, to whom all these names were probably well known, would have guessed that so many of her runners would fail to reach the finishing post. For we are now at the last hurdle, nine years to go at the time of writing, and as far as I can tell, Albert Campion is the only one of her runners still in the field; some people might include Gideon Fell and Sir Henry Merrivale, but a survey of the books available on most paperback counters would not support them. And Sayers left out names which would have been worth betting on: Wimsey, Alleyn, Poirot and Grant. What gave them, out of so many, such stamina?

Only ten years before Sayers wrote those words it was possible for an American professor, herself both knowledgeable and enthusiastic about detective novels, to remark that, 'The detective story is primarily a man's novel . . . and . . . the great bulk of our detective stories today are being written by men.' (Marjorie Nicolson, in *Atlantic Monthly*.)

Anybody knowledgeable and enthusiastic about detective novels today, asked to name British authors whose work has survived since the Golden Age would probably, after Conan Doyle, mention Christie, Sayers, Marsh and Allingham.

It is with a certain unease that a lifelong feminist recognises any but the most objective differences between men and women writers. Since fame and fortune have come equally to writers of both sexes, in this sphere at least there should be no qualitative distinction. Is it merely a coincidence that in this century the most successful British detective novelists have been women? One cannot, after all, postulate statistical trends from such small samples. Yet there were many men writing crime novels at the same time as these women, men who were thought by their contemporaries to be equally skilled and whose books were equally popular.

Arnold Bennett was the *Evening Standard*'s chief book reviewer between 1926 and 1931 and covered an impressive range of topics with good and just judgement. He praised mystery writers who are now quite forgotten, such as D. Maynard Smith and Bruce Graeme. He was told by an 'independent and erudite student of detective fiction' that a book by J. J. Conington *(The Case with Nine Solutions)* was representative and among the best of the school. Who remembers it now? Other enthusiasts regarded John Rhode, Henry Wade and numerous other masculine authors as far superior to Sayers or Christie; Bennett said that he could not force himself ever to finish reading the latter's novels. There are indeed male crime novelists whose work has survived, in print at least, but none has the same popular esteem. In America, the best, and best known, crime writers have been men, and it is their work which the general reader still enjoys, the books of the 'hard-boiled' school of writers such as Spillane, Hammett and Chandler. British men of a slightly later generation have written among the best crime novels ever published, for instance, Michael Innes and Nicholas Blake (C. Day Lewis), but in discussing the original question with several authorities on the subject of crime fiction, I have met with no disagreement on the fact that four or five women represent the most popular writers from the Golden Age of Detective Fiction.

There is considerable disagreement as to the reasons. One contemporary reviewer supposed that men were not writing that kind of book then. Another believed that women were not writing any other kind of book, as he had not heard of the numerous excellent writers like Margaret Kennedy, E. M. Delafield, Angela Thirkell and Storm Jameson, to mention only a few, whose sensitive and literate novels are out of fashion now. A successful thriller writer of the 1970s attributed a book's life to publishers' policy, insisting that the capricious nature of 'blacklists' had little to do with merit. What it has much to do with, however, is popularity; publishers offer what they believe will sell, and books which are not bought are not reprinted. Whatever the reason, the public, not only in Britain and the United States, but in most countries of the world, bought and still buy the novels these women wrote.

So I return to the question: why is it that respectable English women are so good at murder? Inherent in this question are several others. Are English women better at writing about murder than those of other nationalities? Maybe not; but they are certainly more popular. Even Mary Roberts Rinehart, who would be claimed by many American readers as their answer to Agatha Christie, is little known outside the United States. Are English women better at this work than English men? The answer must be, if success and survival are the criteria, that they are. Are they respectable? I shall show that these famous women crime novelists were conventional, conformist and conservative, and that their very adherence to accepted standards in their fantasies made the product of their imaginations attractive to the public. Is murder their preferred subject? Josephine Tey, after all, had her greatest successes with novels about other crimes. Nevertheless, the plot and structure necessary for a murder mystery, and the moral certainties involved in its elucidation, seem to be among the ingredients for success, while the personal reticence the form allows, the barrier which the author can erect between herself and her readers, is apparently desirable for both these readers and these writers. They eschew self-revelation, they dislike the verbal strip-tease of more emotional fiction. Above all, is crime a subject which any self-respecting reader or writer could or should prefer?

To all these questions the following chapters will suggest answers.

Part One

1 Development

Murder and romance, deception and passion, have always been of absorbing interest to those whose own lives lack them. From the time when *Pamela*, the first English prose novel, was published in 1741, readers have wanted and writers have supplied vicarious drama, and by the closing years of the eighteenth century there was no shortage of what a character in Jane Austen's *Northanger Abbey* calls 'horrid mystery novels'. In 1754, Lady Mary Wortley Montagu advised her daughter Lady Bute to oversee her granddaughters' reading:

> Point to them the absurdity often concealed to them under fine expressions . . . I was so much charmed at fourteen with the dialogue of *Henry and Emma* [a verse drama by Matthew Prior] I can say it by heart to this day, without reflecting on the monstrous folly of the story in plain prose, where a young heiress to a fond father is represented as falling in love with a fellow she had only seen as a huntsman, a falconer and a beggar, and who confesses, without any circumstances of excuse, that he is obliged to run his country, having newly committed a murder. She ought reasonably to have supposed him (at best) a highwayman, yet the virtuous virgin resolves to run away with him to live among the banditti, and wait upon his trollop, if she had no other way of enjoying his company. This senseless tale . . . has hurt more girls than were ever injured by the lewdest poems extant.

Such sensational stories were not separated into those which terrified and those which puzzled; the distinction was of no interest until the detective novel became—like any art form past its first youth—the subject of scholarship and analysis.

The first works which would now be classified as 'Detective Stories' were those by Edgar Allan Poe; but there was always literature about crime, whether tales of an interesting rogue's

exploits (like Fielding's *Jonathan Wild*) or 'shockers' like
Matthew Gregory Lewis's *The Monk*, which so disgusted
readers and critics on its first appearance in 1794 that the
publisher insisted on immediate expurgation. In the same year
William Godwin, the husband of Mary Wollstonecraft, and
father of the author of *Frankenstein* (Mary Shelley), published
Caleb Williams, a three-volume novel about a murder with a
theme which has again been popular in recent years—the
corruption of authority and all state institutions. Godwin's
motive in writing was political, but the story, although verbose,
as was characteristic of the time, is dramatic, and the tracking
down of the murderer is relentless. Godwin's anarchical
philosophy was as shocking to his contemporaries as his fellow
writers' frivolity. Even before the era was Victorian, a high-
minded disapproval of fiction was normal. Catherine Morland,
the heroine of *Northanger Abbey*, is taught that gentlemen despise
novels:

> 'Have you read Udolpho, Mr Thorpe?'
> 'Udolpho? Oh Lord, not I. I never read novels. I have something
> else to do . . . novels are all so full of nonsense and stuff.'

Later, Catherine fortunately discovers that not all young men
wish to appear so serious, She has supposed that Mr Tilnet
never reads novels:

> 'Why not?'
> 'Because they are not clever enough for you. Gentlemen read
> better books.'
> 'The person, be it lady or gentleman, who has not pleasure in a
> good novel, must be intolerably stupid. I have read all Mrs
> Radcliffe's works, and most of them with great pleasure. The
> Mysteries of Udolpho, when once I had begun it, I could not lay
> down again; I remember finishing it in two days, my hair standing
> on end the whole time.'

Ann Radcliffe's *The Mysteries of Udolpho*, like her other books,
was a story of mystery and romance; it was in the style of the
first 'Gothic' novel, Horace Walpole's *The Castle of Otranto*. The
recipe for such books requires haunted castles, an element of
the supernatural, ruins by moonlight and pervasive fear; Jane

Austen's heroine insists that her library books should be 'horrid'.

Mrs Radcliffe was proud (in a permissive age) of her propriety, and it is ironic that she should have originated the disreputable 'Byronic' hero, a character drawn from stock by later thriller writers, and doted upon by their readers. Mrs Radcliffe's villain Schedoni has

> something terrible in his air, something almost superhuman. His cowl too, as it threw a shade over the livid features of his face, increased its severe character, and gave an effect to his large and melancholy eye which approached to horror . . . His physiognomy . . . bore traces of passions which seemed to have fixed the features they no longer animated. An habitual gloom and austerity prevailed over the deep lines of his countenance, and his eyes were so piercing that they seemed to penetrate at a single glance into the hearts of men, and to read their most secret thoughts.

Byron must have read this, to have written:

> That brow in furrowed lines had fixed at last
> AND SPAKE OF PASSIONS but of passions past
> A high demeanor, and a glance that took
> Their thoughts from others by a single look;
> And some deep feeling it were vain to trace
> At moments lighted o'er his vivid face.

But there is a major difference between Ann Radcliffe's villain and the Byronic hero, for the latter is rendered the more fascinating by his wickedness. Byron's Gaior and Conrad are tempestuous lovers with thwarted passions and mysterious past histories; they featured in terrific melodramas of love and crime which were written by a handsome young nobleman who was 'mad, bad and dangerous to know'. It is no wonder that their appeal was overwhelming, nor surprising that so many later novelists invented heroes who were handsome and sinister, and whose lives were bedevilled by crimes of the most dramatic kind; and women writers, from the creator of Mr Rochester onwards and downwards, were fascinated by the brute-hero.

Less lovable protagonists took part in the so-called 'Newgate novels' for which there was a vogue between about 1820 and

1840. These tales were usually based on real crimes recounted in the *Annals of Newgate*. Many who read them were genuinely afraid that such literature either foretold or would incite another Terror (as the French Revolution was called) in England, and all the periodicals of the time carried articles discussing the methods and even the desirability of general education if it led to the populace being able to read such subversive literature.

The fashion for these stories about housebreakers, hangmen and highwaymen gradually gave way to the sensational novel typical of the Victorian dramatic writers. Charles Dickens, Wilkie Collins, Charles Reade, and other highly regarded writers of the period, relied for their effects on brutal stimulants to fear. The great writers naturally acquired numerous imitators in whose less powerful hands sensation writing became 'the reproach and abomination' of Victorian popular literature:

> 'There are no less than five murders in this book,' said Arabella, taking up the volume before her. 'Five murders, very interesting cases of slow poisoning, and two elopements, and several faithless wives; and everybody gets into a predicament—into the most awful situations you can conceive; but the hero and heroine—they are both of them poisoned, only they get well again somehow—are married at last, and have a castle left them, and ever so much a year. Oh it is so exciting and beautifully written.'

So speaks Arabella in *Thorneycroft Hall* by Emma Jane Worboise, which came out in 1864. But Miss Worboise's own views are expressed by Arabella's cousin Ellen: 'You must know—your instincts ought to tell you—that such stories are unfit for our reading. What has a young girl to do with such shameful wickedness? I wish all such books were burnt . . .'

An eternal bonfire was in store for the authors as well as the books, according to the Tractarian, Francis Paget, writing in 1868:

> And the writers of these books, aye, of the very foulest of them—authors who have put forward confessions of the darkest profligacy that an utter reprobate could make, and who have degraded women's love into an animal propensity so rabid and so

exacting as to profess an opinion that its gratification will be cheaply purchased at the cost of AN ETERNITY IN HELL—these writers are, some by their own admission, some by internal evidence (where the publication is anonymous) *Women*: and the worst of them, UNMARRIED WOMEN!

Twenty years later, the idea of women writing novels was seen in less apocalyptic terms. Compton Mackenzie said that in his childhood—he was born in 1883—it was something between a joke and an impropriety. In spite of such disapproval, women had been most prolific in the writing of all kinds of fiction throughout the nineteenth century, and before. It was the only way that many of them, particularly those of the middle and upper classes, could hope to make any money. Many chose to hide behind masculine pseudonyms and to reveal their identity and gender only if their work was successful. It is, after all, still true today that reviewers and readers have particular expectations of 'women's novels'.

Many of the women writers of the last century produced a quantity of work whose size must chasten many a modern author. They pushed their quill pens from inkpot to page with an almost unbelievable industry. Anthony Trollope's mother is a good example. She did not start writing until she was nearly fifty, and supported her family on novels which they learnt to assume would be forthcoming at stated intervals, no matter how distracting were the family circumstances. 'The doctor's vials and the ink bottle held equal places in my mother's rooms,' he wrote of a time when not only his sister but also his father and elder brother were dying of consumption. 'She was left alone in a big house outside the town [Bruges] with two Belgian women servants, to nurse three dying patients—the patients being her husband and children—and to write novels for the sustenance of the family.' Frances Trollope wrote in the mornings, before the medical and domestic duties of the day began. Her son later wrote that the best novels of her career were produced at this time.

Reviewers delighted in their scorn for the sensational outpourings of many women 'scribblers'. George Eliot, at least, had earned the right to criticise; as she did in an article for the *Westminster Review* in 1856 called 'Silly novels by lady novelists', one of which she described as a 'wonderful pot-pourri of Almack's, Scotch second sight, Italian brigands, death bed conversions, superior authoresses, Italian mistresses, and attempts at poisoning old ladies'. She decided that 'the ability of a lady novelist to describe actual life and her fellow men is in inverse proportion to her confident eloquence about God and the other world.'

But trash has always been a good fuel to keep the pot boiling, and many novels which seem farcically melodramatic and cloyingly sentimental to us were regarded as full of emotion and feeling when they were written. *East Lynne*, for instance, by Mrs Henry Wood, was enormously popular when it was published in 1861. It was translated into several languages and remained in print until 1930. It is the story of Lady Isobel Vane, who marries the virtuous Mr Carlyle, believes him to be hankering for his first love, succumbs in her unhappiness to the flattery of the villainous Francis Levison and elopes with him. She regrets it immediately, he abandons her, and she is visited with punishments which seem unbearably disproportionate now, and were regarded as quite appropriate then. Lady Isobel's illegitimate child is killed and her own face unrecognisably mutilated in a carriage accident. She punishes herself by returning to her former home disguised as a governess (Madame Vine) and is employed by her former husband and his new wife to teach her own children, who have been told that their mother is dead. She is then obliged to watch her son dying, and to see her old rival take her place as mother and wife.

The painful deathbed scene of the child is followed by the equally prolonged decline of Lady Isobel herself. Her husband recognises her at last, just in time to tell her that he can forgive her, and to arrange for her burial in the family vault. The gloom of the book is slightly alleviated by a well-planned sub-plot involving a mistaken accusation of murder and the eventual conviction of the real criminal, who is, of course, Lady Isobel's heartless seducer. This part of the story includes circumstantial evidence, alibis, missing witnesses and a logical presentation of the case in a good court scene.

East Lynne had been rejected by three London publishers before the firm of Richard Bentley accepted it, although Mrs

Wood's first novel, *Danesbury House*, had already appeared.

Mrs Wood was born Ellen Price in 1814, in Worcester. Her father was a glove manufacturer, and she married a man who, their son said, 'had not a spark of imagination. It was an effort to him to read a novel.' She was an invalid and wrote propped up on a sofa; 'she never knew what it was, not to be in the humour for writing. It was not only that she could always write, but she ever felt a desire to do so—a power urging her whether she would or no.' This power urged her to set out a completely organised scheme: 'Once thought out, plot and incident were never changed; the story, in being written, did not develop fresh views and possibilities. It was not permitted to do so; the author had her matter well in hand—a fixed purpose.'

After *East Lynne*, Mrs Wood wrote many sentimental and slow-moving mysteries, though few jerk as many tears as *East Lynne*. One is *The Master of Greylands*, which is about a lost heir, smugglers, family likenesses, wrongful inheritance, a heroine who is 'a brilliant musician, a fair linguist, and fond of sketching in water colours. With it all, she was very gentle in manner, modest and retiring, as a woman should be.' There is also yet another lady who disguises herself as a governess to gain entry to the family home.

Evidently Mrs Wood herself subscribed to all the Victorian prejudices; and part of the reason for the success of novels of this kind was that their authors confirmed the readers' beliefs. Readers wanted to be shocked, horrified, thrilled and frightened—but not to have their convictions shaken. Reading novels was still regarded as an unworthy occupation, for fiction of any kind was by definition a lie, and far from being the dominating literary form it could be a light diversion only. Children were not allowed to open story books before luncheon, or at all on Sundays. When the London Library was started, Herbert Spencer insisted that no novels but those of George Eliot were worth acquiring for it. At the time no distinction was recognised between crime novels and other novels. Wilkie Collins did not think that *The Moonstone*, which is now accepted as the first detective novel, was different in kind from his other books, or from those of his friends like Charles Dickens. His intention, and that of the (admittedly inferior) women writers in that field, was to excite deep, strong emotions, as does a play in the theatre. He hoped to impart a vivacity and verisimilitude, which he thought had been missing in prose fiction, by concentrating more on incident than on character. These dramatic novels were the more respectable version of the shockers or dime-novels which tried only to induce fear, by showing villainy, violence and crime.

But much of life was villainous, violent and criminal; the dramatic novel portrayed a section of true life, no less than did the novels of 'realism'. Collins was so skilled a writer that even his villains were credible, and Sergeant Cuff, the detective in *The Moonstone*, is a wholly convincing figure. Those industrious and prolific ladies who were Collins' contemporaries, who churned out romantic and mysterious stories, were less able to create plausible characters. Florence Warden, Helen Mathers, Laurence Lynch, Mrs George Corbett, and many others, wrote escape literature and the refuge they offered from reality was in fantasy land.

Mary Elizabeth Braddon (1837–1915) was even more productive than Ellen Wood. She was born in London, the daughter of a solicitor who could not keep a job, and who was so unfaithful to his wife that she left him when Elizabeth was four. In 1857 Elizabeth became an actress; three years later she left the stage in order to write and fell in love with John Maxwell. He was a married publisher, with a wife in a lunatic asylum who died in 1874. But Elizabeth lived with Maxwell, brought up his children, had five of her own, and earned enough from her books to pay off his debts. At the age of twenty-four she published her first novel in serial form in an insolvent magazine called *Robin Goodfellow*, and then in the *Sixpenny Magazine*. It was called *Lady Audley's Secret* and had been inspired by Wilkie Collins' *The Woman in White*. It turned the contemporary ideals as shown in *The Woman in White* upside down. In Collins' book, the blonde heroine is the prototype of the weak, dependent, feminine victim. In Braddon's, the pretty, golden-haired girl whose 'fair face shone like a sunbeam' is the criminal and the bigamist—the complete opposite of the traditional villain.

Elizabeth Braddon became the editor first of *Belgravia* and later of *Mistletoe Bough*, in each of which she published some of her own stories, but she never again was as successful as she had been with that first book, although her publishers called her 'The Queen of the circulating libraries'. Some contemporary critics even accused her of fostering crime because she devised so many original and ingenious ways of breaking the law. Her books are still enjoyable reading to those who can avoid the liberated woman's irritation at the subjugation accepted by virtuous women of the last century. This subordination is rarely questioned by these authors. As I show in later chapters, one of the qualities shared by the most successful crime novelists in the last century, and in the present one, is an acceptance of their society's prejudices. In *Lady Audley's Secret*, for instance, which was published in the same year as *East Lynne*, the reader is apparently expected to sympathise with George Tallboys, who, driven to desperation by poverty, has left his wife and new-born son to go and seek his fortune in Australia. He neither leaves his wife a message nor sends her any for three years, yet on his return he is outraged to find that she has supposed herself abandoned and tried to carve out a new life for herself. Admittedly, she has been rendered instantly odious by setting off without her child—but she left him in her father's care, and sent regular contributions to his upkeep. Later she is revealed as a liar, bigamist and, in the end, would-be murderess, and her eventual punishment is to be confined for life in a Belgian madhouse. The moral is evidently that nothing excuses a woman's infidelity, even to a husband who has apparently gone for ever.

Just as Mrs Wood used more than once the device of having an unrecognisable lady accepted into the family home as a governess, Mrs Braddon's imagination was full of beautiful young women who go to the bad because they cannot bear poverty. Perhaps this is an example of people putting into their fiction what they dare not do in fact. In *Dead Men's Shoes*, the beautiful young protagonist Sybil (she can hardly be called a heroine) leaves the slum in which she is living with her husband. Like Lady Audley, she puts her child out to foster care, and like George Tallboys, her husband goes off to Australia. He comes to fortune by a different route, while Sybil is waiting for an inheritance from an uncle and fending off

eligible proposals. But Sybil does not quite undertake a
bigamous second marriage. Instead, she is suspected of
murdering the rich uncle, and after public exposure (trial
scenes again) and the desperate illness which is so regular a
feature of these novels, she is forgiven and allowed to live
happily ever after with her husband and child.

These novels appealed to the senses—to pity, fear and
horror; and they were bound to be attractive to a complacent
reader who had never been tempted to excess. They are about
mysteries, but not those of a type which a reader could
elucidate, and though they are about crimes, the plots are more
about how the wrongdoer was caught than about his
identification. Motive is also very important, and it is worth
remembering now how much more numerous the motives for
murder were then; release from oppression and monogamy
could only be through somebody's death. No wonder murder
stories, both fictional and true, appealed to 'proper'
females—they may even have found them vicariously
satisfying. The novelist Elizabeth Stephenson wrote in 1864:

> Women of family and position, women who have been brought up
> in polite society, women who pride themselves on the delicacy of
> their sensibilities, who would faint at the sight of a cut finger, and
> go into hysterics if the drowning of a litter of kittens were
> mentioned in their hearing—such women can sit for hours
> listening to the details of a cold-blooded murder.

There is a separate line of novels which engages the intellect
as much as the heart. From Godwin's *Caleb Williams*, which
was perhaps the first book in which the author began at the
final chapter and worked backwards to the beginning, through
the first stories which can definitely be termed detective fiction
—the famous three stories by Edgar Allen Poe—there were
many which featured detectives of some kind, if not actual
detection. But most of the detectives were pursuing an
identified quarry. The identification of the wrongdoer as the
chief-purpose of the story was a different subject, and for some
time after Edgar Allan Poe published his three seminal stories
between 1841 and 1844, it was mostly in France that detective
fiction appeared, from the pens of Eugene Sue, Emile

Gaboriau and Fortuné de Boisgobey, who wrote of deductive methods and inferential reasoning. The use of these processes are as old as the human race; many historians claim that the Bible and classical literature include stories of detection. Obviously the *roman policier* could not appear before a police force existed; the Metropolitan Police Act of 1829 established London's first police force, a few years after the Sûreté Générale had been formed in Paris.

The famous investigator Vidocq published his memoirs in 1829; he was a former criminal who became a detective. A British crime reporter, Angus Bethune Reach, became his friend, and learnt a lot from him; his crime story, *Clement Lorimer* (1849), was the first in which the words 'sleuth-hound' appear. In the 1850s many stories about detectives appeared in Britain in the cheap 'yellowback' edition, among them *Recollections of a Detective Police Officer* by William Russell, 1878; *Revelations of a Private Detective* by Andrew Forester, 1863; and Anonyma's *The Experiences of a Lady Detective*, as well as many other books with similar titles, enough for Wilkie Collins to make his Sergeant Cuff say, 'It is only in books that the officers of a detective force are superior to the weakness of making a mistake.'

It is generally accepted that the first proper detective novel apart from *The Moonstone* was by a woman, the American Anna Katherine Green. As a matter of fact, an earlier one, called *The Dead Letter*, by Seeley Regester, appeared nine years before it, in 1867. Seeley Regester was the pseudonym of Mrs Metta Victoria Fuller Victor, who had been born in Erie, Pennsylvania, in 1831, and who became a prolific writer of dime novels. *The Dead Letter* was her only detective novel and is rarely seen now. *The Leavenworth Case*, however, Anna Katherine Green's book, became a best seller on first publication and remained in print almost until today. On the strength of it, Mrs Green is variously known as the mother, grandmother and godmother of detective fiction. Genealogists impute fatherhood to Edgar Allan Poe.

The Leavenworth Case was published nine years before the first Sherlock Holmes story; it had a soundly worked-out plot, a police detective called Ebenezer Gryce, who appears in later books by the same author, and a suitable list of suspects among whom the suspicion of murder circulates; any description of the book makes it sound a total cliché now, but it was new and original when it first came out.

A rich old man, Mr Leavenworth, is murdered in the library of his luxurious New York house, just as he is about to sign his new will; there are beautiful daughters, a dignified butler, an enigmatic male private secretary, all the qualifications, in fact, for what was later to become the typical 'body in the library' type of book. Agatha Christie mentions that her sister read *The Leavenworth Case* aloud to her when she was a girl, and it seems to have had a deep and formative influence on her imagination.

Anna Katherine Green had published a book of poems and a verse play before her first book, but the prose of *The Leavenworth Case*, which is in many ways very heavy going, does not make readers regret that she never achieved what she always said was her real ambition, to be a professional poet. She was born in 1846 in Brooklyn, New York, the daughter of a well-known criminal lawyer of the time. She was educated at a boarding school (Ripley Female College, Vermont) and married a man who designed and manufactured furniture, called Charles Rohlfs. They had three children, and lived in Buffalo, New York State, until her death at the age of ninety in 1935.

Her upbringing by a lawyer who evidently discussed his cases at home had given Anna Katherine Green a considerable familiarity with criminal law, and with crime. The narrator of *The Leavenworth Case* is a young lawyer, Everett Raymond, who was the first to compete, as an amateur, with a professional detective in fiction. The professional is

> Mr Ebenezer Gryce, one of our city detectives . . . He was not the thin, wiry individual with a shrewd eye that seemed to plunge into the core of your being and pounce at once upon its hidden secret that you are doubtless expecting to see. Mr Gryce was a portly, comfortable personage with an eye that never pounced, that did not even rest—on you. If it rested anywhere, it was always on some insignificant object in your vicinity, some vase, inkstand, button or book . . .

He could never, as the narrator says, pass as a gentleman. When he is asked whom he suspects of the murder, he replies

'Everyone and nobody. It is not for me to suspect but to detect.' He is a solid, competent, hard-working cop, not unlike Inspector Cuff, or Bucket of *Bleak House*—the original honest and unexciting police detective who had appeared in 1853. Gryce does his work of detecting, not suspecting, with the help of 'Mr Q' who is frequently made to peer through key holes, listen at doors and generally do the more degrading chores of detection. Mr Gryce's final self-satisfaction also sets a precedent:

> 'Well, that is the best day's work I ever did! Your congratulations, Mr Raymond, upon the success of the most daring game ever played in a detective's office.'
>
> I looked at the triumphant countenance of Mr Gryce in amazement. 'What do you mean?' I cried. 'Did you plan all this?'
>
> 'Did I plan it?' he repeated. 'Could I stand here, seeing how things have turned out, if I had not? Mr Raymond, let us be comfortable. You are a gentleman, but we can well shake hands over this. I have never known such a satisfactory conclusion to a bad piece of business in all my professional career.

In some later books—for Green uses him in thirteen of the forty books she wrote during her long career—Gryce, by then an octogenarian, is assisted by the original nosy-parkering spinster, Miss Amelia Butterworth, who shows may of the characteristics later to reappear in Miss Marple, Miss Silver and others. Miss Butterworth is an upper-class, unmarried woman, whose training in decorum conflicts with her eagerness to interfere in other peoples' affairs. Some of her victims describe her as a meddlesome old maid; in *The Affair Next Door* she asks, 'Did they realise at first glance that I was destined to prove a thorn in the side of everyone connected with this matter for days to come?'

In fact, Anna Katherine Green invented a form, and prototypes of characters which were to become a standard in detective fiction for many years. Her popularity lasted for a long time, and her inventions were original. That said, one is obliged to add that her books are not, in other ways, good. Her style is melodramatic and forced, and includes the moralising which most of her contemporaries thought indispensable in fiction. It seems extraordinary that the British Prime Minister

Stanley Baldwin, speaking at the Thanksgiving Day dinner of
the American Society in London in 1928, should have called
The Leavenworth Case his favourite detective story at a time when
so many better ones had superseded it; though since he was
also the 'onlie begetter' of the success of Mary Webb's *Precious
Bane*, his judgement was perhaps sounder in politics than in
literature. Arnold Bennett was prompted to reread *The
Leavenworth Case* by Baldwin's statement, and found it long-
winded, clumsy, maladroit and sentimental. But as a young
man, it had enthralled him. All one can say now is that *The
Leavenworth Case* is clearly one of the books which cannot be
judged by the standards of a later generation.

Anna Katherine Green continued to publish mystery novels
for the rest of her life, but the genre was revolutionised by the
first appearance of Sherlock Holmes in 1887. As a French
commentator said, 'With the entry onto the stage of Sherlock
Holmes, the dawn of the logicians arose onto the sinister
empire of crime.' Ratiocination became the method of
discovery, and eccentricity the keynote of the thinker. A
contemporary reporter welcomed Holmes: 'we were fast
becoming weary of the representative of the old school; he was
at his best a very ordinary mortal . . .'

Holmes was anything but a very ordinary mortal, and he set
the precedent for detectives with marked peculiarities, quite
different from such as Cuff, Bucket and Gryce. It was this
abnormality which, by creating an imaginative reality of its
own, allowed the detective story to escape into a world so
complete that it has survived in the imaginations of its readers
ever since. It was the adherence in all particulars to the
plausibilities of everyday life which rendered the books about
Holmes's predecessors mortal; they were neither novels of
realism—in which serious crime must have a limited place, and
in which greater perception of rounded character is required—
nor of fantasy. As Robert Louis Stevenson wrote in his
comment to *The Wrecker*:

> We had long been at once attracted and repelled by that very
> modern form of the police novel or mystery story . . . attracted by
> its peculiar interest when done, and the peculiar difficulties that
> attend its execution; repelled by that appearance of insincerity and

shallowness of tone, which seems its inevitable drawback. For the mind of the reader, always bent to pick up clues, receives no impression of reality or life . . . and the books remain enthralling but insignificant, like a game of chess, not a work of human art.

Stevenson was refering to the many detective stories which appeared in Britain and the United States in the second half of the nineteenth century. Very few are remembered or worth remembering now, except by collectors and enthusiasts; some merit a place in the histories of the genre, either for their original features, like R. Austin Freeman's detective, Dr Thorndyke, whose fictional methods were actually copied by the real police, or for their freakish popularity, like *The Mystery of the Hansom Cab*, by Fergus Hume, one of the inexplicable best sellers of all time which seems virtually unreadable now.

By the end of the century, the fashion in detective novels was for those whose plots relied on scientific evidence, but these were convincing only if the writer understood at least a little of what he was writing about. It is now customary to say that as women were denied education at the time they were naturally unable to achieve success in that field, and were obliged to use plots which relied upon the application of common sense, on the feminine eye for small details, such as the changes in a household's routine, and on the quick ear for a child's innocent observations. While it is true that many of the books women wrote relied then, and perhaps still rely, on an intuitive or logical skill in assessing the implications of unusual circumstances, it cannot be true that the women authors applied these methods *faute de mieux*. Both in England and in America most towns had good schools for girls which taught them the subjects their brothers were simultaneously learning; the 1970s and 1980s mark the centenary celebrations of numerous girls' high schools. Any woman who had learnt to use a library and had access to one would have been as well able as a male writer to acquire the small amount of technical expertise required for the 'scientific' detective novel.

In fact, many women, as well as many men, were writing for the by then profitable market in detective stories. Most of their books, whether founded upon intuitions or upon scientifically material clues, are unenticing for the modern reader. 'The rivals of Sherlock Holmes' are period pieces. The increasing use of circulating libraries, both subscription and public, and the growing number of cheap editions readily available, meant that there were many writers and readers of books which are now as forgotten as our own contemporary best sellers will soon be.

Florence Warden was still writing in the 1890s, as were most of the popular providers of three-volume novels like Mrs Henry Wood, Miss Braddon, the very prolific Helen Mathers, the American Mrs Murdoch van Deventer—who wrote as Lawrence Lynch—Catherine Louisa Purkis, whose detective was the nondescript Quakerish Loveday Brooke, and Mrs L. T. Meade.

Elizabeth Thomasine Meade wrote more than two hundred and fifty books for girls, many short stories for the *Strand* magazine, and several mystery novels. She lived from 1854 to 1914, and was married to Alfred Toulmin Smith. She overcame the problem of her ignorance of scientific matters by collaborating with Clifford Halifax on various books featuring medical detection (*Stories from the Diary of a Doctor*, 1894 and 1896), and with 'Robert Eustace', who was later to collaborate with Dorothy L. Sayers. With Eustace, L. T. Meade wrote the first book to feature a female gang leader, Madame Koluchy, the head of a dangerous secret society: 'the brain had conceived and the body had executed some of the most malignant designs against mankind that the world has ever known.' Madame Koluchy was a kidnapper, bank robber, blackmailer and murderer, to mention only a few of her crimes, and she was the first criminal in fiction to hide behind the useful disguise of a beauty therapist. The villainess of *The Sorceress of the Strand* specialises in only one crime, murder, but she is even more sinister than Madame Koluchy.

Equally well known for a long while was Carolyn Wells, who wrote eighty-two mystery novels, mostly featuring her detective Fleming Stone. Carolyn Wells, who was born in New Jersey in about 1870, became totally deaf after an attack of scarlet fever when she was six, but she was well educated and widely travelled. She married a publisher, Hadwin Houghton, and they lived in New York. Her first crime novel was published in 1909; she edited mystery anthologies and wrote the first treatise on the subject, *The Technique of the Mystery Story*. It is a tough-minded and caustic book, surprisingly unlike Carolyn Wells's own novels which are, bluntly, implausible and foolish. As Barzun and Taylor remark about *The Mystery of the Sycamore*, it is the 'worst cock and bull story ever put together by a rational human being'. They might have said more, but for the fact that 'this gentle American lady' was obviously, in private life, a delightful and impressive woman of whom her colleagues were fond. She did not, by the way, consider either reading or writing detective fiction until she came across the works of Anna Katherine Green, in 1910.

The Baroness Orczy is remembered today for her novels about the Scarlet Pimpernel. The idea for him had come to her, she believed, by direct inspiration, and he was a real and serious person in her life. Born into a Hungarian family which traced its ancestry back to the Teutonic Knights of the tenth century, Emmuska Orczy's first years were spent on the family estates, where she remembered the feudal life style with changeless admiration. One of her earliest memories, however, was of the peasants setting fire to the steam mill which her father had installed in his attempts to modernise their methods of work. The fire destroyed the standing crops and much of the family's property. (The episode remained vivid in her mind, although she had been only three at the time, and she described it in graphic detail later in one of her historical novels.) After this, the family moved to Budapest, then to Brussels, Paris, and finally London, when Emmuska was fifteen. Her father was a well-known composer and musician, a friend of Franz Liszt. Emmuska only began to learn English when the family moved to London, but all her writing is in that language. She had hoped to be a painter, and enrolled at the Heatherly School of Art where she met her husband, Montague Barstow. Both were to exhibit their work at the Royal Academy.

If Emmuska Orczy's reputation rested only on her crime stories it would be slight. Her own real passion was for Sir Percy Blakeney, the Scarlet Pimpernel, whom her readers loved even if the critics did not. Her short stories about Lady Molly of Scotland Yard are perhaps worth reading for their period flavour; Lady Molly Robertson Kirk, whose adventures are told by a female assistant suffering from an advanced case of heroine-worship, first appears in 1910: 'Well, you know, some say she is the daughter of a duke, others that she was born in the gutter and that the handle has been soldered onto her name in order to give her style and influence. I could say a lot, of course, but my lips are sealed,' is the beginning of the first story.

In a later story we find that her husband, Captain Hubert de Mazareen, was wrongly convicted of murder, and after a recommendation to mercy had been sentenced to twenty years' penal servitude. But 'the love she bore him triumphed over all. They did keep their marriage a secret, but she remained faithful to him in every thought or feeling within her, and loyal to him with her whole soul.' After five years Lady Molly succeeds in proving her husband's innocence, and gives up her connection with the police.

Far more interesting are the stories about 'The Old Man in the Corner', written between 1905 and 1909, and in this character Baroness Orczy invented the first armchair detective. The stories are of apparently baffling mysteries which the old man solves with more twisting than reasoning, but they are simply told, and show the author's talent for presenting entertaining situations. In her autobiography, *Links in the Chain of Life*, the author tells us how she came to think of this character. She and her husband were on their way home in a horse bus, past Westbourne Park Station and over the canal:

> It was while we were lumbering over the bridge that I had an inspiration, I simply can't call it anything else, for it meant a good deal to me for some time after that. The fog had descended in all its grim faced abomination. The horses were going at foot pace. Through the darkness and the fog one could just vaguely distinguish the turbid water of the Cut, and the dim outline of a barge slowly drawing out from one of the arches. All so dark, so gloomy, so silent and mysterious, and the thought came to me of the many deeds of darkness that could be (that were probably) accomplished under this cover of fog and gloom.
>
> It was out of that first thought, and from that grim background of murkiness which could almost be felt, that the whole concept of a series of stories of detection and crime came to my mind. I had never thought of crime and detection before but I did then. All I knew of the subject was what I read in the newspapers; the crime,

the coroner's inquest, the police court and all the rest. But as soon as I got home I broached the matter to my husband, as I always did. He liked the idea and thought that if not written in too 'sanguifulminous' a way the stories might be very successful. He was nothing if not practical, and the first advice he gave me was to try and think of an original character—yes, *original*, he insisted, around whose personality I could build my stories of crime.

That personality must in no way be reminiscent of Sherlock Holmes, then at the height of that interesting gentleman's popularity. And I must 'say it as shouldn't' that the 'Old Man in the Corner' as I conceived him, was in no way reminiscent of any other character in detective fiction. I thought of him even before I embarked on that popular series of stories, of him and his big checked ulster, of his horn rimmed spectacles, his cracked voice and dribbling nose, but above all of his lean bony fingers fidgeting, always fidgeting with a bit of string.

In the last story the old man, who has always exercised his deductive talents in conversation with a young journalist, Polly Burton, is broken of this habit, in a neat device whereby the author got rid of a 'running character' of whom she had grown tired:

'[The murderer] was never seen or heard of again?' asked Polly.

'He has disappeared off the face of the earth. The police are searching for him, and some day perhaps they will find him—then society will be rid of one of the most ingenious men of the age.'

He was watching her through his great bone rimmed spectacles, and she could see the knuckles of his bony hands, just above the top of the table, fidgeting, fidgeting, fidgeting, till she wondered if there existed another set of fingers in the world which could undo the knots his lean ones made in that tiresome piece of string.

Then suddenly—the whole thing stood before her—Mrs Owen lying dead in the snow beside her open window; one of them with a broken sash line, tied up most scientifically with a piece of string. She remembered the talk there had been at the time about this improvised sash line . . .

'If I were you,' she said, without daring to look into the corner where he sat, 'I would break myself of the habit of perpetually making knots in a piece of string.'

He did not reply, and at last Polly ventured to look up—the corner was empty . . . She has never set eyes on the man in the corner from that day to this.

Baroness Orczy never wrote any more crime stories except for two not very successful novels in the 1920s. By then her style seemed more suited to the historical novels she in any case preferred. She and her husband moved to live in Monaco, where he died during World War II and she shortly afterwards.

A contemporary of Baroness Orczy was Mrs Marie Belloc Lowndes, who wrote a number of short stories about a detective whose prophetic name was Hercules Popeau. A sister of Hilaire Belloc, Marie was genuinely interested in crime and in literature, and had been a protegée of Robert Browning. Hilaire and Marie Belloc were the children of a French father and an English mother who was active in the struggle for the emancipation of women. Louis Belloc died young, and Bessie, his widow, took her children back to England, where they were brought up, with frequent visits to France. Marie's only formal education consisted of two years at a convent school, but she was to write well-organised books in a pleasant, easy English. Her most famous book is a fictional treatment of the case of Jack the Ripper—*The Lodger* (1911). It is about a murderer who leaves notes signed 'The Avenger' beside his victims' bodies. His landlord and landlady separately become suspicious of him, but neither can bear to voice the thoughts which might lose them his rent. The plot is contrived, in that the landlord's friend happens to be a policeman who drops in to keep them informed about the progress of the police investigation, but the book is full of atmosphere and tension and the author is good at developing her characters and the relationships between them.

One of Marie Belloc Lowndes' few novels not based on a real crime is *The Terriford Mystery* (1913). This is a gripping period story in which a girl goes to perilous lengths to free her fiancé from the suspicion of having murdered his first wife. There are some irritating flaws in the technique of detection—people who could have answered them are not asked the vital questions, and it is too obvious that the nice characters are innocent—but this is the basic difficulty with crime novels: if the characters are too nice, the reader will not wish to suspect them; if we know too little about them, we are not reading about real people. This was a problem which became very clear in the post-war period.

Even before World War I, however, many features of the

detective novel had already become clichés. An eccentric detective had seemed a startling innovation in 1887 when Conan Doyle introduced Sherlock Holmes.

In his autobiography, *Those Days*, E. C. Bentley wrote, 'Sometime in the year 1910, it occurred to me that it would be a good idea to write a detective story of a new sort . . .' Bentley did not like the exaggerated unreality of Holmes's character, nor the many imitations of him who had been made so unlike life. He also disliked the extreme seriousness of Holmes, and all the mock Holmeses.

'It should be possible,' he decided 'to write a detective story where the detective was recognisable as a human being, and was not quite so much the "heavy sleuth".'

Bentley made a list of the ingredients which seemed essential to a detective story by the year 1910: a millionaire—murdered, of course; a police detective who fails where the gifted amateur succeeds; an apparently perfect alibi; some fussing about in a car, with at least one incident in which the law of the land and the safety of human beings are treated as entirely negligible by the quite sympathetic character at the wheel; a crew of regulation suspects, to include the victim's widow, his secretary, his wife's maid, his butler, and a person who had quarrelled openly with him; and love interest.

All these requirements—except, obviously, the dashing around in fast cars—had been invented by Ann Katherine Green. She was still alive and working at the time (she died only in 1935) but did not repeat her first successful formula with her subsequent books, and the other female writers of the period, both in England and America, produced mystery novels quite different from those upon which Bentley based his recipe. The English writers were sticking to the mixture of romance and suspense which appealed to their circulating-library subscribers, and those who approached the detective story were not, in the strict sense of the term, 'respectable English ladies' like their heirs. Anna Katherine Green, of course, was American, as was a writer whose career began in 1908 and continued for half a century, Mary Roberts Rinehart. Emmuska Orczy was Hungarian by birth, Marie Belloc Lowndes, French. Perhaps because no successor to Anna Katherine Green had put a female name to a detective novel of his type, E. C. Bentley was told by an American publisher's reader: 'It impresses me as essentially a man's story. But there may be a big audience for a man's detective story.' Statistics do not relate whether *Trent's Last Case* appealed exclusively to the male reader. Bentley himself was very surprised at the idea.

Bentley intended to write a kind of skit, but *Trent's Last Case* is regarded as 'one of the few masterpieces of detective fiction' and its author as the regenerator of the long detective novel in England, who gave a model for the post-war renaissance. It is a remarkable book for its time, not least in the final twist which shows that the amateur got it wrong and the police detective was right. Unfortunately, to readers who are familiar with later books, *Trent's Last Case* is dreadfully dull, in spite of the literate and natural style in which it is written. On the other hand, there is no doubt that it was the first of a new kind of detective novel, produced in the Golden Age of detective fiction, after the end of World War I.

2 A Kind of Vice?

'The reading of detective novels,' wrote Edmund Wilson, 'is simply a kind of vice.' He equated it with the drug habit—addictive, wasteful of time and degrading to the intellect. He thus demonstrated the scorn for popular taste which is characteristic of those who take it upon themselves to judge the recreations of others. For centuries, prophets of doom have defined corruptions to which they are smugly immune. As early as the seventeenth century, critics were denouncing the spread of shoddy, sentimental fiction; in 1801 Wordsworth was dismayed at how 'bad reading blunts the discriminating powers of the mind, and unfitting it for all voluntary exertion, reduces it to a stage of almost savage torpor.' A little later, S. T. Coleridge wrote:

> where the reading of novels prevails as a habit, it occasions in time the utter destruction of the powers of the mind. It is such an utter loss to the reader that it is not so much to be called pass time as kill time; it conveys no trustworthy information as to facts, it produces no improvement of the intellect, but fills the mind with a mawkish and morbid sensibility which is directly hostile to the cultivation, invigoration and enlargement of the nobler faculties of the understanding.

Carlyle's pejorative phrase was 'universal shoddy'.

In 1851, *The Times*, discussing the new bookstalls provided at railway stations by W. H. Smith, thundered, 'every addition to the stock was positively made on the assumption that persons of the better class who constitute the larger portion of railway readers lose their accustomed taste the moment they enter the station.' At the time, the popular works stocked in those bookstalls were by such authors as Bulwer Lytton and Captain Marryat, though all entertainment literature was included in the denunciations. In the same year a select committee reported to Parliament that for their Sabbath edification the labouring classes read 'the foulest filth of all literary matter . . . robbery was reported merely as a skilful sleight of hand, murder as nothing else but heroism, and seduction and prostitution as being anything else but blamable.' How the members of the committee must have suffered during their research!

In 1874 it was stated in *Temple Bar* that the reading of such literature, 'by reason both of its quality and quantity, has led to a deterioration of the human species, physically, mentally and morally . . .' The writer, revelling in his perception of mankind's decline, announced that the human race would very soon be divided between cretins and invalids—all as a result of inferior literature. It is amusing to compare this comment with what the man who discovered the evolution of species was to write. Charles Darwin, when looking back over his life, said:

> Up to the age of thirty, or beyond it, poetry of many kinds, such as the works of Milton, Gray, Byron, Wordsworth, Coleridge and Shelley, gave me great pleasure, and even as a schoolboy I took intense delight in Shakespeare, especially in the historical plays. I have also said that formerly pictures gave me considerable, and music very great delight. But now for many years I cannot endure to read a line of poetry; I have tried lately to read Shakespeare and found it so intolerably dull that it nauseated me. I have also almost lost any taste for pictures or music . . . on the other hand, novels which are works of the imagination, though not of a very high order, have been for years a wonderful relief and pleasure to me, and I often bless all novelists.

How different from a correspondent in the *Evening Standard* of 1891: 'Many are the crimes brought about by the disordered imagination of a reader of sensational and often immoral rubbish, while many a home is neglected and uncared for owing to the all absorbed novel reading wife.' Others called the public libraries a greater curse than public houses in being the cause of wasted lives. In that world anything nice must be naughty; but the disgust for sensational literature survived after Victorian puritanism was itself derided.

In a famous outpouring of intellectual snobbery published in

1932, *Fiction and the Reading Public*, Q. D. Leavis discussed the deterioration she traced in standards since the Industrial Revolution. In the 'old order' people either had such interesting lives that they had no need to escape boredom by reading, or there was so homogeneous a reading public in the eighteenth century that all its members were equally able to appreciate the merits of real literature. The quotations above show that those who lived before the Industrial Revolution did not think themselves in such an intellectual paradise, and the most cursory knowledge of social history must surely indicate that the high-minded and like-minded population of Mrs Leavis's imagination had never existed. She supposed that the books available to the general public in the eighteenth century were good because the popular writers were in touch with the best work of their age, whereas the writers of the early twentieth century did not change in their courses because Joyce, Woolf, and Lawrence had written. 'A taste for novel reading as opposed to a taste for literature is not altogether desirable,' she remarked. Modern fiction unfitted its readers, she said, for any novel which required 'readjustment'. Popular novels substituted an emotional code which was inferior to the traditional code of the illiterate and she went on to say that the new ethics promulgated by modern fiction produced a social atmosphere unfavourable to the aspirations of a minority; 'the great novelists of the day pass out of the reader's field of vision.' Mrs Leavis thought that a readership, uncorrupted in the eighteenth century, only a little degraded in the nineteenth (since anyone who read Dickens, whom she regarded as second rate, could also read George Eliot), was severely stratified by the twentieth, when there was an unbridgeable gap between Marie Corelli and Henry James. The reading capacity of the general public had never been so low.

Such criticisms really distil into a disapproval of the century of the common man. Literacy, increasing in the nineteenth century and widespread, in theory at least, after the Education Acts of 1870, had made the pleasure of escaping through the printed word available to readers whose lives gave them cause to welcome it. 'What saved the lower middle class public for some time from a drug addiction to fiction was the simple fact of the exorbitant price of novels.' The opening of the fiction

market to the general public was a blow to serious reading, for
Mrs Leavis was sure that the lowest common denominator of
taste prevailed and, what was more, that enjoying bad books
destroyed the capacity to appreciate good ones. She was not, as
we have seen, a pioneer in this form of obloquy, and in
ignoring the complaints of her predecessors, which showed that
the past was not so ideal as she supposed, she also ignored the
answers given to them—not that they would have changed her
mind. But the onlooker, beginning to feel ashamed to enjoy
unimproving but entertaining novels, may be comforted to
know that they have been defended by respectable authorities.

Sir Walter Scott, for example, knew that there had never
been a homogeneous reading public. In his own home town,
Edinburgh, the first circulating library in the British Isles had
been started early in the eighteenth century and, naturally, was
at once held responsible for moral decline. 'All the villainous,
profane and obscene books and plays . . . are got down from
London by Allan Ramsay and lent out for an easy price to
young boys, servant weemin of the better sort, and gentlemen,
and vice and obscenity dreadfully propagated . . . by these,
wickedness of all kinds are propagate among the youth of all
sorts.'

Of course, it was in Scott's own interest to defend fiction.
'Excluding from consideration those infamous works, which
address themselves directly to awakening the grosser passions
of our nature, we are inclined to think the worst evil to be
apprehended from the general perusal of novels is that the
habit is apt to generate an indisposition to real history and
useful literature.' He was not alone in regarding some of the
works published in his day as infamous. *The Monk* by Matthew
Gregory Lewis, which was published in 1796, was a tale of
devilry and depravity, spiced by murder, rape, torture and
indecency. It had horrified even Byron.

In an address to the subscribers of the Windsor and Eton
Public Library, Herschel said in 1833 that 'reading transports
[the working man] into a livelier and gayer and more diver-
sified and interesting scene, and while he enjoys himself there
he may forget the evils of the present moment, fully as much as
if he were ever so drunk.' For as the correspondent to the
Evening Standard, quoted above (p. 40), perceived, fiction and

alcohol could serve the same purpose. Remembering the miseries of many workers in that era, one can hardly grudge them oblivion. By the time the *Evening Standard* printed those letters, most Free Libraries estimated that between sixty-five and ninety per cent of the books in circulation were, in fact, fiction.

In 1864 a Society for Pure Literature was flourishing, with many members united in a fight to suppress popular books. For as Wilkie Collins had pointed out, 'the readers who rank by millions will be the readers who give the widest reputations, who return the richest rewards, and who will therefore command the services of the best writers of their time.' Collins must have been delighted to hear what was not intended as a compliment: 'Why, your novels are read in every back kitchen in England.'

The members of the Society for Pure Literature would not have guessed that Dickens (the Edgar Wallace of his day, Queenie Leavis called him) would one day be regarded as improving literature and pressed upon the attention of school and university students. But the Society was fighting a losing battle against the tide of the impure. During the 1840s and 1850s, the development of the 'yellowback' railway novels had created a radical difference between the cost of a new novel and a reprint, and made those cheap editions available to people who were not rich. This also made things less easy for the circulating libraries, though they continued to exercise a disproportionate influence on the publication of hardbacks. If Mr Mudie did not stock a novel in his branches, it was doomed; publishers always had to ask themselves, 'What will Mudie think of this one?' In the 1860s W. H. Smith, who were running railway bookstalls, started lending books, but they also had a virtual monopoly on the sale of books at stations and were able to take full advantage of the new opportunity of supplying a mass reading market which had been created by literacy, leisure, a little pocket money and a longing for escape.

By 1887 the *Edinburgh Review* reported that the sale of sensation novels in serial form exceeded two million copies a week. Adventure and melodrama were best sellers, just as three-quarters of a century before the Newgate Calendar and the Malefactors' Bloody Register had sold to gratify that human interest. H. M. Criminal Statistics, hardly a volume of light reading, sold well for the same reason. Throughout the nineteenth century fiction was always more popular than fact. The same can be said today; in 1969 a survey in Sheffield showed that fifty-three per cent of the books lent by public libraries were fiction, and by then the flood of cheap paperbacks had made light reading a universally available indulgence. A sociological survey of young people showed, with one of sociology's typical revelations of the obvious, that modern fiction should be seen as being in competition with other provisions for filling in leisure time, and that young people read in bed to get away from reality. But getting away from reality is exactly what the pundits have always deplored.

Theirs is the attitude of the jailer, who will not permit escape into an artificial world: the purpose of the novel is not to be a refuge from life, but to help the reader to deal less inadequately with it. Anything else is the purest waste of time, particularly unforgivable in people like lawyers, doctors, businessmen, academics and clergymen, who apparently formed the backbone of the detective-story public, and in the last century would have been the guardians of the public conscience in the matter of mental self indulgence. Life should be real, earnest and unrelieved. Mrs Leavis was appalled that a library assistant should have pinpointed the emptiness and lack of meaning in the common reader's life by explaining, 'if a woman is taken up with a house all day, she doesn't want tales about married problems or misunderstood wives—she knows enough about those already; she can't be bothered with dialect after a day's work, and historical novels aren't alive enough. What she enjoys is something that is possible but outside her own experience.' Mrs Leavis had no patience with the effect of this kind of novel reading on the general public. She thought it would 'work upon and solidify her prejudice', and 'debase the emotional currency by touching grossly on fine issues'. Elsewhere she assumed that the habit of fantasising led inevitably to maladjustment in later life.

It is worth taking some notice of Q. D. Leavis' comments because they are typical of highbrow criticism of light fiction and because she and her husband, F. R. Leavis, were so immensely influential upon generations of later literary critics, publishers and teachers. Her objections are, in essence, two:

first, that reading bad novels disinclines and disables the reader from appreciating good ones; secondly, that it unsuits the reader for real life. A quarter of a century later much the same was said about the new medium of escape: 'There is a good deal of evidence to suggest that cinema and television foster a kind of escapist day dreaming which is likely to be emotionally exhausting and crippling to apprehensions of the real world,' wrote G. H. Bantock in the *Pelican Guide to English Literature*; and no contemporary reader will need to be reminded of similar animadversions on the television of today. It is not a universal view, even among scholars. In *The Profession of English Letters*, J. W. Saunders believed that 'giving the public what it wants breeds its own ennui; people tire of entertainment which merely feeds stock responses, and which fails to satisfy properly, deeply, imaginatively, their curiosity about the workings of human nature; ultimately then . . . people will turn from the weaker literature which merely skims the shallows of life, to the writers who have new perspectives and deep experience to offer.' This is more optimistic, but still the view of one who despises popular fiction. 'The problem is to persuade more people to be content with looking at themselves, to be interested in becoming more secure, more human, more alive, and to break the hold of mass entertainment which satisfies the more strident demands of human nature to escape from itself and thus go to sleep.'

This inward-lookingness of the twentieth-century novel, this concentration on psychological reality, is exactly what the readers of 'genre' fiction avoid: 'When reality falls short,' says Saunders, 'we turn to art and fiction.' Precisely; and the reality falling short is not that of human relationships but of dramatic event. As Bulwer Lytton said in 1832: 'It is exactly from our unacquaintance with crime, viz., from the restless and mysterious curiosity it provokes, that we feel a dread pleasure in marvelling at its details.' It is those without adventurous lives who wish to read about them. May it even be that those whose exclusive attention is devoted to the emotions (in their reading) are deprived in that sphere in their lives? Charles Dickens' reply to the critic of people who preferred sensation novels was, 'Good God, what would you have of them?'

What they would have of them is resignation to the external

monotony of life and concentration on higher things, whatever contemporary wisdom decrees they currently are. The nineteenth-century Society for Pure Literature wished fiction to propagate religious principles, and dreaded the association of a mass reading public with low-grade fiction; they saw it as a social problem, to be countered with the rival attraction of depressing, soporific tracts often disseminated by the churches. Presumably modern reformers wish to encourage an appreciation of art rather than religion. It is not made clear, and never has been, why readers are assumed to be unable to enjoy sensation, seek escape, admire art and remember religion all at the same time. A prominent spokesman for the new puritanism is David Holbrook: 'The truth is that our adult culture at large nowadays is a desert, an impoverishment, a disgrace . . . the spreading psychic spinelessness, inculcated by the pressures of the phantasy projection industry . . .'

It seems to be almost impossible for a novel to have both critical and commercial success. Malcolm Bradbury, whose own books are, in fact, an exception to prove this rule, said that 'a large part of minority literature is now written for the critic and the students whom he teaches . . . Many of our most important writers are aware of belonging to a literary cultural minority.'

It is enough to make a writer of entertainment novels shrivel. Though the detective story was regarded by Mrs Leavis as marginally less deplorable than other light fiction since it made the reader think, if nothing else, a crime novelist can hardly plead that in mitigation. Most of those who deplore light fiction, far from excepting crime novels, regard them as among the most offensive, and Howard Spring, himself not above hoping that his readers would be entertained, wrote in 1938, 'the mountains of detective novels and thrillers that industrious and uninspired moles of writers push up year by year are injurious and mentally devitalising to those who read them, because more often than not those who read them read nothing else.' Not even books by Howard Spring, perhaps?

Crime novelists are in the front line facing the attack. Even those who do not approach the intellectual superiority of Q. D. Leavis are well aware that it is proper to scorn the thriller. In the last century writers were not divided into mainstream novelists and the rest, though there were plenty of attacks on sensationalism. Nowadays the crime novel is a separate product, to be listed apart from other novels in publishers' catalogues, and reviewed in the statutory four lines at the bottom of a column which has devoted all its space to one or two 'serious' novels. This is the fate which crime novelists take for granted. Occasionally reviewers pathetically protest that some of the best contemporary writing, and the most interesting characterisation, is thereby dismissed.

In 1944, Raymond Chandler wrote of the

> essential irritation to the writer, which is the knowledge that however well and expertly he writes a mystery story, it will be treated in one paragraph, while a column and a half of respectful attention will be given to any fourth-rate ill-constructed, mock serious account of the life of a bunch of cotton pickers in the Deep South . . . the Anglo Saxons think first of the subject matter, and second, if at all, of the quality.

Chandler was commenting equally on American and British practice; a previous literary editor of the *New Statesman* ceased publishing reviews of crime novels at all because he could not bring himself to prepare copy for such trivia. His attitude was not untypical of his profession.

Often crime novelists are tempted to try to achieve recognition as serious writers—some perhaps because they feel like Conan Doyle, who complained that Sherlock Holmes took his mind from higher things. Few are successful. Agatha Christie became slushy when she wrote as Mary Westmacott. Margery Allingham's *The Dance of the Years* was a boring failure. John le Carré lost his edge and bite when he wrote *The Naive and Sentimental Lover*. Dorothy L. Sayers, ambitious for fame as a linguist and a theologian, is remembered by all but an enthusiastic few as the creator of Lord Peter Wimsey. Ngaio Marsh was endowed with the title of Dame for her services not to literature but to the theatre, but it is for the former that she is, and will remain, famous. (Conversely, many writers of other kinds of book tried their hands at one detective story just to see whether they could manage it—for instance, Arnold Bennett, J. B. Priestley and Hugh Walpole.)

Even its practitioners seem to accept that the crime thriller cannot be an important novel, or a good novel, for it does not, or at least until recently did not, aim at subtle character drawing for its own sake, at exciting the reader's aesthetic sensibilities, at revealing sociological detail, or at any purpose which might be called instructive. Its defenders call it not a novel, but a tale, making the distinction that the novel probes the soul and appeals to the emotions, while the tale unfolds a story and appeals to curiosity, wonder and the love of ingenuity. Or, as Raymond Chandler put it in a much-quoted passage from an article deriding the conventional detective novel, 'It [in this case, a book by Sayers, but his words apply to all writers in her field] was second grade literature because it was not about the things which could make first grade literature.'

Some writer of the classical period of the detective story, when the rules were very strict about what they could do, hoped that even within that framework they could create a novel rather than a tale; after all, the sonnet form, or the rhyming couplet, did not necessarily enforce mediocrity on the poets who obeyed their rules. Dorothy Sayers wanted to use the mystery form to write worthwhile novels, and many crime writers in the modern period, less interested in whodunnit than in why-he-did-it, have concentrated on human motivation as much as any mainstream writer. Indeed, it is sometimes difficult to understand the categorisation of such books as crime stories, when *Crime and Punishment* or *The Eustace Diamonds* are not so classified. But the uncertainty is greater than it was in the twenties and thirties, when practitioners did adhere to the kind of rules which the members of The Detection Club vowed to obey at quasi-religious ceremonies. They forswore the use of Divine Revelation, Mumbo Jumbo, Jiggery Pokery, Coincidence, The Act of God, and the concealment of vital clues from the reader.

The decade of the 1930s is regarded as the Golden Age of the detective story proper. It was pronounced dead by Somerset Maugham in 1952—'The story of deduction is dead'—and by Jacques Barzun in 1955: 'We moderns have in our time witnessed the greatness and fall of a genre—the detective story . . . The end has come; the genre is extinct, though some noble practitioners live on.' He said that a genre dies long before it

disappears, and compared the detective novel with the obsolete
heroic couplet or madrigal. It may have seemed, in 1955, that
the only good practitioners of the detective story then writing
were those who had produced their best work thirty years
before. But since then the corpse has revived. The detective
story is alive and well and living in the bookshops of the world.
A new generation of writers are describing characters whose
actions are dictated by their personalities not by requirements
of the plot, but the stories are technically within the rigid
detective form, with a beginning, a middle and an end, a fairly
posed problem and a plausible solution. These are writers, like
some survivors of the previous generation, whose work is
popular, in print, and enjoyed by a public which is not aware
that it should despise the mystery story, or regard it as a fossil.
There is still a large following for the tale.

Most commentators accept this fact as evidence simply of the
bad taste of the general public. In a tacit, circular argument,
popularity itself is used as an indicator of mediocrity. Certainly
the kind of success which is purely a marketing phenomenon
proves nothing but the power of advertising. Many books have
been pushed and plugged and sold in stackfuls one month and
forgotten the next. When a book is treated like soap powder, its
bubbles are as ephemeral. It is not with such artificial success
that we are concerned. But if a novel has attracted readers for
years it must have some quality which human beings want. If
Agatha Christie is the writer whose books have sold more
copies all over the world than those of any other writer, then,
rather than assuming that the world-wide public has degraded
tastes, surely it would be more logical to accept that she was
meeting a universal, spontaneous need, which is not recognised
by the critics and editors who reflect and form educated taste.

This is a problem which has interested both readers, and
authors, who are frequently asked why on earth they devote
their talents to this particular field. Of course the simple
answer is that in this aspect, if no other, crime pays. Dorothy
Sayers claimed that she wrote thrillers solely as money makers.
Margery Allingham wrote what would sell, Ngaio Marsh
supported her theatrical interests through her pen, and Agatha
Christie, who was at first surprised to be paid for indulging a
harmless hobby, soon grew to depend upon her earnings.

The answer, however, begs the question. There are other equally profitable themes. Romantic fiction writers and historical novelists have chosen their particular forms of pot boiling not simply because they can command thereby world-wide sales, but because they have a passionate belief in their importance. 'A total commitment,' as Rachel Anderson put it in her book about them, *The Purple Heart Throbs*, 'to dotty ideals which gave that prose style its power, emotional drive and luxuriant vitality.' 'I know it was useless to try and write with a view to what the public might like; the only thing one can do is to write what one wants to write and hope for the best', said Dorothy L. Sayers, about *Gaudy Night*. The money motive exists, as it existed for writers as diverse as Elizabeth Gaskell and Evelyn Waugh, but it is not necessarily either the only or the chief one. After all, Marsh and Christie wrote their first stories just for fun, and Allingham's crime novels, her 'right-hand books', were those she really wanted to write, as opposed to the 'left-hand' work with which, at the beginning of her career, she earned her living. Josephine Tey called her crime novels her 'yearly knitting'. But the impulse to write for writing's sake does not come only to those who produce what the world regards as art; and the need to push the pen faster for cash has resulted in many fine works of literature.

It is naturally gratifying when a writer can earn a living at the work he or she wants to do anyway, and it is easy to use that as the excuse and answer to the remark made so often to crime novelists by outsiders: 'Oh, you write mysteries? Of course I never read them.'

The fact is that crime writers write them because they do (or at some time did) read them. Agatha Christie, having been introduced to the work of Conan Doyle and Anna Katherine Green by her elder sister, regarded herself as a connoisseur of detective stories when she decided, years before actually getting down to it, that she could write one too. Dorothy Sayers had soaked herself in 'Dead Eye Dick' and Arsène Lupin stories during the months she spent teaching in France and England. Ngaio Marsh said that she was not a great addict of detective fiction when she started writing *A Man Lay Dead*, but she had read quite widely in the field, and on the day she started writing had sat at home all day reading a thriller mystery. It is, therefore, surely reasonable to assert that people write what they like reading.

Kingsley Amis's dictum about readers perhaps also applies to writers:

> The major arts, including prime literary forms like poetry or the novel of society, can perhaps be validly approached out of pure, or mere, intellectual curiosity. The minor genres, such as science fiction, jazz, the western and the detective story, can (I think) only be deeply appreciated and properly understood by the addict, the bulk consumer who was drawn to the stuff in late childhood for reasons he could not have explained then and would have a lot of trouble explaining now.

It is interesting to note in this context that Graham Greene believes that his vocation to write about the 'dangerous edge of things' (Browning's words, much quoted by serious crime novelists) was determined by his childhood reading of such writers as R. L. Stevenson, Anthony Hope and Rider Haggard (*The Listener*, 4 October 1979). Dennis Wheatley, another immensely popular thriller writer, whose ingredients include snobbery and violence, as well as history and romance, wrote that in his teens he devoured historical romances and spy stories, such as those by Stanley Weyman, A.E.W. Mason, E. Phillips Oppenheim, William le Queux, Dumas and Baroness Orczy.

It is not simply to keep up with what the opposition is doing that crime writers read crime novels; and most of the good crime novelists have been eager readers of their rivals' work. Margery Allingham read widely in the field, and thought that Agatha Christie had 'the liveliest intelligence in the business'. She also much admired Josephine Tey, but did not particularly enjoy the work of Dorothy Sayers. Sayers herself had a catholic taste in reading, and could not help applying her scholar's mind even to the genre in which she affected to be ashamed to work, so she became an authority on the types and history of crime novels; her view was that the problem puzzle story filled the vacuum for the work-exhausted brain whose owner did not care to turn to religion, morals or sentiment for recreation. Later, Raymond Williams, from the standpoint of the critic, also said that the kind of serious attention required by serious literature is not always possible, personally or socially; and he pointed out that modern ways of living 'Allow neither attention or rest, but just a permanent unfocussed restlessness.' Dorothy Sayers once scornfully said that contemporary literature was steeped in self-pity, and, long after she had ceased to write it, when asked why she was not interested in modern fiction, replied:

> As I grow older and older
> And totter towards the tomb
> I find that I care less and less
> Who goes to bed with whom.

Not caring who goes to bed with whom is one aspect of the fact that crime novelists do not regard the emotions as inevitably paramount; they are interested in more of life than relationships between individuals, which have been so prominent a subject of mainstream fiction. Readers enjoy the act of concentration, as well as the emotional rewards provided by other kinds of fiction. As Barzun and Taylor crisply phrase it, 'To think is human too.'

The pleasures of ratiocination, however great, are not the only ones provided by detective novels. In the related thrillers and spy stories, which are usually all lumped together and usually enjoyed by the same readers, the exercise of reason is almost completely subordinate to the excitement of unexpected events and the interest of exotic backgrounds. There is now an increasing proportion of thrillers, and of psychological crime novels, to those with deductive plots. It may be that this is due to the changes in scientific knowledge. When deductions could be explained as comprehensively as Holmes's listed varieties of cigar ash, or Thorndyke's analysis of poison, there were clues upon which a reader's own mind could work. But the specialisation and mechanisation of analytical techniques do not leave much room for the human sleuth. The very refinements of science which gave birth to the classic detective novel and were just within the grasp of the non-scientist have now reached the stage where they are not suitable material for reader, or even hero, participation. Even the 'police procedural' story tends to be either uninteresting (because of its technicalities) or unconvincing.

Most writers prefer to look much deeper than the human taste for reasoning to explain the appeal of the crime novel. They see in it the successor to fairy stories (Graham Greene calls them 'the modern fairy tales'), to morality plays, and to myths about scapegoats and law breakers. Julian Symons said, 'the crime novel at its best is a modern version of an old morality play, or a sort of mirror, which when we look in it shows us a face naked with lust, greed, avarice and violence.'

The appeal of this is masochistic indeed, and other commentators have said that the satisfaction derives from the fixing of the guilt for sin, not on our own mirror images, but on somebody else. With the identification or death of the villain the reader is thought to experience a moral calm, the peace of mind which comes from a series of events which has been logically completed, with no loose ends, no unfulfilled obligations, and above all, no vicarious guilt for the reader.

Margery Allingham came to believe as she looked back on the years of her writing career, that the mystery had become the Folk Literature of the twentieth century, and was a modern version of the medieval mystery play, those pantomines of personified Vice and Virtue. She thought that in the same way the morality play stated an elementary theory of right or wrong to ordinary people terrified by the uncertainties and threats of their own era so does the modern mystery; the plague was once as terrifying as the bomb is now.

Others use a similar rationalisation, and assert that the spectacle of crime and punishment purges civilised man of fear and guilt, and that the modern myth of the crime novel offers him the animal indulgence of the chase and the kill. This is the opposite, in fact, of the theory expressed by some writers about modern crime—for instance, about the Moors Murderers, Brady and Hindley—that we are all guilty.

Jacques Barzun regards all such rationalisations as pretentious nonsense. He may well be right, though perhaps only as regards the subdivision of the crime novel to which he has a fanatical and exclusive devotion—the pure tale about 'finding out'. Otherwise, leaving aside the question of those deeper fulfilments regarded as indispensable by readers who want the best or nothing in the field of fiction, there is surely a human instinct to be interested and excited by the abnormal, by danger, by mystery, by anything, in short, which is not part of the daily round. It is because crime stories are about things which do not happen to most of us that we like reading them. It is unlikely that criminals or policemen enjoy them, except for a good laugh at their inaccuracies, or that victims enjoy them at all. Indeed, it is a common feature of the writers of crime stories that they have no personal experience at all of crime and detection. There are a very few exceptions, however—usually police officers who have turned to crime writing—including the American Dorothy Uhnak and François-Eugene Vidocq, whose not wholly factual memoirs inspired both Edgar Allan Poe and Emile Gaboriau. Vidocq was a notorious criminal who was later appointed head of the criminal investigation department of the French police.

It is here that one of the common features, and explanations, of the English lady's success with murder lies: she writes something which is, for her, fantasy. Whether it is the glamorous fantasy of the dashing hero, or of the dashing hero's girlfriend, the kind of romantic day-dreaming different only in kind from that of any Mitty, or whether it is the unfounded fantasy of something nasty in the woodshed, the English lady is producing a work derived in its most vital parts entirely from imagination. None of the mystery writers whose success has been lasting met with crime or criminals during her career.

Why should people choose to imagine what in real life must give rise to a mixture of tension, misery and fear? It must be because they are always conscious of the 'dangerous edge of things' from their own standpoint of personal security. It is a more creative manifestation of the urge to look for burglars under the bed. Many people live their lives out oblivious of the potential horrors which surround them, but others, among whom the crime novelists are numbered, always remember that it is a thin barrier between their own comfortable lives and chaos. Perhaps the more comfortable the lives, the less personal the experience of viciousness, then the greater the fear. For 'the dark is always more frightening than what it conceals.'

Fear as an ingredient is more consciously mixed with the thriller than with the detective novel. In this the thriller is the more direct descendant of the 'Gothic' type of novel. As Sir Walter Scott had said about Mrs Radcliffe:

The species of romance which Mrs Radcliffe introduced bears the same relationship to the novel as melodrama to drama. It does not appeal to the judgement by deep delineations of human feeling, or to the passions by deep pathos, or to the fancy by light touches about life and manners, or to mirth by representations of the ludicrous and humourous.

Yet such books had, Scott explained, a deep and powerful effect by appealing to the passion of *fear*. This they achieved by describing external incident:

> . . . while the characters of the agents, like the figures in many landscapes, are subordinate to the scene in which they are placed. The persons bear, not the features of individuals, but of the class to which they belong—if they are dressed in the proper clothes and speak the appropriate language, then the audience need not laugh or weep at them . . . they are in some sort as fabulous as fairies or ogres.

Scott said that the test should be 'whether Mrs Radcliffe's writing, as a separate and distinct species, possesses merit and affords pleasure . . . Curiosity and a lurking love of mystery, are more widely diffused among humanity than either a genuine taste for the comic, or true feeling for the pathetic.'

Many of the writers who followed Ann Radcliffe aimed pointedly at this human curiosity and love of mystery; their novels included poisonings, elopements, murders (as Arabella listed in *Thorneycroft Hall*) and often added abandoned children, the trusty standby of indistinguishable twins, and the final resolution of suicide. As a writer in *The Athenaeum* put it in 1875, 'our modern novelists have abandoned the gallows, and suicide is almost inevitably the penalty.' The readers were eager; and their mentors carried on disapproving. One wrote in *Blackwood's* in 1890, 'All criminal romance leaves an unpleasant and unwholesome flavour behind,' and he complained that the reader felt morally worse after reading such books. No doubt he believed it was just as well that the genre was doomed: 'Considering the difficulty of hitting upon any fancies that are decently fresh, we are bound to say that not a few of them show considerable dexterity and ingenuity. But surely this sensational business must soon come to an end, not to be suspended for half a century or so. Of sensation, when it is degenerated to melodrama and burlesque, there must surely come satiety at the last'. Like so many of the critics who foresaw the death of the crime novel, this writer was premature; fear has remained a major ingredient of sensational fiction and Geoffrey Household probably spoke for many others in his profession when in 1979 he said on television 'I want to give you fear.'

Whether readers want to fear 'because it's so nice to stop again', or because they welcome the verbalisation of their own inarticulate terrors, is not clear. Equally curious is the notion that the identification of a criminal will in itself end the fear, for in detective novels, the villain's end makes a very final resolution. Many detective writers have tried to combine terror and logic. A. E. W. Mason, the once very popular creator of Inspector Hanaud, said in 1931 that he wanted to combine 'the crime story which produces a shiver with the detective story that aims at a surprise', and he has been followed by many others who try both to mystify and to chill spines.

No doubt readers like to suppose that in life's next chapter, as in fiction's, the triumph of truth and reason, order and law, will signify the end of misery. This may be why detective novels were so unexpectedly popular during the war, with their implication of anarchy's permanent defeat. At the height of the Nazi blitz in 1940, special 'raid libraries' were established at the entrance to shelters. Borrowers wanted, almost exclusively, detective stories.

The appeal to fear, and to a belief in the power of order, may seem equally unsuited to the chaotic world of the twentieth century. It is far easier to understand the appeal of the detective novel's settings. For the more fantastic the events, the less credible the characters, the more closely the superficial details stick to fact. The crime novel has been chosen by many exiles as the most evocative reminder of their home. Somerset Maugham always chose detective novels for his light reading on his travels; Cyril Connolly, homesick in the south of France, passed his time 'walking with Inspector French round the Mumbles, gazing down winter estuaries, making innumerable railway journeys, exploring Rochester with Thorndike, going with Mr. Fletcher to country towns, till I could find my way in any of them to the Doctor's pleasant

Georgian house, the rectory, the spinster's cottage, the eccentric lawyer's office . . . ' He thought that these books were the last repository of the countryside, their local colour beautiful as well as useful; and from reading a large number of such books, he retained in his mind, apart from these pleasant landscapes, 'mash—a kind of bran mash, a great packing case of bran with here an arm and there an ear—a weapon or a corpse sticking out of it . . .'

In the post-Doyle period, the non-metropolitan parts of the British Isles were preferred for detective novels and far from cities being the natural setting, as J. G. Cawelti claims, most stories took place in very different places from Holmes's foggy London or Marlowe and Spade's 'downtown'. As Sherlock Holmes himself said, 'It is my belief, Watson, founded upon my experience, that the lowest and vilest alleys in London do not present a more dreadful record of sin than does the smiling and beautiful countryside . . . Think of the deeds of hellish cruelty, the hidden wickedness which may go on, year in, year out, in such places, and none the wiser . . . '

Some of the most successful detective novels have been set in a bounded geographical area containing a closed list of suspects. The advertising agency in *Murder Must Advertise*, the hospital in *Green for Danger*, the fashion house in *The Fashion in Shrouds* are all unforgettably realised, and many a girl has set her sights on Oxford after reading the description in *Gaudy Night* which Somerville's dons found so unflattering. It is not simply the physical details which create the scene; the minutiae of daily life are equally noticeable. What more will most of us ever wish to know about forensic laboratories than we learn from P. D. James's *Death of an Expert Witness*, or about campanology than *The Nine Tailors* tells us? It is natural for writers to make use of their special knowledge, and inevitable that they should indulge their particular enthusiasms. Thus those who do not share Ngaio Marsh's passion for the theatre may feel that she tells them more about it than they ever wanted to know, and too many of Michael Innes's books may be set in decayed country mansions, but the essence of a corpus of work by a single author is often a completely unified world. If the aristocracy of Great Britain do not live as Michael Innes makes out, then at least in a hundred years' time everyone will believe that they did. No doubt Agatha Christie's world of country towns and traditional villages, with rich men in their castellated villas and poor men at their gates, will be taken as the very distillation of mid-twentieth-century England. In some parts of the world it already is, and where the clues and crimes are forgotten, their settings survive.

The clues, the crimes and the settings, inseparably, are attractive, and not only to English exiles like Cyril Connolly; their appeal transcends national boundaries. The complaint that these books merely reinforce the least creditable prejudices of the readers, which is levelled not only at Agatha Christie but at most of the best-selling crime novelists of her day, is expressed most cogently, though not uniquely, by Colin Watson in *Snobbery with Violence*. He believes that every best seller echoes the readers' private desires and opinions, so that when Agatha Christie or Dorothy L. Sayers wrote something which seems to be racialist or anti-semitic, they were expressing their readers' own attitudes, hence the popularity of their books. He does not explain why they are so widely read in Israel and in Black Africa.

Certainly there can be no disagreement with the view that the crime novel reflects—rather than tries to alter—the society in which and for which it is written. Writers of light fiction have rarely set out to be social reformers, and the writers of the twenties and thirties in Britain and America lived at a time when most people longed to find political peace and stability, and believed in the value of settled habit, conforming morals, and the stratified, hierarchical society which still existed. The gradual post-war increase of large-scale organised crime, of political terrorism, of carelessness about individual life, is reflected in fiction. Even before the war the hard-boiled novels of Chandler and Hammett drew little moral distinction between the criminal and the detective, and this attitude is increasingly common today. A random sample of current 'crime novels' recently received for review by the present writer shows that the vast majority have been thrillers in which both the good guys and the bad guys are equally ready to kill in the course of their work and equally unlikely to give the act a moment's thought afterwards. (Hardly any of these books seem to be written by women.)

Between the wars, however, Colin Watson says, the middle classes did not want dispatches from beyond the frontier of their own experience; elsewhere he says that novels such as the spy stories by E. Phillips Oppenheim and the thrillers by Sapper offered wish-fulfilment both to the readers and the author. While not necessarily sharing Watson's distaste for the general reader (as Edmund Crispin said in his review of *Snobbery with Violence*, 'the poor old middle classes have been at it again'), one must obviously agree that crime novelists neither could, nor wished to, nor perhaps should, offer new moral ideas to their readers. As Barzun said about obtrusive psychological insights offered instead of material information, 'when I hunger for "real characters" I am satisfied by nothing less than Stendhal, Balzac, Meredith, James, Dickens, Hardy or Joyce. When I want to read about the psychology of a murderer I go to Dostoevsky, Buchner, Victor Hugo, Stevenson or Shakespeare. I do not want it from Miss Mary Limpet or Mr. Sterling Brass who write in the "I Did It" and the "I Done It" manners respectively.' And he might well have added that he did not go to crime stories for propaganda or moral improvement.

It is distasteful to realise that the middle classes of the 1930s wanted their villains to be wily orientals or Huns or Jews. It would be agreeable to be able to say that writers whose work one otherwise enjoys held views which were more liberal than the crowd's. But the reflections of archaic prejudices which we detect in detective novels are not mirrored by the worldwide audience the books still attract today. The fact is that these writers, in setting improbable events in realistic surroundings, took over all the details of those surroundings, and if they wrote about middle-class life they put in middle-class prejudices. This will make them all the more useful to future sociologists—to whom propaganda would be of only negative use—but it is not the reason for their success.

Watson complains that the poverty between the wars was something to which the middle classes were purposely blind. Surely it is more likely that they turned to light literature to rest their eyes from it. But it is true, however, that few writers of crime stories knew much about poverty in working-class surroundings. They set their work in environments which were familiar to them and wrote about the worlds they knew. Agatha Christie was herself an upper-middle-class country lady who shared her neighbours' prejudices; Margery Allingham skated, like her novels, between prosperous rural stability and the world of creative artists; Sayers' pervasive atmosphere of High-Church convention, leavened by London offices and glimpses of artistic and political dissent, reflected the world she lived in herself.

The re-creation of familiar or interesting places; the supposed intimacy with a class whose doings have always been thought interesting by outsiders; the reminder of unarticulated fears; the invitation to think rather than to feel: all these are expressions of the readers' own desires, and the writers'. One could provide for the other exactly what was wanted. The events take place in a world literally copied from reality; the fantasy lies in those events, and in their protagonist the running hero, who is perhaps the major reason for the continuing popularity of these books.

3 Detective Heroes

To the inventor of Lord Peter Wimsey, the detective was 'the protector of the weak . . . the true successor of Roland and Lancelot'. Margery Allingham thought that 'the knight errant is romance's eternal hero, the rescuer, the dragon slayer, the wanderer in search of other peoples' troubles. When he became a displaced person, he went into hiding, and lived on disguised as Nero Wolfe and Archie, as Poirot, as Peter Wimsey, as Reggie Fortune, Philo Vance and Perry Mason, as the Good Fairy Private Eye, in fact . . . an unlikely sprite.'

In pinpointing the romantic, mythological quality of their detective heroes, Allingham and Sayers identified the common feature of the crime novels which survive. It appears as well in other series which have retained their popularity with the general public, for instance, C. S. Forester's Hornblower series, John Buchan's adventures of Richard Hannay, even Wodehouse's Wooster and Jeeves, and romances by such authors as Heyer and Cartland, whose heroes—all gorgeous brutes by different names—are always the same person.

What these long-lived heroes have in common is not merely that they have appeared in several books; there have been many 'series detectives' who have been forgotten. They must attract affection, either of a romantic or a filial kind, and they must show an almost magical power, which makes them superior to the uncertainties and inefficiencies of everyday life. The true hero restores order without doubting that it is right and necessary. He undertakes the responsibilities of others, to whom he is superior by reason of his physical courage, or his mental agility—or both.

This is no place for speculation about mankind's longing for a saviour, we must merely accept that it is a human characteristic on both religious and secular planes. From earliest times, legends of a hero's courage and resourcefulness have been integral to man's imaginative life. Every society has produced them, from the ancient Greeks and Romans to the early Irish and other Celtic races, the Teutonic peoples of the Heroic Age, and western Europe's age of medieval chivalry. Every literature has its own tales of supermen.

In our own time, the knight errant can most easily be recognised in thrillers. Characters like James Bond exist to adventure and suffer, in order to save the rest of the citizens from the need to do either. Their purpose is to restore order to a threatened community. In thrillers the only individual who matters is the hero himself. The threat is to a larger community and often, in modern thrillers, to the whole world, or at the very least to 'society as we know it'.

The hero of a detective novel comes to the rescue of one, or a few people. Like the knight in medieval chivalry, he undertakes single combat on behalf of a single victim—Perseus or St George, Andromeda or the maiden, a dragon, whether real or symbolical—this triangle of the hero, the innocent and the aggressor is constantly repeated.

With greater sophistication the myth changes, and with a greater emphasis on science and understanding, the hero's methods are refined. It is no longer enough for the man in shining armour to ride up, unsheath his sword and fight: he must *think*. In this way, while the conventionally physical hero continued to be glorified, and in many thrillers still is, a character appeared in fiction whose function was heroic, but whose appearance and methods were not. The dragon became a criminal, the maiden usually an accused or threatened innocent; the intellectual hero began, in these detective stories, as a police detective of minimal glamour.

The detective's public image was originally little different from that of the criminal. Both appeared to the average citizen as dangerous and suspect, or, in the case of the ancients employed as members of the Watch, as useless. Henry Fielding, who was not only a novelist but also a reforming magistrate and responsible for establishing the Bow Street Runners, called them, in *Amelia* (1751):

these poor old decrepit people, who are from their want of bodily strength, rendered incapable of getting a livelihood by work. These men, armed only with a pole which some of them are scarce able to lift, are to secure the persons and houses of His Majesty's subjects from the attacks of gangs of young, stout, desperate and well armed villains . . . If the poor old fellows should run away from such enemies, no one I think can wonder, unless it be that they were able to make their escape.

Such officers of the Watch were obviously unable to detect or arrest the majority of criminals, and a system developed of setting a thief to catch a thief. A reward was paid for the capture and successful prosecution of highwaymen and, later, of those who committed other crimes against property. Public officials and private citizens were equally entitled to such rewards, with the result that in the eighteenth and early nineteenth century detectives were really nothing more than spies or informers, for only those who associated with criminals could acquire the information with which to earn the rewards. Corruption was thus built into the system. Furthermore, it was worth the informer's while to wait until his target committed a serious crime, for the scale of the payment increased with the seriousness of the offence; also there was an evident inducement to perjury since the witness had a financial stake in the conviction. Not only members of the public, but even Bow Street Runners, came to trial in those days on charges of conspiracy and even of incitement to robbery so that they could arrest the robbers.

The master criminal Jonathan Wild embodied the double aspect of thief and detective in a spectacular way. He was famous as a thief-catcher, and in the role of public servant was consulted by the victims of robberies. He styled himself 'The Thief Taker General of Great Britain and Ireland' and ran a 'Lost Property Office' through which stolen goods were restored to their owners. In fact, he organised the thefts which he later claimed to investigate, and used his Lost Property Office to dispose of the loot. He was eventually arrested and hanged in 1725, and his story inspired both Gay's *Beggars' Opera* (1727) and Fielding's novel *Jonathan Wild the Great* (1743).

At this period, then, the detective was seen by the public as more of a rogue than a hero, and the criminal seemed to be of greater intrinsic interest than the law enforcer. After the Metropolitan Police Act of 1829, public attitudes gradually changed. From that time on popular fiction dealt with Police Detectives, usually in the form of 'true life memoirs'.

The *Memoirs of Vidocq* were very influential and popular both in France and, in translation, in England, where they were first published in 1828. Vidocq was a 'poacher turned gamekeeper' considered by his contemporaries as the French Jonathan Wild, although he was not simultaneously thief and thief-taker, but first one then the other. Vidocq set the pattern followed by later crime novelists in which the criminal and his hunter are inextricably intertwined. It appears in the 'tough' American crime novels of the first half of the twentieth century, and now in all countries where crime stories are written, in realistic, tough crime, or police procedural stories.

Vidocq also possessed the knack of being able to disguise himself unrecognisably. His autobiography tells of his use of false wrinkles, wigs, hair dyes, mock blisters, scars and moustaches. *The Times* of London said that he could even disguise his stature: 'by some strange process connected with his physical formation he has the faculty of contracting his height several inches, and in this diminished state to walk about, jump, etc.'

The *Memoirs of Vidocq* were well known to Edgar Allan Poe who, in his three proper detective stories, was the first to use what later became the convention, the omniscient amateur detective 'of an excellent—indeed, of an illustrious family'. The adventures of the brilliant Chevalier C. Auguste Dupin are recounted by an admiring, obtuse companion. Indeed, the superiority of the talented amateur to a professional was one of Poe's themes. Dupin says (in the 'Rue Morgue'):

> The Parisian police, so much extolled for their acumen, are cunning, but no more. Vidocq, for example, was a good guesser, and a persevering man. But without educated thought, he erred continually by the very intensity of his investigations. He impaired his vision by holding the object too close. He might see, perhaps, one or two points with unusual clearness, but in so doing he, necessarily, lost sight of the matter as a whole. Thus there is such a thing as being too profound.

This treatment of the police as incompetent blunderers in comparison with the amateur detective is of course a theme which ran, and runs, through detective fiction; from Sherlock Holmes's condescension to Inspector Lestrade, to Poirot's relationship with Japp, and Wimsey's patronising of Inspector Sugg, it is a familiar pattern.

The first novel in which a police detective is himself the hero had, however, preceded Vidocq and Poe. *Richmond, or Scenes from the Life of a Bow Street Runner*, written by Thomas Gaspey and published anonymously, appeared in 1827. Richmond is as much the protector of the weak and innocent as he is a thief-taker, and he is the first fictional detective to play the 'knight errant' role, being motivated by pity for the victims of the crime he is sent to investigate, and feeling himself sufficiently rewarded by the satisfaction of having righted a wrong. Richmond was a Bow Street Runner. His successors in fiction were members of the Metropolitan police.

By the 1850s, newspaper readers were familiar with the work of professional detectives, particularly after the much-publicised O'Connor murder case of 1849 in which Frederick and Maria Manning were arrested as a result of police investigations.

William Russell, whose fictionalised recollections appeared in Chambers' *Edinburgh Journal* between 1849 and 1856, invented a police detective as hero who, like Richmond, regarded himself as the protector of the helpless. By 1863, Hawkshaw, the Great Detective, appears in *The Ticket of Leave Man*, by Tom Taylor, in the guise of a philanthropist who is dedicated to defending the innocent and to reinforcing society's assumptions.

The first novel in which a policeman is shown both realistically and sympathetically is Charles Dickens' *Bleak House*. Dickens had great admiration for the police force; he spent much time studying its work and wrote journalistic articles about it in *Household Words*. He clearly hoped to give the detective a heroic status in the reader's mind. The famous Inspector Field was his model—both in appearance and working methods—for Inspector Bucket in *Bleak House*; Dickens even gave him some of Field's characteristic gestures, such as his using his fat forefinger to emphasise his words.

Bleak House, although in précis a most sensational novel with all the usual ingredients of missing wills and guilty secrets, is of course much more than that; it is an important description of a society and the tensions in it. Here it is necessary only to consider Inspector Bucket, who is the first in a long line of fictional detectives who seem stolid and unremarkable:

> Mr. Snagsby is dismayed to see, standing with an attentive face between himself and the lawyer, a little distance from the table, a person with a hat and stick in his hand, who was not there when he himself came in, and has not since entered by the door or either of the windows. There is a press in the room, but its hinges have not creaked, nor has a step been audible upon the floor. Yet this third person stands there, with his attentive face and his hat and stick in his hands and his hands behind him, a composed and quiet listener. He is a stoutly built, steady-looking, sharp-eyed man in black, of about middle-age. Except that he looks at Mr. Snagsby as if he were going to take his portrait, there is nothing very remarkable about him at first sight but his ghostly manner of appearing.

Elsewhere Bucket is described as a 'sharp-eyed man—a quick keen man—and he takes in everybody's look at him, all at once, individually and collectively, in a manner that stamps him as a remarkable man'.

Bucket is in the habit of proclaiming, 'I am Inspector Bucket of the Yard, I am', a foretaste of the vanity which his fictional heirs are wont to display. He also is the first detective, of the many in later fiction, not only to arrest and handcuff a suspect who is later shown to be innocent, but also to assemble an audience, which includes the criminal, to whom he explains the actions and reasoning by which he has been able to identify the guilty party.

Bucket incarnates bourgeois values and lower-middle-class respectability; his very ordinariness was no doubt reassuring to Dickens' readers. At the same time he uses powers which are far from ordinary or realistic, for instance, that of moving with uncanny ease between places. As the narrator says, 'Time and place cannot bind Mr Bucket'; and between the classes of what was a very stratified society, he shows 'adaptability to all grades'. He also achieves a deep insight into the thoughts of others—he 'dips down into the bottom of [Mr Snagsby's] mind.'

Bucket exemplifies what was to become a literary stereotype, copied or developed by other nineteenth-century writers, most of whom are now forgotten. But by the time that Jules Verne was writing *Round the World in Eighty Days* (1873) he could assume that policemen of this kind were typical of English society and that his Inspector Fix of Scotland Yard would be accepted as such by his readers.

The fictional policemen tended to be lower middle class, unremarkable in appearance, conscientious and shrewd; examples appear in, among other works, Mrs Henry Wood's *Mrs Halliburton's Troubles* (1862) and M. E. Braddon's *Henry Dunbar* (1864). But the only other such character to be remembered a century later is Wilkie Collins' Sergeant Cuff. Cuff appears in only one book, *The Moonstone*, which centres around the disappearance of a unique diamond which was stolen by a British soldier from an image of an Indian god, comes into the possession of Rachel Verinder, and disappears in mysterious circumstances.

Cuff has various amiable idiosyncracies. He talks irrelevantly about the cultivation of roses, and makes remarks which imply conclusions the reader cannot quite follow. He is underpaid, badly treated, competent in disguise and interestingly fallible. Unlike the detectives who boast of their triumphs, Cuff says at the end of the book:

> There's only one thing to be said about the matter, on my side I completely mistook my case. How any man living was to have seen things in their true light, in such a situation as mine was at the time, I don't profess to know. But that doesn't alter the facts as they stand. I own that I made a mess of it. Not the first mess, Mr Blake, which has distinguished my professional career. It's only in books that the officers of the detective force are superior to the weakness of making a mistake.

Like Bucket, Cuff was based on a real policeman—Inspector Jonathan Whicher of the Metropolitan Police Detectives' department. Whicher had been known as the Prince of Detectives, but his reputation suffered when he arrested Constance Kent for the murder of her small brother. She was

acquitted, amid much publicity. In physical details the real and
the invented policeman were not alike, but Cuff is given the
keen-eyed perceptiveness essential to a good detective:

> A fly from the station drove up as I reached the lodge; and out got
> a grizzled elderly man so lean that he looked as if he had not got an
> ounce of flesh on his bones in any part of him. He was dressed all
> in decent black, with a white cravat round his neck. His face was as
> sharp as a hatchet, and the skin of it was as yellow and dry and
> withered as an autumn leaf. His eyes, of a steely light grey, had a
> very disconcerting trick, when they encountered your eyes, of
> looking as if they expected something more from you than you
> were aware of yourself. His walk was soft; his voice was
> melancholy; his long, lanky fingers were hooked like claws. He
> might have been a parson, or an undertaker—or anything else you
> like, except what he really was.

Cuff lives still, less for his own personality than because the
book in which he appears is a classic. T. S. Eliot called it, 'the
first, the longest and the best of modern English detective
novels'. Cuff does not display the uncommon, almost magical
powers given to other detectives, though he did evoke both fear
and respect from the characters in the novel.

Collins himself admired the works of Emile Gaboriau, a
French contemporary whose books are verbose and
melodramatic, but ingenious in the detective techniques used.
The police have never been esteemed in France, least of all in
Gaboriau's day. The narrator in *Le Petit Vieux de Batignolles*
says:

> This was the first time in my life that I crossed the threshold of the
> Prefecture of Police, against which I had hitherto been quite as
> prejudiced as any Parisian. Those who study social questions may
> well ask how it happens that the French police are so generally
> hated and despised. Even the ordinary street policeman is the
> object of aversion; and the detective is loathed as intensely as if he
> were some monstrous horror, in lieu of generally being a most
> useful servant of society.

In spite of this, Gaboriau created an agent of the Sûreté,
Lecoq, who is not unlike Vidocq. Like him, he is a master of
disguise, and like all the best heroes in fiction, he is capable of
brilliantly logical and intuitive deduction. He is also extremely

vain, although the amateur, Pere Tabaret, appears to be more brilliant than he.

Later writers returned to Poe's formula, and made their inefficient police detectives plod through the plot, while the best work was done by amateurs or private detectives. Quite often the amateur was also the hero of the romantic strand of the plot. His courage and wit sort out the mystery and win the fair maiden at one stroke. The policeman is duped and sometimes even doped. In *The House on the Marsh* (1884) by Florence Warden, Inspector Maynard of Scotland Yard is given a drugged drink by the master criminal he has been sent to catch. He is found in a stupor by another officer:

> The other detective shook him and glanced at the wine.
> 'Drugged,' he said shortly.
> With a few vigorous shakes he succeeded in rousing Maynard, and when he began to look round him in a dazed way, the other said sharply—
> 'Pretty fellow you are to be hoodwinked like that, and drink and sleep quietly under the very roof of one of the greatest scoundrels unhung!'
> 'Who?' the other said, startled. 'Mr Rayner?'
> 'Mr Rayner! Yes, Mr Rayner, to simple folk like you; but to me and every thief taker that knows his business— the missing forger, James Woodfall!'

With policeman like these, amateurs were clearly needed, if only to make the policemen look foolish. When Sherlock Holmes appeared in 1887, in *A Study in Scarlet*, he was to set the pattern for detective heroes for generations to come. No other character in fiction can have given rise to as much parody, imitation and consideration as he.

When Conan Doyle invented the character, with whom in later years he was to grow very bored, he had already published several short stories and written a frequently rejected full-length novel. He was a debt-ridden young doctor with an ailing wife. It occurred to him to base the character of a detective on that of his professor at Edinburgh University, Joseph Bell:

> Gaboriau had rather attracted me by the neat dove-tailing of his plots, and Poe's masterful detective, M. Dupin, had from

childhood been one of my heroes. But could I bring an addition of my own? I thought of my old teacher, Joe Bell, of his eagle face, of his curious ways, of his eerie trick of spotting details. If he were a detective he would surely reduce this fascinating but unorganised business to something nearer to an exact science. I would try if I could get this effect . . . It is all very well to say that a man is clever, but the reader wants to see examples of it, such examples as Bell gave us every day in the wards. The idea amused me . . .

The idea amused the reading public, too. Doyle, who was himself a typical Victorian in his emotions, his imperialism and his philistinism, invented a character who outraged Victorian convention in his behaviour, but who, on account of his superior qualities, was forgiven.

Sherlock Holmes is a gentleman with polished manners and at ease in the most exalted company; he was the first detective to be socially acceptable to the upper classes, for detection was vulgar work, and only an outsider, like Holmes or Poirot, or an aristocrat, could plausibly transcend social barriers. He is knowledgeable in a variety of fields, having written monographs on such subjects as tobacco and the Polyphonic Motets of Lassus; however, he declines to burden his mind with irrelevant information, and Watson has to admit that Holmes is wholly ignorant of literature, astronomy and philosophy. Holmes plays the violin, is an experimental scientist, and a genius at disguising himself. He has fits of depression in which he lies on a sofa for days on end hardly speaking or moving, and he injects himself with cocaine, 'as a protest against the monotony of existence'.

Conan Doyle had created a superman, who alone could help those who appealed to him. He used Poe and Gaboriau's formula of having his hero's exploits recounted by an admirer, in this case Watson, and he included policemen who were repeatedly baffled by Holmes's genius. Holmes became the archetype of the detective hero, and the standard by which his successors would be judged.

Even in his own time, Holmes had many fictional rivals. In the words of Hugh Greene, who edited an anthology with the title *The Rivals of Sherlock Holmes*, 'some were honest men, some were formidable. From Holborn and the Temple in the East, to Richmond in the West, they dominated the criminal underworld of late Victorian and Edwardian London, sometimes rescuing their clients, sometimes eliminating them . . .'

In 1928 Agatha Christie was able to publish a novel (*Partners in Crime*) in which she parodied the behaviour of detectives whose characters must have been familiar to her readers. In the same year, Dorothy L. Sayers was to list, in her introduction to a collection of detective stories, many heirs to Dupin, whose doings were chronicled by 'admiring and thickheaded' friends. Other publishers produced books with such titles as 'Fifty Famous Detectives of Fiction'; but few of them are famous now.

F. Austin Freeman, for instance, is regarded by Hugh Greene as one of the best detective-story writers of all time and Raymond Chandler said that he had no equal in his genre. His detective was the handsome Dr Thorndyke, whose stooge was Dr Jarvis, and to whom Superintendent Miller, an unimaginative policeman, turned for enlightenment. Freeman was a surgeon himself and, like Conan Doyle, modelled his detective on one of his own teachers, Dr Alfred Swayne Taylor, a professor of Medical Jurisprudence. Apparently Freeman made all the experiments he was to describe in his books himself. Thorndyke is a forensic scientist, and some of his fictional methods were later put into use by the police. Like Holmes, Thorndyke remains superior to emotion, but his character is undefined, and perhaps because it is much less fantastic than that of Holmes's is much less interesting. He is given, like Holmes, to didactic patronising: ' "Now, my dear Jervis," said Thorndyke, shaking an admonitory forefinger at me, "don't, I pray you, give way to mental indolence. You have these few facts that I have mentioned. Consider them separately and collectively, and in their relation to the circumstances. Don't attempt to suck my brain when you have an excellent brain of your own to suck." '

Another 'superman' detective was the blind Max Carrados, who used his exceptionally acute sense of smell and hearing to compensate, and more than compensate, for his lack of sight. The stories, by the author of the Kai Lung books, Ernest Bramah Smith, were regarded as exceptionally attractive in their day (they appeared between 1914 and 1924) but are only of historical interest now, as are Arthur Morrison's Martin Hewitt stories; Hewitt was in his day remarkable mainly for being unremarkable—both in appearance and in ability.

Equally well known in the early years of the century was a French Inspector of the Sûreté called Hanaud, who appeared in several novels by A. E. W. Mason. Howard Haycraft regarded Hanaud's adventures as 'among the most subtly conceived and described in the genre', and Mason himself, who had been both a Member of Parliament and the civilian Chief of British Naval Intelligence, had ambitions to write a thriller which was also worth reading as a novel. Many commentators think that he succeeded. Hanaud is a tall, burly man who looks 'like a prosperous comedian' and uses as his 'Watson' his friend Ricardo.

After the war, there were many popular and busy fictional police detectives. Julian Symons aptly used the adjective 'humdrum' for the books in which most of them appeared. They read now like the written equivalent of pictures 'painted by numbers'. The best of them is probably Freeman Wills Crofts' Inspector French, but his activities will appeal mainly to readers with an interest in timetables and organisational detail, for he is a methodical, conscientious, uninteresting character.

The un-eccentric amateur—as opposed to the Holmesian figure with identifying peculiarities—appeared first in E. C. Bentley's Philip Trent, who was presented as a well-known artist, respected by the police and the press. The three books in which he featured are still regarded with respect and affection by authorities on the genre. What seemed so original when first read was copied by so many later writers that Philip Trent is now almost forgotten, along with most of his imitators; but it was pointed out by Barbara Reynolds in 1977 that much of Lord Peter Wimsey is based on Philip Trent. She quotes from a manuscript draft of a talk by Dorothy L. Sayers which she found in the archives at Wheaton College, Illinois:

> I suppose everybody has at least heard of *Trent's Last Case*. It holds a very special place in the history of detective fiction. If you were so lucky as to read it today for the first time you would recognise it at once as a tale of unusual brilliance and charm, but you could

have no idea how startlingly original it seemed when it first appeared. It shook the little world of the mystery novel like a revolution, and nothing was ever quite the same again. Every detective writer of today owes something, consciously or unconsciously, to its liberating and inspiring influence.

What Sayers herself owed to its influence was the idea for her detective; Trent and Wimsey as Barbara Reynolds points out, 'are found to be so like each other as to seem almost blood relations.' Sayers also said that Wimsey was like Trent 'but with a touch of Bertie Wooster as well', and she made many conscious verbal gestures to remind herself and her more perceptive readers of the resemblance. Trent quotes poetry, speaks French fluently, whistles under his breath, is cheerful and lively, and serious beneath a veneer of frivolity; also he falls instantly and desperately in love with a female suspect, Mrs Manderson. In 1934, Sayers wrote, 'E. C. Bentley's Trent, in a single masterpiece, established the detective's right of a liberal education, and a sincere personal emotion. His conversation and his love affair, for the first time in detective history, breathed the air of poetry.'

Trent was the first of many similar amateurs. Roger Sheringham, one of A. B. Cox's characters, began as a skit on others, but when his readers took him seriously, the author was forced to tone him down; H. C. Bailey's hero was Reggie Fortune and Philip Macdonald wrote about Anthony Gethryn. None of their contemporaries would have expected these names to sink into oblivion while others survived. A. A. Milne wrote a novel called *The Red House Mystery* (1922) which is usually, incomprehensibly, described as a major work in the field; its amateur hero was called Anthony Gillingham. All these characters were in the same tradition as Trent. They are perceptive, sympathetic, inoffensive; they are all, in contrast to their pre-World War I colleagues, very ordinary indeed—so ordinary as to be uninteresting. Nobody could wish to re-read one of their adventures, perhaps because the element of fantasy or wish fulfilment is completely missing.

At the height of the careers of Campion, Poirot, Wimsey, and the other amateur detectives, fewer than one hundred murders and major crimes took place in Britain each year, and of those not many presented such features as would appeal to the readers of fiction. George Orwell complained of 'the decline of the English Murder' after the mid-twenties—meaning real-life murders. He did not believe that modern murder cases would be remembered and studied in the same way as 'the old domestic poisoning dramas, product of a stable society where all the prevailing hypocrisy did at least ensure that crimes as serious as murder should have strong emotions behind them.' But even at its 'best period' the middle-class murder (or at least, the one identified as unnatural death) was a tiny proportion of what was in any case a low total.

In none of these cases is it recorded that any part was played by amateur or private detectives in the investigation. Of course, most crime novelists were well aware of this, and Ngaio Marsh was not alone in making her hero a member of the regular police force. But by far the majority of the many crime novels published before the last war featured non-police detectives. Since the war the fashion has been to invent heroes who are also policemen, perhaps partly to avoid the implausibility of laymen being repeatedly involved in crime, but it is noticeable even now that these police officers, Innes's Appleby, James's Dalgleish, for instance, tend to find themselves investigating crimes for which other policemen are technically responsible, and whose routine they are consequently spared. This trick enables the author to keep her detective in the same position as the amateur, that of an individual plunged alone into the murk of mysterious crime. When policemen heroes are convincingly rendered they are too like real life to become fantasy-heroes. As one of them, Nicolas Freeling's Van der Valk, says, 'It is only in books that one finds the brilliant amateur detective. Real policemen are obstinate and hard-headed, are slow and literal minded, are frequently mean and nearly always narrow: they have to be. They are part of the administrative machine, a tool of government control . . . '

The tough hero of the Chandler school, much admired by many perceptive people, is profoundly unattractive and uninteresting to others in his cynical, world-weary guise of the good lone guy in a population of bastards. His descendant, the hero-loner, the James Bond figure, although as dislikable personally, is disguised by the glamour of his gadgetry and his surroundings. Chandler's man must go down his mean streets in unrelieved squalor.

Chandler had always despised the amateur detective of the Golden Age. He wrote in 1950, 'He wouldn't do even when his brother was a duke, and he had a title and was a classical scholar of considerable attainments . . . The private eye is admittedly an exaggeration—a fantasy. But at least he's an exaggeration of the possible.' Chandler did not accept that his own 'hard-boiled' stories depended on quite as much suspension of disbelief as the soft-boiled European ones. He developed and expanded the convention in which a poor, disreputable man, calling himself a private eye, would take on a criminal gang or a corrupt administration on behalf of an individual client; the private eye would often work without pay, undergo acute physical suffering, drink, drive and survive. What is this if not the story of the hero, the maiden and the dragon? Chandler's own detective has survived, and so have those he most deplored for their lack of realism. Chandler himself realised as clearly as any mystery writer ever has, that his detective was a modern knight, a redeemer:

In everything that can be called art there is a quality of redemption . . . Down these mean streets a man must go who is not himself mean, who is neither tarnished nor afraid. The detective on this kind of story must be such a man. He is the hero, he is everything. He must be a complete man and a common man and yet an unusual man. He must be, to use a rather weathered phrase, a man of honour . . . He is a relatively poor man, or he would not be a detective at all. He is a common man or he could not go among common people. He has a sense of character or he would not know his job. He will take no man's money dishonestly and no man's insolence without a due and dispassionate revenge. He is a lonely man, and his pride is that you will treat him as a proud man, or be very sorry you ever saw him. He talks as the man of his age talks, that is, with rude wit, a lively sense of the grotesque, a disgust for sham and a contempt for pettiness . . . He must be the best man in the world, and a good enough man for any world.

Philip Marlowe's adventures appeared between 1939 and 1965, after the Golden Age of detective fiction was over, but his continuation of the superman formula reinforced the theory that an appealing running hero, loved by his creator, is the clue to survival. For Chandler loved Marlowe; as Julian Symons says: 'Philip Marlowe becomes with each book more a piece of wish fulfilment, an idealised concept of Marlowe himself, a strictly literary conception.' If Chandler had been a woman writing the same books, would Symons have accused her, as he did Dorothy Sayers, of falling in love with her hero?

Most of the detective heroes of the pre-war period, unloved and forgotten, emphasise the achievement of those of their contemporaries who have names the general reader knows. In a class of his own is Father Brown. He worked within the framework of more conventional protagonists—all solved problems which had baffled lesser men, protected innocence, were merciless with guilt, and accepted the prohibitions of society. But Father Brown's originality of method, and Chesterton's poetic narrative, make it hard to equate this detective with any of the plodding or frivolous young men, or with the scientific and reliable older ones. Brown represents the 'little man', and he works on a mixture of faith, shrewdness and intuition. He represents the commonplace. He is utterly unremarkable. 'His short figure, his short sighted and undistinguished countenance, his rather rusty black clerical clothes, could pass through any crowd in his own country without being noticed as anything unusual.' The methods of story telling, the plots, Father Brown himself, all depend heavily on paradox, and too many stories read at a sitting may surfeit the reader both with this device and with Chesterton's flamboyant fancy. In his own way, Father Brown is an archetypal rescuer of the threatened innocent but no maiden saved by this hero would wish to imagine him rewarded with her hand in marriage—a defect shared by Hercule Poirot.

Poirot first appears as old and retired—he often calls himself 'Old Papa Poirot' although he is unencumbered by any family. He died aged, at a rough computation, 133 years—a mythological character indeed.

Having been well soaked in the Sherlock Holmes tradition, Agatha Christie had naturally invented a detective with a stooge, and equally naturally, one who was the opposite in every superficial characteristic from Holmes. ' "I don't know what I'd imagined," ' says the narrator of one of Poirot's triumphs (*Murder in Mesopotamia*):

> Something rather like Sherlock Holmes—long and lean, with a keen clever face. Of course I knew he was a foreigner, but I hadn't expected him to be quite as foreign as he was, if you know what I mean. When you saw him you just wanted to laugh. He was like something on the stage, or at the pictures. To begin with he wasn't above five feet tall. I should think—an odd, plump man, quite old, with an enormous moustache and a head like an egg. He looked like a hairdresser in a comic play.

Sherlock Holmes was tall, one hundred per cent English, thin, clean-shaven, untidy, drug-taking and interested in the honey bee. Hercule Poirot had a mania for order and symmetry, a faith in the power of the brain, 'the little grey cells', and a taste for drinking tisanes and sirops (like his creator, he did not like alcohol) which seems as unsuitable for a Gallic gourmet as a retirement interest in the cultivation of vegetable marrows. His list of characteristics identifies him as a mythological figure, a *deus ex machina* who was certainly as unreal to his author as he is to his readers. He served as a machine for detection, and any other collection of characteristics would have done as well, for his personality does not affect the action, except for the fact that Poirot's solutions are usually arrived at after so many additional murders that a CID man would have been demoted to the uniformed branch, and point duty.

Agatha Christie had wanted to have a detective of a kind who had not appeared before:

> I remember our Belgian refugees. We had quite a colony of Belgian refugees living in the parish . . . why not make my detective a Belgian? I thought. There were all types of refugees. How about a refugee police officer? A retired police officer. Not too young a one. What a mistake I made there. The result is that my fictional detective must really be well over a hundred by now. Anyway, I settled on a Belgian detective. I allowed him slowly to

grow into his part. He should have been an Inspector, so that he would have a certain knowledge of crime. He would be meticulous, very tidy, I thought to myself, as I cleared away a good many untidy odds and ends in my own bedroom. A tidy little man. I could see him as a tidy little man, always arranging things, liking things in pairs, liking things square instead of round. And he should be very brainy—he should have little grey cells of the mind—that was a good phrase: I must remember that . . . Hercule Poirot. That was all right—settled, thank goodness.

Settled he remained. Sherlock Holmes was to grow from Doyle's original conception, developing some mannerisms and shedding others, and finding emotion in an originally cold temperament. But Poirot was caught like a fly in amber, from the moment of his conception. However, although Christie avoided giving Poirot any more personality, allowing him a function but no character, this did not prevent him from becoming a figure in the imagination of her readers. He became so much part of the folklore of detection that nameless references could be made to him in other writers' work, and readers would be expected to understand. For instance, in *Hamlet, Revenge!*, by Michael Innes (1937), a pushy female suggests calling in '. . . a very good man whose name I forget, a foreigner and very conceited—but, they say, very reliable.'

Poirot was indeed reliable—his intuitive methods always resulted in the downfall of the guilty, if not in the protection of all the innocent. His methods are not those of a plodding, routine detective, even if they bear a superficial resemblance to them. He does not bother with many timetables or complications of research; he does not use the scientific methods of a Thorndyke or the routine of an Inspector French. Hercule Poirot says ' "I do not run to and fro, making journeys and agitating myself. My work is done within—here." He tapped his forehead significantly.'

In *Lord Edgware Dies*, he says:

I have noticed that when we work on a case together, you are always urging me on to physical action, Hastings. You wish me to measure footprints, to analyse cigarette ash, to prostrate myself on my stomach for the examination of detail. You never realise that by lying back in an armchair with the eyes closed one can come nearer to the solution of any problem. One sees them with the eyes of the mind.'

'I don't' [Hastings] said. 'When I lie back in an armchair with my eyes closed one thing happens to me and one thing only.'

'I have noticed it,' said Poirot. 'It is strange. At such moments the brain should be working feverishly, not sinking into sluggish repose. The mental activity, it is so interesting, so stimulating! The employment of the little grey cells is a mental pleasure. They, and only they, can be trusted to lead on through fog to the truth.'

Poirot claimed that everything was susceptible to rational enquiry. In this he differed from his creator, who had a certain fondness for the mystical, and indulged it in the short stories about Mr Satterthwaite and the mysterious Mr Harley Quin. To Poirot everything was explicable. 'The power of the human brain, Hastings, is almost unlimited.' He regarded organisation and method as the prerequisites for full use of that brain. Symmetry in all things, was his aim, even in interior decoration, and in the disposition of ornaments upon a mantlepiece.

It may have been this passion for order and reason, common to all fictional detectives but particularly emphasised in Poirot, which reinforced his popularity during the chaos of the war. It is then that his role of magical rescuer would be especially desirable. How his readers must have longed to rub a lamp and summon such a genie to solve their problems.

As a rescuer, Poirot acts as 'the knight in shining armour'. In his personality, he was more likely to evoke irritation than adoration. He was invented during an era when xenophobia seemed less disgraceful than it does now, and many of the people he meets on the page, as well as many who read about him, despise the manifestations of foreignness. It was regarded as amusing for a man to act the music-hall Frenchman. He wore the clothes of a cad (or an outsider), with patent leather boots, dyed hair, waxed moustaches; he interspersed his broken English with simple French words—such as an elementary education might have taught his English readers—and the caricature is reinforced by his inability to master simple English idioms. He does un-British things like listening at keyholes, reading other people's letters, and above all, boasting. He belongs to the breed of detective who keep their deductions to themselves until the last chapter, sometimes hinting at them in a tantalising way. As Captain Hastings, his aide in the earlier books, complains, 'You make all these confounded mysteries and it's useless asking you to explain. You always like keeping something up your sleeve.'

Poirot is always the father, not the lover, figure. He gives the other characters little talks and good advice, showing a comforting ability to 'Put dolly back together again', and a paternal superiority. 'Mademoiselle, I beseech you, do not do what you are doing,' he says in *Death on the Nile* ' . . . Do not open your heart to evil . . . because if you do, evil will come. Yes, very surely, evil will come. It will enter in, and make its home within you, and after a little while it will no longer be possible to drive it out.'

Obviously, apart from the fortuitous resemblance between Poirot and Christie's second husband, Max Mallowan, there can be no suggestion that Poirot presented himself to Agatha Christie as an ideal. But one might appropriately note the parallels between the work of an archaeologist and that of a detective. Both assemble material evidence from which they will make deductions. Both must be very precise about detail, and perceive tiny clues. Both make intuitive assumptions about human behaviour. Both are essentially detached from the subject of their research.

Poirot is no 'pin-up'. Newsboys will not gasp hoarsely, as they do in Ngaio Marsh's work, 'Handsome Alleyn'. Girls in the stories will never have a crush on him. He neither falls in love, nor loves. One cannot make out a case for any emotional relationship between him and his author.

Peter Wimsey, on the other hand, has been accepted by many commentators as the expression of Dorothy Sayers' own desires. 'The short stories suggest,' said Julian Symons 'that Dorothy Sayers might have been a better and livelier crime writer if she had not fallen in love with her detective.'

'Dorothy Sayers has been castigated, with some justification, for falling in love with her Wimsey,' Ngaio Marsh wrote. 'To do so may have been an error in taste and of judgement.'

P. D. James said, in a BBC series about crime writers, 'By the time she wrote *Gaudy Night*, Miss Sayers, like her alter ego [ie Harriet Vane], had become dangerously enamoured of her aristocratic sleuth. This is an occupational hazard for the female writer . . .'

The original Wimsey would have been hard for an intellectual woman like D. L. Sayers to fall in love with. He was a 'silly ass' par excellence, in spite of his remarkable expertise in a wide variety of fields. He is attributed with specialist knowledge of music, wine, history, bibliography, and of course, English, French and classical literature, from all of which he quotes lavishly. The intellectual qualities are more emphasised in the later books, as the caricature of the aristocrat diminishes. He begins as a facetious man who tries to seem a fool. By the later books he is revealed as a trouble shooter for the Foreign Office, trusted by, and influential upon governments. Flippancy has been a feature of the English hero since Robin Hood teased the Sheriff of Nottingham with his mocking repartee. In a book about thriller heroes, *The Durable Desperadoes*, William Vivian Butler concludes, I think rightly: 'Anyone who has ever fallen deeply under the spell of the desperadoes, especially in childhood, carries at the back of his mind a rogue ideal of piratical nonchalance. He is forever suspicious of pomposity, subservience, and solemnity . . .'

Sayers has been much criticised for her snobbery in choosing to make her detective a titled aristocrat. With benefit of hindsight, it was perhaps a tactless decision for a work designed to be popular in a society which is supposed to disapprove of hereditary privilege, and in which the only acceptable snobbery is inverted. But contemporary critics should remember that in 1922, when *Whose Body?* appeared, the British were not yet freed from the nineteenth-century respect for the upper classes. It should also be noted that half a century on, outside the world of the writers, intellectuals and bound-breakers who set social trends, the English still love lords. Rural communities in the British Isles still automatically regard the local person with a title as ipso facto important; Lady This is still invited to open fêtes and govern schools, Lord That still lends his name to appeal committees and boards of management.

Sayers had been brought up in a rural parish in East Anglia and she must certainly have known what respect a title attracted to the least worthy holder of one. She may have grown out of such emotions herself, although there is no reason to suppose that a High Anglican Conservative would ever have done so, but her readers would have accepted without question that Lord Peter had easier access to police and witnesses than Mr Wimsey would have done. The critics are being unreasonable and anachronistic in denying the existence (deplorable though it was) of a stratified and class-conscious society.

Even if Sayers had known how much other writers and critics would dislike a rich lord, she must have realised that the title and money would make the life of an amateur detective much easier, and in a way, much more plausible. It spared her having to invent a reason for his being able to find the time to poke his nose into other people's affairs because he did not theoretically have to be elsewhere earning his living. She was not the only writer to regard a gentleman of leisure as a suitable adventurer. Dornford Yates, with Pleydell, Sapper with Bulldog Drummond, and John Buchan with Richard Hannay, all used the same device. When amateurs had jobs, they were usually freelances—like Philip Trent, who was a painter—but their work never seemed very time-consuming.

Only one of Sayers' novels, *Clouds of Witness*, is actually concerned with the aristocracy. Even this book, in which Wimsey's brother, the Duke of Denver, is accused of murder, is not set in a grand house, but in a quite modest 'shooting box'. A stately home appears only in the last novel, *Busman's Honeymoon*. And there are very few titled characters in the novels, compared with those of other detective novelists, and very few settings which are even 'upper class'. Christie, Allingham and Marsh all make far more use of large houses and titled people and the kind of life they were popularly supposed to lead.

Wimsey's physical appearance is far from heroic, though it too is gradually toned down. 'Tow haired, supercilious looking blighter . . . cross between Ralph Lynn and Bertie Wooster', says a character in *Murder Must Advertise*, and elsewhere Sayers wrote—surely to her own later embarrassment—'his primrose coloured hair was so exquisite a work of art that to eclipse it with his glossy hat was like shutting up the sun in a shrine of polished jet.' He has a 'parrot profile' and the only part of his own appearance of which he is proud are his long-fingered hands. He wears a monocle, carries a stick; he has a light, drawling voice and 'a ready babble of speech'. By the time that Harriet Vane admits to loving him, in *Gaudy Night*, he has a much more serious appearance and manner. If he was seen at a dog show 'giving the perfect imitation of the silly-ass-about-town', he must have been either frightfully bored or detecting something. 'I know that frivolous mood, and it's mostly camouflage—but one doesn't always know for what,' Harriet says. By this time, when he says 'Hullo -ullo' it is 'a faint echo of the old frivolous manner'. He is, Harriet realises, a middle-aged man.

Sayers had realised that if she were to continue writing about Peter Wimsey—in successive books she got closer to her own target of detective stories which were also novels—she would have to 'perform a major operation' on Peter Wimsey. So, 'I laid him firmly on the operating table and chipped away at his internal mechanism through three longish books.' She knew that this alteration would be necessary when Peter met Harriet. Harriet was too 'real' a person to be united convincingly with the puppet which the early Wimsey seemed to be. When she first invented him, Sayers had not realised that 'any character that remains static except for a repertory of tricks and attitudes is bound to become a monstrous weariness to his maker in the course of eight or nine volumes'. This was a problem which other writers also had to face. Perhaps only Margery Allingham, of those who worked in this field, was really successful in solving it.

For the early Peter Wimsey wealth and brains were not sufficient endowments. His heroic qualities were emphasised by making him display remarkable physical prowess.

He is a famous cricketer, and had played for Oxford at Lords. He was a courageous officer during the war, admired by his men: 'A regular good officer', one of his corporals says many years later, and goes on to tell affectionate anecdotes about his behaviour. He was buried alive in a dug-out, and had a nervous breakdown after the war, cured only by the calm treatment of his servant Bunter. Even at the age of forty-five he is able, when an impetuous young man launches a blow at his head, to catch the wrist 'in an iron grip'. In *Murder Must*

Advertise, he drives flawlessly at a great speed, climbs high trees and—in a harlequin's fancy dress—shins up a statue in the centre of a pool:

> Up and up went the slim chequered figure, dripping and glittering like a fantastic water-creature. He caught the edge of the upper basin with his hands, swung for a moment and lifted. Even at that moment, Willis felt a pang of reluctant admiration. It was the easy, unfettered motion of the athlete, a display of muscular strength without jerk or effort. Then his knee was on the basin. He was up and climbing, upon the bronze cupid. Yet another moment and he was kneeling upon the figure's stooped shoulders—standing upright upon them, the spray of the fountain blowing about him . . . Soon he dives, though the water is shallow and there are warnings that he will break his neck. The slim body shot down through the spray, struck the surface with scarcely a splash and slid through the water like a fish. Willis caught his breath. It was perfectly done. It was magnificent . . .

(Compare a story called *The Flying Stars*, from *The Innocence of Father Brown* (1911) by G. K. Chesterton. Flambeau has intruded upon a Christmas party disguised as a harlequin, to steal some jewels. Later Father Brown finds him in the garden, still disguised, leaping from tree to tree. D. L. Sayers always derived her mental images from the printed page.) In this adventure of Wimsey's the lady in the case did not find Wimsey desirable. She senses that he is thinking of a hanged man, and fears him. But Harriet Vane was to find that he was the perfect lover, as a succession of Viennese singers and other spectacular ladies vouchsafed. All in all, by the time that Dorothy Sayers had finished with him, there was nothing he could not do.

In this perfection, and in his freedom from the mundane worries of other people, lay his appeal for Sayers' readers, and perhaps for her. She was to write in 1936 that she deliberately gave him a large income—'after all, it cost me nothing and at that time I was particularly hard up and it gave me pleasure to spend his fortune for him. When I was dissatisfied with my single unfurnished room, I took a luxurious flat for him in Piccadilly. When my cheap rug got a hole in it, I ordered him an Aubusson carpet. When I had no money to pay my bus fare I presented him with a Daimler Double Six, upholstered in a style of sober magnificence, and when I felt dull I let him drive it . . .' This was straight fantasy; whether the other attributes of Lord Peter Wimsey were equally imaginary has been a subject for much speculation. Various friends and acquaintances of Dorothy Sayers have been identified as his model, including John Cournos, who had emigrated from Russia as a child, and after serving in the Foreign Office during the war, became a writer. 'Cournos, if anyone, was the prototype of Wimsey,' says Janet Hitchman, but she also suggests that Eric Whelpton, who met Dorothy Sayers at Oxford in 1919, might have been the origin of Wimsey, and Whelpton himself apparently believed this too. But he said in 1976, when he was eighty-two, that he had never read any of the Peter Wimsey books.

It is a pleasant game to trace the origins of fictional characters, and each player can find evidence for his or her guesses, since novelists almost invariably, and indeed, inevitably, draw on their own experiences, and often, unconsciously, use traits of the people whom they know. Many writers are surprised on rereading their books years later to realise that sayings or characteristics which they thought they were inventing had come into their minds from memory, not imagination.

It is commonly said, too, that every character—from the one-line parlourmaid to the hero and heroine—reflects the author, that nothing comes to the page but from within the writer's self. There is probably some truth in this too but, as Sayers herself wrote (*In the Mind of the Maker*), 'Well meaning readers who try to identify the writer with his characters or to excavate the author's personality and opinions from his books are frequently astonished by the ferocious rudeness with which the author himself salutes these efforts at re-absorbing his work into himself. They are an assault on the independence of his creatures, which he very properly resents . . .'

It is indeed proper to resent such identification. A far more plausible case was made by Barbara Reynolds when she drew attention to the likenesses between Wimsey and E. C. Bentley and Philip Trent. She gives proper weight to the influence on a well-read writer of books as opposed to people. 'Dorothy Sayers was a *literary* writer, that is, a writer who loved literature, and whose imagination was nurtured by the fantasy worlds of other writers.' What can be less surprising, after all, than a writer whose own academic education had been in the literature of medieval romance should invent so heroic a protagonist for her own books?

The original knight of chivalry showed no fear; presumably he was not supposed even to feel it. One of the common features of the twentieth-century substitute is the apparent sangfroid with which he greets danger. We are not made party to his thought processes about his emotions. Even those detective heroes who are quite fully characterised in other ways are seen from the outside. The feelings we know of are only those they articulate, except in rare books, like the one in which Albert Campion is suffering from loss of memory, and events are shown through his bemused eyes. With memory, reticence returns. We are rarely told what Wimsey thinks, or Alleyn, or Poirot, unless they express their feelings to other characters. These heroes are not beset by the uncertainties, the worries, the feelings of inadequacy, from which their readers suffer, and which do appear in some detail in the tales of the next generation of detectives. P. D. James's Adam Dalgleish, for example, is a fully formed character. He searches his own conscience, as well as the mysterious circumstances. But Peter Wimsey is a fully realised character only in his last book, *Busman's Honeymoon*: 'by bringing him fully to life, his creator killed him off,' says Barbara Reynolds. Even then, he is seen through Harriet's eyes. The only introspection we perceive is what he puts into words, his adoration for Harriet, and, in the end, his torment while he waits for the execution of the murderer he has been instrumental in convicting. Perhaps, to be worshipful, a fictional character must remain apart; the reader must never understand all.

Albert Campion is a character who remains enigmatic, and he is much less of a superman—rather like Wimsey in appearance, but even less given to explanation or self-analysis. So much about him is left unexplained or undescribed that it is hard to imagine how inventor or reader could fall in love with him. We do not even have any amorous scenes between him and the girl who, through several books, progresses from being a schoolgirl admirer, to fiancée, to wife, and eventually is the middle-aged mother of his adult son. So much is left unsaid. We know nothing of Campion's interests or habits, of his thoughts or his motives.

Albert Campion had 'a pale and somewhat vacant face . . . sleek yellow hair was brushed back from a high forehead and pale blue eyes were hidden behind enormous horn rimmed spectacles.' In *Sweet Danger*, Campion is recognised by one of his friends as he is masquerading as royalty in a French hotel. The friend, Guffy Randall, reflects:

> After all, it might almost be true; that was the beauty of Campion. One never knew where he was going to turn up next—at the Third Levee, or swinging from a chandelier, as someone once said. As Guffy crossed the vestibule, he had time to consider Campion. After all, even he, probably one of that young man's oldest friends, knew really very little about him. Campion was not his name; but then it is not considered decent for the younger son of such a family to pursue such a peculiar calling under his own title. As to the precise nature of the calling, Guffy was a little fogged. Campion himself had once described it as 'Universal Uncle and Deputy Adventurer.' All things considered, that probably summed him up . . .

It is never made clear why Campion's real name is not well known. In later books we discover that it is Rudolph, and that the surname begins with a K. But in more than one book characters appear who went to school with him, when he could hardly have been of an age to insist on anonymity. In *Police at the Funeral*, the formidable Great Aunt Caroline says to him, 'And now, let me look at you, Rudolph. You're not much like your dear grandmother, but I can see the first family in you.' Later she assures him, 'Very old ladies only gossip among themselves . . . I must say that I quite agree with your people in theory, but after all, as long as that impossible brother of yours is alive, the family responsibilities are being shouldered, and I see no reason why you shouldn't call yourself what you like.'

Is the implication that Campion, with his immaculate form, pale straight hair and 'habitual expression of contented idiocy' is a younger brother of, perhaps, the then Prince of Wales? Margery Allingham once confided to another crime novelist that his destiny was to inherit the throne. Perhaps she saw, and meant us to see, a cross between the Duke of York (later George VI) and Rudolph Rassendyll.

Campion is enigmatic in his interests, achievement and behaviour; one could guess what he reads and thinks, but his historian does not tell us. He is reluctant to carry firearms, and prefers blunt instruments; he is a character who remains vague, but, unlike Hercule Poirot, he seems a complete personality all the same. By the time he is middle-aged, Campion is solemnised, and capable of partaking in the more serious affairs which his creator was writing about by then. He has inherited his family responsibilities, whatever they are; he has been offered the governership of an island colony—'the last remaining civilised place in the world, and the weather is so good for children,' he is assured. 'You'll have great authority without ever having to show it, which is so tedious, real wealth, experienced service and the finest quail shooting in existence.' Even his grandfather would have considered the position suitable for him, but he will have to leave his manservant, the uninhibited Lugg, behind. Campion does not in the end allow himself to be shunted off into the higher ceremonial (all this occurs in *More Work for the Undertaker*, 1949) and in the books which follow he seems to be at work for the secret service as he had been during the war.

As 'deputy adventurer' Campion is entirely reliable, and fits the image of the magical righter-of-wrongs to perfection. Whether he is lovable, or was lovable to Margery Allingham, is another matter.

In the case of Roderick Alleyn, the inhuman perfection he displays is, in a way, superfluous. Although he, like Wimsey and Campion, was from an upper-class background, he earns his living as a policeman, and all he really needs to do is his job. But in none of the books is there any reference to his salary, to his professional squabbles and struggles for promotion, or to any of the dissatisfactions which most employees occasionally experience. Being a professional, he is properly concerned with the mysteries which rather artificially involve the amateur detective. He has experts to do the technical jobs which

Campion rarely seems to need, and which Wimsey and Bunter cleverly manage between them. Alleyn is supported by an apparently ageless team, who deal with fingerprints, photographs and post mortems. Otherwise, the fact that he is an official, instead of an amateur detective, makes little difference to his presentation. He has outstanding good looks, like a Spanish grandee, as we are repeatedly told; he is attractive to many women, all of whom he politely rebuffs, except for the one who for several books rebuffs him. He caps quotations and appreciates great paintings in a manner which novelists suppose to be typical of the educated classes.

To Ngaio Marsh, Alleyn was 'very real indeed'. She never succumbed to falling in love with him, she wrote, but grew to like him 'as an old friend':

> I even dare to think he has developed third dimensionally in my company. We have travelled widely: in a night express through the North Island of New Zealand, and among the geysers, boiling mud and snow clad mountains of that country. We have cruised along English canals and walked through the streets and monuments of Rome. His duties have taken us to an island off the coast of Normandy and the backstage regions of several theatres. He has sailed with a psychopathic homicide from Tilbury to Cape Town, and has made arrests in at least three country houses, one hospital, a church, a canal boat and a pub. Small wonder, perhaps that we have both broadened our outlook under the pressure of these undertakings.

It is easy to imagine that a lifelong companion of her own invention would be good company on the travels of an unmarried woman.

Alleyn is an optimist, and it is in this that he most differs from Wimsey and Campion. Wimsey is haunted by the hideous experiences he shared with all his generation in the trenches of World War I. Towards the end of the series of books, his remembered horror is replaced by the anticipated one of the next war. Campion skates, if not explicitly, on a thin layer of civilisation. Like Allingham herself, he was too young to be involved personally in the war, but he has her insecurity and mistrust of public affairs. In all except the first lighthearted books, the reader is aware of lurking danger and evil.

Roderick Alleyn has more superficial reactions. He expresses neither ethical doubts nor political fears, nor does he have ghastly memories. He is agreeable and urbane, and perhaps less the man his creator would choose to love, than the one she would have liked to be.

His career started in the Foreign Office—'from 1919 to 1920, Alleyn's youthful and speculative gaze had followed tail coated figures hurrying with discretion through the labyrinths of diplomatic corridors.' We are not told his feelings about the police force, nor why he chose that work. Only once does he threaten to leave the service—if he is forced to suspect Agatha Troy, with whom he has fallen in love, of murder. It is during that case (*Artists in Crime*, 1938) that he says, 'I detest my job. For the first time I despise and detest it.' The emotion is short lived and apparently not repeated, though once he and Agatha Troy are married he is careful to shield her from details of his distasteful work. What seems strange is that he should be supposed to be happy in it. He is, after all, so extremely fastidious both about material objects and about people. One cannot imagine him doing any of the work which the more realistic novels and plays of the 1960s and 1970s have taught us are part of the policeman's life. For instance, any form of violence seems completely alien to him. There is only one fight in the books, in *Spinsters in Jeopardy*, and it is a very clean one. 'There was, for Alleyn, a sort of pleasure in this fight. "I needn't worry. For once I needn't worry," he thought. "For once the final arbitrament is as simple as this. I'm fitter than he is." ' He had been exceedingly provoked in this case by the kidnapping of his own small son. One can but be impressed that even in these circumstances, fighting body to body with the disgusting, naked Dr Baradi, he should have retained command of such vocabulary. Usually, however, Alleyn avoids the seamier side of a metropolitan policeman's work. Perhaps the painfully worshipful Inspector Fox shields him from it. It is hard to believe in him as a serving policeman, if we try to do so, but as Margery Allingham once said, 'it is a very sour world when the romantic heroes masquerade as policemen in uniform.'

Uniformed or not, these were romantic heroes, with the sales appeal of familiarity; all publishers beg their crime novelists to stick to a 'running hero'. Curiously, some of these characters are still heroic to readers who could be their great-grandchildren (Campion and Alleyn were both born in the early years of the century, Wimsey would be ancient by now, and Poirot long since dead), while others, equally popular in their day, are hardly known. Dr Thorndyke, Reggie Fortune, Philo Vance and Inspector Hanaud are unfamiliar names to modern readers, yet those names which have survived appeal to all classes, not merely to the educated classes who were, D. L. Sayers said in the 1930s, the only readers of good mystery fiction. She thought then that the mystery was in danger of losing touch with the common man and becoming 'a caviar banquet for the cultured', because of the separation of fine writing from common feeling. She particularly regretted that writers presented puzzles without living characters, and felt that the lack of life and colour, as well as the increasing technicality of detection and crime, prevented the novel from being read in both kitchen and study. She listed the books which she thought would survive, which 'strike that interior note of essential mysteriousness which is part of the nature of things,' but her examples from the twentieth century by Bentley, Freeman, Van Dine and Bramah Smith have permanent places only in the memories of experts. It is the creature of feminine fantasy who has survived.

I do not suggest that these writers fell in love with their creations. In my view they created the kind of men they would like to fall in love with, or perhaps, to be. As Gwen Raverat, another woman of their period, had written (in *Period Piece*), in her dreams she was always a young man. Because these women were so typical of the society in which and for which they wrote, because they accepted the prejudices and ideals common to their readers, their own fantasies expressed those of less articulate people—to be, or to be loved by, or to be rescued by, a 'verray parfit gentil knight'.

4 Heroines

The terminology of Women's Liberation implies that its policies are new inventions. However, feminism, 'the woman question' and the movement towards women's suffrage antedate modern egalitarianism by quite long enough for it to be strange that nearly all the successful detectives in fiction have been male. There were female detectives, but they were oddities, invented for effect, like the detectives who were blind, or crippled, or eccentric. A woman was expected to evoke a faint surprise. Even today, more than a century after the appearance of the first woman detective in fiction, the thriller still almost invariably has a hero not a heroine; often he has a girl, often the girl is tougher even than he is; but there is an odour of market research about them, as though the author has submitted to public expectation. The women in such stories never seem quite to belong in them.

Jenni Calder writes, in *Heroes*, that fiction does provide 'female spies, and female agents, female soldiers and female guerillas, and female astronauts, but most of them [are] no more than imitations of men—and often puppets of men . . . what is lacking is charisma, leadership, individualism, and more practically, a sense of professionalism . . . probably most of the people most women most admire are men, which suggests the obvious, that the qualities traditionally thought of as heroic have also been traditionally thought of as male.'

There is an exact parallel with the behaviour of women, in a post-liberation era, in the un-heroic professions of business and government. There seems so far to be little attempt to modify the assumptions and practices created over centuries by men, instead women adopt them uncritically and competitively. The definition of qualities deemed admirable, useful or heroic, must change before equality can be anything but an illusion.

Writers of crime novels, however, can hardly be expected to lead opinion; indeed, if they want success they must do the opposite—reflect the prejudices and aspirations of the reader. Naturally the authors who first wrote about women detectives carefully maintained their modesty and femininity.

The two earliest examples are *The Experiences of a Lady Detective* by 'Anonyma', which appeared in 1861 (or 1864: bibliographers disagree) and told of the adventures of a Mrs Paschal, and *The Female Detective* (1864) by Andrew Forester. These ladies had turned to detection as one of the few possible ways to make a living, and they expect their femininity to be useful; they have a natural propensity to eavesdrop and snoop. These books were original in their day, but make a sticky read now, for they have been overtaken by fashion and time.

An excellent brief history of the women detectives of fiction appears as the introduction to Michele B. Slung's anthology, *Crime on Her Mind*. She lists thirty-four women detectives who had appeared by the end of World War I, of whom at least twenty were in the last century.

It was important for these women not to alienate the interest of their readers. They were as feminine as contemporary prejudices required, and this limitation on their behaviour is now a limitation on our pleasure in reading about them. In Michele B. Slung's words: 'The authors themselves never seem to be quite certain of their creation, intent as they are on playing up the novelty of such a peculiar figure, often abandoning her in mid career and finishing her off, not at the Reichenbach Falls, but at the matrimonial altar, in order to reassure the Victorian public of her ultimate femaleness.'

M. McDonnell Bodkin wrote stories about a female detective, Dora Myrl, and another series about Paul Beck, the 'rule of the thumb detective'. He married the two of them off; but usually the female detective married the suspect, who was often a lover whom she had freed from unjust suspicion by her own deductive efforts. Most of these stories were written by women, and an implicit comment is made on their standard by Hugh Greene in his anthologies about 'the rivals of Sherlock Holmes', in which Lady Molly of Scotland Yard is the only female sleuth, and Baroness Orczy and L. T. Meade (with Robert Eustace) are the only two female authors.

Even in the Golden Age of detective fiction when women had the vote, entered professions and expected equality, a properly investigating woman was still apparently implausible. Women had been employed by the Metropolitan Police since 1905, or, if one is to include the two women put in charge of female prisoners, since 1883. They had been practising as doctors since the middle of the nineteenth century; the first woman to be called to the English Bar, Helena Normanton, was admitted to the Middle Temple within hours of the passing of the Sex Disqualification (Removal) Act of 1919, was called to the Bar in 1921, and was the first woman to be briefed in the High Court in 1922. Yet women detectives were still abnormal; of those who did appear, few have retained any hold on public affection, and those who have survived are, unlike the male equivalent, those with the least glamour. Very few are professional detectives, though Edgar Wallace did include in his enormous list of publications two girls who worked at Scotland Yard, one of whom, Leslie Maughan, like E. Phillips Oppenheim's Lucy Mott, was related to a senior official there. F. Tennyson Jesse had a heroine called Solange Fontaine who was the daughter of a consultant to the French Sûreté, but her methods were far less practical than his must have been. Solange frequently insisted that the real clues to the solution of a crime were in the characters of the people involved rather than in the minutiae of material evidence studied by other detectives, and she was gifted with an ability which Mrs Tennyson Jesse believed she had herself, an extra spiritual sense which warned her of evil.

The best female detectives, whose adventures are still read with pleasure, are those descended from that invention of Anna Katharine Green, Miss Amelia Butterworth. Patricia Wentworth's Miss Maud Silver became one of the chief exponents of the deductive talents of elderly spinsters.

Patricia Wentworth was born Dora Amy Elles in 1878, the daughter of an Indian Army General. She was a true child of the Raj; educated in England, she returned to India to marry Lieutenant Colonel George Dillon. Her first published work appeared in the *Punjab Civil and Military Gazette*. Her first novel, a romance set in the French Revolution, won a prize of two hundred and fifty guineas in 1911, and for many years she wrote historical romances to support her daughter and stepsons, for her husband died in 1906. On his death she returned to England, and in 1920 married another Lieutenant Colonel, George Turnbull. They lived in Camberley, a suitably military environment, and her husband concerned himself closely with her writing. She dictated to him, and he sometimes rearranged and altered what she had said. She published two volumes of poetry, and her first mystery story, *The Astonishing Adventure of Jane Smith*, appeared in 1923.

Patricia Wentworth died in 1961. Her work had attracted many admirers, and reviewers were unusually complimentary about her productivity and competence. Many of her books are still in print, or have been republished. Connoisseurs of the form, however, regard her 'damsel in distress' stories as anodyne, girlish and trivial, and in spite of the fact that she wrote more than eighty books, she is ignored by the experts; Julian Symons, for instance, does not even mention her in his history. She once said that her aim was to present 'ordinary convincing human characters in extraordinary situations', but her characters are sadly shallow, and her situations rarely convince.

The first book which featured Miss Silver appeared in 1928; it was nine years before the next one came out, but eventually Miss Silver was the detective in thirty-two mystery stories. She remains unchanged throughout. She began and ended her career as an elderly retired governess, and was one of the very few detectives ever to have a fan club of her own. Her methods are observation and inference from experience; she sits listening, watching and continuously knitting coatees or bootees for some relative's new baby. Her often delphic statements are preceded by 'a gentle cough'. She has her 'leg work' done by several devoted police officers who address her, like Queen Victoria, as 'Dear Ma'am':

Spinster Miss Silver certainly was, and had never desired to be otherwise. With a most indulgent heart towards young lovers, and a proper regard for the holy estate of matrimony, she never regretted her own independent position. Aunt to (Inspector) Frank Abbott she was not, but the tie between them was a strong one. His irreverent sense of humour was continually delighted by her idiosyncracies, the primness of her appearance, her fringe, her beaded slippers, her quotations from Lord Tennyson, the rapid play of the knitting needles in her small, competent hands, her moral maxims, and the inflexibility of her principles.

Wentworth saw Miss Silver as 'The Victorian Standard Applied. The Moral Pointed. Penetrating Analysis of Character. And all served up with the true Tennysonian garnish' (*Out of the Past*, 1955).

Her role is usually to smooth out the course of true love between a gormless girl, called something odd like Lyndall, or Lisle (surely more evocative of stockings than glamour when *Danger Point* came out in 1942), or Carmona, and a strong silent man with a name like Dale, Garth or Craig, who had been wrongly accused or suspected of shocking crimes. The girls are gentle and sensitive, and they rush, or rather, wander, into a danger which they have been specifically warned to avoid.

These novels are part of a familiar sub-section of the mystery category, memorably entitled 'Had I But Known'. They are about heroines whose adventures are related with a regular punctuation of hindsight: 'Had I but known then what I know now . . .'

It was Ogden Nash who coined the phrase.

Personally I don't care whether a detective story writer was educated in night school or day school
So long as he doesn't belong to the H.I.B.K. school.
The H.I.B.K. being a device to which too many detective story writers are prone;
Namely the Had-I-But-Known . . .
Had I But Known Narrators are the ones who hear a stealthy creak at midnight in the tower where the body lies and, instead of locking their door or arousing the drowsy policeman posted outside their room, sneak off by themselves to the tower and suddenly they hear a breath exhaled behind them,
And they have no time to scream, they know nothing else till the men from the DA's office come in next morning and find them.
Had I But Knowners are quick to assume the prerogatives of the Deity,
For they will suppress evidence that doesn't suit their theories with appalling spontaneity,
And when the killer is finally trapped into a confession by some

elaborate device if the Had I But Knowners some hundred pages later than if they hadn't held their knowledge aloof,

Why, they say, why Inspector, I knew all along it was he, but I couldn't tell you, you would have laughed at me unless I had absolute proof . . .

In *The Spinster Detective*, Nash expressed it more succinctly:

> Had she told the dicks
> How she got in that fix,
> I would be much apter
> To read the last chapter.

Barzun and Taylor say that these books were evidently written for feminine readers, and Symons beleives they were specifically for maiden aunts. It is not the fact that the main protagonist was usually female, nor even that such books are usually written by women, which give rise to this judgement, but the fact that their plots are usually based on domestic life, with families fluttering ineffectually around its minor disarrangements. Indeed the genre is equally irritating to most women critics; Dorothy L. Sayers hinted at her own scorn in *Gaudy Night*, when Harriet remembers Peter saying: 'The heroines of thrillers deserve all they get. When a mysterious voice rings them up and says it is Scotland Yard, they never think of ringing back to verify the call. Hence the prevalence of kidnapping.'

The American Mary Roberts Rinehart was an early and important exponent of this type of novel. American readers see her as their answer to Agatha Christie, their equivalent 'respectable woman who is good at murder'. But her books were never very well known outside the United States, although some were published in Europe, and some are still in print. The American writers whose crime stories survive in world-wide esteem are not respectable women, but men writing about tough, hard-boiled dicks, of whose lives such authors as Spillane and Hammett had personal experience. Nowadays the authorities regard their work as being of literary significance.

Mary Roberts Rinehart never thought of herself as a crime novelist; her straight novels, journalism and short stories were of far greater importance to her, but she realised, rightly, that it was as a mystery writer that she was famous in her lifetime, and expected to be remembered. Her own life story was impressive and may have contributed to the success of her reputation as a writer, for unlike most British writers she was concerned with public affairs, and also had considerable personal experience of the dark and violent side of life.

She had been born in Pittsburgh in 1876, where her family was poor but not poverty stricken. Her mother was a dressmaker and her father a salesman of sewing machines. He was also an inventor, but though he apparently had several ideas which made other people rich, he never seems to have benefited from them himself, and when Mary was in her teens he shot himself. Mary's childhood was happy, though she retained vivid memories of several horrors, beginning with her abduction by (and escape from) a strange woman when she was five. During her childhood she experienced the death of her best friend from scarlet fever, the mutilation of another friend by the first trolley car in the town, a stampede of wild bulls through Pittsburgh, the murder of the butcher's wife by her daughter with one of the butcher's axes, and the disastrous floods of the Allegheny and Monongahela rivers. Her later thrillers included little that was so horrible.

Mary had hoped to be a doctor but there was no money to pay for the training, and at the age of sixteen she enrolled as a trainee nurse. She was introduced to a world 'so new, so strange, and at times so terrible that even now it hurts me to remember it,' she wrote nearly forty years later. This early experience of illness and death entirely changed her outlook on life. She encountered all the horrors of the unreformed hospitals of the time where surgeons still called antisepsis 'poppycock', and where death was slow and terrible, illness painful and rarely relieved. 'In two years of this contact with life as it is at its rawest and hardest, my young illusions began to go. Thereafter and always I have built such dreams as I have dreamed, such romances as I have written, on a basic foundation of reality, stark and naked reality.'

During her training Mary met and, at the end of it, when she was nineteen, married Dr Stanley Rinehart. By the time she was twenty-five she had three sons, had undergone three operations, and taken on the care of her ailing mother. She began to write when she was convalescing from one of her numerous illnesses, at the suggestion of her nurse, and very soon she found herself churning out the words for money; her husband, who was not earning much in general practice, had gambled and lost all his savings on the stock exchange. All her life Mary was determined that her own work should come second to her role as a wife and mother. She wrote for half an hour here, half an hour there, between heating the baby's bottle, nursing sick children, running her house with no help, and working in her husband's dispensary. At the end of one year as a writer she had sold forty-five stories and novelettes. Her industry was prodigious all her life. But she did not use her own experiences in her stories. Her crimes were sanitised for her readers' protection, and in her fiction, virtue was triumphant, wrongdoing punished. She was not prepared to publish one single line which would be unsuitable for a child's eyes.

Before World War I, the Rineharts spent three years in Austria, Germany and London. When war broke out in Europe Mary crossed the Atlantic again as a special correspondent for the *Saturday Evening Post*. She toured the war zones of France and Belgium for three weeks, the first woman observer to do so, and on her return to America worked feverishly to try to alert her country to the tragedy in Europe; she sat on commissions, wrote articles, lectured and debated. When America joined the war she urged other mothers to send their sons to it.

She was famous by that time, for her books had been successful and she was also known as a playwright. Reviewers said of her first published novel, *The Circular Staircase* (1908), that she had made the first advance in the technique of the crime story since Edgar Allan Poe. The story relates the terrifying mysteries which surround a middle-aged spinster, Rachel Innes, on holiday with her nephew and niece in a rented house. It was filmed in 1915, and later, as *The Bat* (1920), adapted for the stage. The author said afterwards that it had been intended as a skit on the usual solemn crime story, but readers took it perfectly seriously, a common fate of would-be satirists of detective fiction. Its recipe was repeated many times not only by Mary Roberts Rinehart herself, but by numerous imitators.

The ingredients nearly always include a female protagonist, often the first-person narrator, who is 'plucky' (an appropriately dated adjective), loyal and foolhardy. She has only to be advised to be careful, to be found on the next dark night creeping alone, without having told anyone what she was doing, into danger. If she finds a murder weapon, she naturally assumes that it will incriminate her nearest and dearest, and rather inefficiently hides it (as in *The Episode of the Wandering Knife*, 1949). If she hears footsteps in the attic of a supposedly empty house, she puts on a wrapper and barges in on the baddy. If she suspects that illicit visitors are in her house at night (like the narrator of *The Confession*, 1925), she does not tell the police, but tries to stay awake and keep watch over the bannisters. The complicated plots, on which Mary Roberts Rinehart prided herself, include coincidence and accident, blunders and errors, which mar the logic necessary for a good detective novel. The psychological flaws are more serious; only too often the murderer is the least likely in terms of character as well as clue. These defects, however, have not affected the popularity of such books. Their ability to involve the reader—especially, perhaps, a female reader who can identify with the imperilled heroine—seems to compensate for the failures of logic. None of the characters attracts particular interest or sympathy and each is supremely unmemorable. The books are also very repetitive; one quotation from *The Wall* (1938) is typical of them all:

> It was that evening that I found what turned out to be a clue. It looked small and unimportant then, but I have wondered since how much death and downright agony of soul could have been prevented had we known its secret at the time. It sounds absurd, I know, to say that a brown coat button could have solved our crimes, or prevented two of them. Yet in a way it is true. Had we known who lost it, and why . . .

The books are nearly all set in a stratum of society which the dressmaker's daughter had come to know. The adventures take place in mansions in New England, in brownstone houses in New York, in holiday houses furnished with exotic luxuries;

the gardens have lotus ponds and gazebos, the houses have ballrooms and servants' halls. The characters are the masters and mistresses, and the staff, or the 'help', are faithful and featureless. It is the American version of the English never-never land. But like Christie, Rinehart lived in it herself. Her profits were soon so substantial that she could move her family into a mansion outside Pittsburgh, on a bluff overlooking the river; soon she was forced to go back to town each day to write undisturbed in a dark office because domestic life was so distracting. When their sons left for college, the Rineharts moved to Washington, where Mary became a political hostess. Stanley Rinehart died in 1932, and she then moved to New York, where she lived until her death in 1958 in a large apartment on Park Avenue. She had written successfully for over half a century and through her efforts with her pen become influential in other spheres. She was proud (if surprised) that men in important positions chose her work for their leisure reading. 'I myself have been read by every recent president', she wrote in the year before her death, 'with the exception of Calvin Coolidge, and even he may have had his off moments. I have been scolded by Theodore Roosevelt, praised by Woodrow Wilson, and had a book made overnight for Herbert Hoover, using the galleys to cut and bind.'

Of the many other American writers who specialised in the 'Had I But Known' sphere, Mignon G. Eberhart is perhaps the best known, but none has achieved world-wide fame. Too many readers are irritated by the foolishness of the characters in such books. It is not only the detective who should display some shrewdness, which Wentworth's Maud Silver, and Rinehart's Miss Pinkerton do, but also at least some of the people whose problems they are investigating. Agatha Christie's Miss Jane Marple never dealt with such witless idiots. Nor did Miss Marple become as bland as Maud Silver, whom superficially she closely resembles, even though she did mellow, after her first appearance as an astringent, self-righteous old woman in *Murder at the Vicarage* (1930).

Miss Marple had been born at an advanced age, springing like a goddess, fully armed, from her creator's head. Her personality changed, perhaps smoothed by success, until she became a knowledgeable, observant, lovable old lady, always

knitting fluffy garments for some collateral descendant. She
had followed Maud Silver's first appearance after two years,
but even before Miss Silver, Dorothy L. Sayers had justified
such characters when she presented an assistant to Lord Peter
Wimsey, Miss Alexandra Katherine Climpson, in *Unnatural
Death* (1927):

> 'Miss Climpson,' said Lord Peter, 'is a manifestation of the
> wasteful way this country is run. Look at electricity. Look at water
> power. Look at the tides. Look at the sun. Millions of power units
> being given off into space every minute. Thousands of old maids,
> simply bursting with useful energy, forced by our stupid social
> system into hydros and hotels and hostels and posts as
> companions, where their magnificent gossip powers and units of
> inquisitiveness are allowed to dissipate themselves, or even
> become harmful to the community, while the ratepayers' money is
> spent on getting work for which those women are providentially
> fitted inefficiently carried out by ill-equipped policemen . . . And
> then bright young men write nasty little books called "Elderly
> Women", and "On the Edge of the Explosion", and the
> drunkards make songs upon 'em, poor things.'
>   'You mean that Miss Climpson is a kind of enquiry agent for
> you?'
>   'She is my ears and my tongue,' said Lord Peter dramatically,
> 'and especially my nose. She asks the questions which a young
> man could not put without a blush . . . People want questions
> asked? Whom do they send? A man with large flat feet and a
> notebook . . . I send a lady with a long woolly jumper on knitting
> needles and jingly things round her neck. Of course she asks
> questions. Everybody expects it.'

They expected it of Miss Marple and Miss Silver too.
   The curiosity potential seems to have been assumed only in
single women. Was it because any married woman was
expected to devote her attention to her family? After all,
Agatha Christie's own experience of perceptive, inquisitive old
women was clearly that of her two grandmothers and their old
lady cronies. Like Agatha's grandmother, Miss Marple always
expected the worst of everyone, and was always proved right.
'I've known one or two like him,' the grandmother would say,
predicting dishonesty from some young man. 'I am reminded
so much,' Miss Marple would say, 'of Mrs. Smith's little

housemaid at home in St Mary Mead,' or, elsewhere, of 'the Lauriston's parlourmaid . . .' She would explain that it was a good many years ago, but 'nevertheless, human nature was very much the same then as it is now. Mistakes are made for much the same reasons.' Everything Miss Marple saw reminded her of some event at home in St Mary Mead. Using her experience derived from that quiet life, she drew parallels of stupidity and knavery.

During the thirties it was plausible that these ladies had the time to sit around minding other peoples' business, and that they should be so unremarkable that suspects would betray themselves in front of them. The nosy old spinster was a necessary feature of village life. Another profession which gave its practitioners good opportunities for seeing what was going on was that of the now almost extinct 'private nurse'. Mary Roberts Rinehart and Mignon G. Eberhart had the same idea. Rinehart's nurse was Hilda Adams—nicknamed 'Miss Pinkerton' after the famous private detective agency—who believed that illness followed crime, and that while tending the one, she could solve the other. Nurse Sarah Keate appeared in several of Mignon G. Eberhart's books for the same reason.

Since the thirties other professions have opened to women, which has made it just possible, if not probable, for them to be repeatedly concerned with crime. Some of the modern women sleuths have actually been police officers, or at least, private detectives, but the only female series detective who is still going strong after fifty years is Gladys Mitchell's Mrs Bradley, Consultant Psychiatrist to the Home Office.

Gladys Mitchell has been extremely prolific, publishing books under the names of Malcolm Torrie and Stephen Hockaby, and her fifty-seventh in her own name in 1980. Her first detective novel, *Speedy Death*, came in 1929. Her heroine Mrs (later Dame) Beatrice Lestrange Bradley is the modern equivalent of a witch, and boasts that one of her ancestors was burned at the stake. She was middle-aged when first introduced and is not yet old; she has a distinguished son, who cannot be young himself, having earned a knighthood. Her assistant, Mrs Laura Gavin, who matures rather more than her employer, marries a police officer during the course of the series, and has a son. Laura Gavin does the donkey work while

Dame Beatrice uses her brains and experience, demonstrating an uncanny insight into human behaviour allied to her expertise in Freudian psychology. She is regularly described as 'saurian' or as resembling a lizard, a crocodile or an alligator. Laura addresses her as 'Mrs Croc'. She is benign and omniscient. She is rich enough to have a cook and a chauffeur for her Rolls Royce and important enough for her name to impress provincial policemen.

Gladys Mitchell is a woman of wide interests and many qualifications. She was born in 1901, near Oxford, and went to London University. She then worked for many years as a teacher of English, History and Physical Education. Her own particular interests have been psychology and witchcraft, and both are recurrent subjects in her novels. Her England is not class-ridden and changeless. She has always set her books in places of contemporary interest, like a progressive school at the time when A. S. Neill was scandalising public opinion at Summerhill, and her environments have changed with the times. Perhaps she would have been more popular if she had been more of a snob and less of a realist, for her books have not achieved the massive following of some of her colleagues, although they are all interesting and well written.

None of these elderly lady heroines has been the type of character to attract a fantasising readership. They are all very prosaic, their sense nothing if not common. They are neither glamorous, like most detective heroes, nor magical like, for instance, Poirot. It was only during the 1960s and 1970s that women adventurers began to appear who might fire their readers' imaginations. But even in a liberated era, it is probably true that women can happily fantasise about being men, or being the girlfriend of a superman; they can identify with heroes, and admire them, while few men will ever imagine themselves in the place of a young and pretty female, let alone an aunt-figure. In any case, the most effective detectives are in early middle age, and women's liberation has not yet rendered a grey-haired woman as attractive as a grey-haired man. If women past their first youth are unmarried, they are thought failures; if married, they are supposed to be back home with the kids, not out in the world detecting.

The female characters in detective fiction whom readers

have loved and identified with, have been, not detectives, but detectives' girlfriends.

It was not only women writers who gave their heroes high-powered companions. Michael Innes presented Inspector Appleby with the tough sculptor Judith; Nicholas Blake's Strangeways also lived with a woman sculptor, after the death of his explorer-wife. Agatha Christie must be excluded here, for Hastings' girlfriends, and Mrs Beresford—the female half of the pair known as 'Tommy and Tuppence'—are embarrassingly fatuous. But the painter Agatha Troy, who married Marsh's Roderick Alleyn, and the aircraft designer Amanda Fitton, provided by Margery Allingham for Albert Campion, are both attractive, while many would say that Harriet Vane is quite as interesting a character as Wimsey himself.

The feminist appeal of able women should not be under-estimated. Peter Wimsey was not expressing merely a peculiar yearning of his peculiar inventor when he thought, 'It would be great fun' to have a wife who wrote books, 'So much more interesting than the ordinary kind that is only keen on clothes and people.'

Of course there must be a good deal of straight wish-fulfilment when a full-time woman writer has the professional women in her books treated with a deference, with an acceptance of the objective value of their work, which can rarely be quite part of her own everyday life. Inspector Alleyn did not wince when introduced as his wife's husband; Amanda Campion's work took precedence over housekeeping and Peter Wimsey was emphatic that Harriet's writing was not to be interupted by domestic trivia. All their authors must sometimes have wished for a similar consideration; Dorothy Sayers for one must have resented the ancillary role her husband expected her to play in the home. Yet professionally she regarded gender as irrelevant. 'I am occasionally desired by congenital imbeciles and the editors of magazines to say something about the writing of detective fiction "from the woman's point of view",' she said in *Unpopular Opinions*. 'To such demands one can only say, "Go away and don't be silly. You might as well ask what is the female angle on an equilateral triangle." '

I wonder whether Sayers would have said the same today,

after a period of uncensored publishing of novels which have, in their explicitness about violence, perversion and obscenity, surely been unprecedented in publishing history. It is immediately apparent to a contemporary reviewer of crime fiction that there *is* a difference between the male and the female angle. At the centre, in this as in everything, the distinction is blurred. Many men offer reflective mysteries, a few women—a very few women—write violent thrillers. But even when Sayers was writing, there was a discernible qualitative difference between mysteries written by male and female writers. Raymond Chandler thought it was because women are more patient and observant. It must be in that difference, indefinable as it is, that the quality which ensures survival lies. It is not in the blatant femininity of such books as the Had-I-But-Known type, for the foolish virgins around whom those dramas revolve rapidly become uninteresting. They are obviously going to grow into the pathetic middle-aged women who are also stock figures in that kind of fiction, the clinging mother, the ailing wife, the disaster-prone widow.

The characters of the detectives' wives are much more memorable, yet, unwilling as a feminist may be to admit it, less realistic. They are all too perfect; they fulfil the traditional roles of women, achieving their success without sacrificing their femininity, and they never resent the difficulties their double roles entail. And they are all so successful. Harriet is sufficiently well known as a writer for her every action to be noticed by intrusive reporters; Agatha Troy's paintings hang in the place of honour in millionaires' houses, and the fact that the millionaire has had the good taste to acquire them is often used as a clue to his character. Even Nicholas Blake's Georgia is one of the three most famous explorers in the world. Next, one observes how little these women's work interferes with their domestic commitments. Troy is an attentive and devoted mother. Amanda sits embroidering the word 'Sheriff' in large letters on her small son's shirt when the action opens in *Tiger in the Smoke*. Even Harriet becomes domesticated; she is found sewing for her three sons at the opening of the story called *Tallboys*. It is as though the authors were anxious to show that their characters are quite ordinary, even if brilliant. (There is a fascinating contrast here with the heroines of the inter-war straight novels by women for whom careers are incompatible with love and sex. For instance, in *Dusty Answer* by Rosamund Lehmann, Judith is baffled by the combination of her own talents and her personal life; and in *A House in Paris* by Elizabeth Bowen an unsuccessful female painter chooses passion, and later domesticity, rather than her profession. *Four Frightened People* by E. Arnot Robertson and *South Riding* by Winifred Holtby are among countless other possible examples.)

There is a certain artificiality in the choice of professions for the heroines which implies that a completely independent woman, one whose work would really not leave her time for sewing, would not have been attractive to these authors. After all, they had been educated as members of The Second Sex. In the character of Val Ferris, Campion's sister, Margery Allingham was perhaps expressing her own desires and her own difficulties. Val is a famous dress designer who is in love with Amanda's boss, Alan Dell; during the course of *The Fashion in Shrouds*, Dell has a brief affair with another woman. I quote the whole of Val's speech, because it is an interesting and rare representation of what a clever, sexy woman thought in 1938; it rings very true:

> I envy those women who just love normally and nobly with their bodies . . . then they're only engulfed by a sort of lovely high tragedy. The hero persists. That's at least decent. Once you cultivate your mind you lay youself open to low tragedy, the mingy, dirty little tragedy of making an ass of yourself over an ordinary poor little bloke. Female women love so abjectly that a reasonable hard-working mind becomes a responsibility. It's a cruelty that shouldn't have to be endured. I tell you I'd rather die than have to face it that he was neither better nor even more intelligent than I am.

In the end Val finds happiness by surrendering her career to marry her cleverer man. She is referred to in later books, but does not reappear. It was not so easy to deal with the running hero's running heroine.

'A good detective never gets married,' Raymond Chandler said; he would presumably not have meant that matrimony prevents a detective from being good. It was the getting married which interfered, in his view, with the drive of detective novels, and the courtship, the intrusion into the plot of irrelevant sexual and emotional distractions. (Yet he told Ian Fleming that in the last book he started to write, just before he died, he was going to have Marlowe marry a French Countess—quoted in Newquist, *Counterpoint*.) The famous, indeed immortal, detectives who are good husbands have wives who are dimly seen as part of their complete equipment: Maigret, Sergeant Cuff, the humdrum husbands of the Golden Age novel, all return to domestic comforts, to well-cooked meals and warmed slippers, to an occasional shrewd suggestion from their helpmeets. Such wives are part of the serious detective novel's furniture. They attract neither interest nor attention.

It is when the detective's work is distracted by a female that the critics disapprove, and that the reading public rejoice. Raymond Chandler's view was that 'love interest nearly always weakens a mystery because it introduces a type of suspense that is antagonistic to the detective's struggle to solve the problem.' But publishers and readers demanded love interest, and only gradually, during the thirties, learnt to dispense with it. For a long time it was essential for a happy young couple to be united by the last page, and by many writers the convention was satisfied in a most perfunctory way, with secondary characters whose roles as lovers were evident from the moment of their introduction and who seemed to have little other function in the story. Austin Freeman was one writer who included a pair of young lovers—that most boring of theatrical and literary formulae—without interfering with the process of crime and detection at all; Ngaio Marsh still includes such a pair in most of her books, now that Alleyn and Troy are long since superannuated in the role.

It is far more satisfactory when the love story is a necessary part of the whole plot, and Wilkie Collins showed very early on how this was possible. He was one of the very few Victorian novelists who could portray sensible women with any kind of conviction. *The Woman in White* has a heroine whose initiative and drive make her seem like a different species from the usual dismal girl of the period. In *The Moonstone*, the love of Rachel Verinder and Rosanna Spearman for the same man, Franklin

Blake, is the pivot of the whole plot; for both knew that he had taken the diamond, and both were determined to conceal the knowledge. E. C. Bentley, too, made Trent's love for Mrs Manderson an integral and necessary part of his plot in *Trent's Last Case*. Dorothy L. Sayers was much influenced by this, as well as other aspects of the book; she felt it gave a lead in the right direction, towards a more profound treatment of the emotions in detective novels. She did eventually try herself to combine passionate love and detective fever, but when she first produced Harriet, just as when Marsh and Allingham first invented Troy and Amanda, true love, or at least, permanent love, was far from her mind.

At first the heroes were fancy free, or at least flitting, like Albert Campion, who fancied a different girl in each of his first few adventures. The trouble is that a series hero who is allowed to mature in other ways must either prove to be a selfish bastard, who really does play the sexual and emotional field, like, for instance, James Bond; or eventually, he must fix his affection on one particular girl and sooner or later marry her. Only Agatha Christie avoided this problem because Poirot was never marriageable in the first place; so Christie never needed to change her initial opinion, that the love interest was 'a terrible bore in detective stories. Love, I felt, belonged to romantic stories. To force a love motif into what should be a scientific process went much against the grain.'

But Sayers, Marsh and Allingham never saw themselves as conducting scientific processes; their characters grew to need wives. Josephine Tey's Alan Grant was attracted by different witnesses and suspects in successive books, but he did not go on for long enough for her to face the real problem—that of making what was an acceptable detachment in a young man, something less than an uncomfortable coldness of heart in an older one.

Certainly all these writers believed at first that 'a detective married was a detective marred' as Sayers put it. Alleyn and Wimsey conducted their early cases uninvolved, and the Joyces and Biddies whom Campion lost to more dynamic lovers represented little more than perfunctory flirtations.

'Of all the hazards which threaten the detective of fiction, I doubt if there is one more likely to be lethal than matrimony.

Taking a wife is a serious step for any man, but for him it can
be lethal,' Allingham remarked, and Marsh said that her agent
and publishers were deeply dismayed when Troy finally
accepted Roderick Alleyn. It had taken Alleyn several books,
but we do not hear much about his courtship. Peter's wooing of
Harriet is even more prolonged, and as for Albert Campion,
the only way that Margery Allingham could find to make him
overcome his inhibitions about asking Amanda to marry him
was to have him concussed throughout a whole book; in
Traitor's Purse he went around punch drunk for seventeen
chapters.

All these heroes are supremely gentlemanly, the very
opposite of that other figure of female fantasy, the sheik who
sweeps his girls off willy nilly on a charger. It is natural for a
busy career woman to hesitate about marriage, for many
reasons, but the detective heroines did so for an inordinately
long time and their lovers show phenomenal self-restraint. The
girls are chaste too—or uninterested. Yet once married they
are happy. It is all very strange.

Troy and Amanda take the place of the detective's stooge,
both before and after marriage; Amanda even calls herself
Campion's lieutenant. She had first met him when she was still
a schoolgirl and surprised him, seven years later, by
reappearing in his life as a beautiful and elegant woman. She is
small, thin, with red curls, toffee-coloured eyes and a
triangular smile. Her most attractive quality is an inspired
common sense, and the practicality proper for a highly
qualified engineer. Troy Alleyn is practical too, but plays a less
active part in Alleyn's detection. He meets her first on a sea
voyage from the South Pacific back to Britain:

> She stood for a moment staring back towards Fiji. Her hands
> gripped the shoulder straps of her paint box. The light breeze
> whipped back her short dark hair, revealing the contour of the
> skull and the delicate bones of the face. The temples were slightly
> hollow, the cheek bones showed, the dark blue eyes were deep set
> under the thin ridge of the brows. The sun caught the olive skin
> with its smudge of green paint and gave it warmth. There was a
> kind of spare gallantry about her.

The expression 'spare gallantry' often reappears, just as the comparison of Alleyn to a monk or a grandee does. Marsh was painting word pictures, but they are not easy for the reader to interpret, and this reader at least has never understood what 'spare gallantry' can be. However, it was something which made Alleyn fall instantly in love. He spends the rest of the book (*Artists in Crime*) solving a murder case at Troy's studio in England, and it ends with Troy admitting that she nearly loves him. 'Then,' said Alleyn, 'I shall allow myself to hope a little.' His hopes are realised and Troy grows old along with Roderick. But in the end, she and Amanda Campion are only ancillary characters. Neither takes the leading part in any book, though each is from time to time the spur to action, providing plausible reasons for her husband to be involved in matters not quite within his normal sphere. For instance, it is a holiday in the South of France with his family which takes Alleyn into the action in *Spinsters in Jeopardy*; it is Amanda who urges Campion on in *The Fashion in Shrouds*. Each eventually has one son, and Ricky Alleyn and Rupert Campion make brief appearances too. Amanda Campion and Troy Alleyn are agreeable and civilised women, and probably exactly what not only their authors, but also their female readers, wished to be.

Harriet Vane, on the other hand, by far the most fully realised of the three, is, in externals at least, an idealised self-portrait of her author, not so much of what she wished to be, as what she rather thought she was. Harriet differs in two major particulars from Dorothy, in precisely the two features of her life which Dorothy might have wished were different. Harriet was not married to a husband about whom she had to be forbearing and who demanded domestic attentions while grudging her success; Harriet was physically attractive.

Dorothy Sayers gave Harriet new attributes, not the wealth and status with which she endowed Wimsey, but an emotional life which Dorothy herself was without, of which, indeed, she was really incapable. She gave Harriet an impulsive heart and an abililty to surrender to her emotions. She was intended to be the antithesis of Peter, who could 'enjoy practically everything that comes along—while it's happening. Only I have to keep on doing things, because if I once stop, it all seems a lot of rot.'

Harriet's personality is not fully developed or exposed until

Gaudy Night, but several books before that her life style has been described. It is full of revealing details about Dorothy's own (or what Dorothy would like her own to be). Harriet lived the life of an independent woman; her flat, like Dorothy's own first one, was in Mecklenburgh Square; she had a secretary; her social life is in the inter-war equivalent of bed-sitter land. She is used to voice Dorothy's own thoughts; for instance, it is amusing to read (in *Gaudy Night*) the account of a crime novelist's plight when confronted by a meticulous reader. Harriet is being complimented by a don at Shrewsbury College:

> 'Do let me say how much I enjoyed your last book. I thought it quite the best thing you'd done—though of course I'm not competent to form an opinion from the scientific point of view. I was discussing it with Professor Higgins, who is quite a devotee of yours, and he said it suggested a most interesting possibility which had not before occurred to him. He wasn't quite sure whether it would work, but he would do his best to find out. Tell me, what did you have to go upon?'
>
> 'Well, I got a pretty good opinion,' said Harriet, feeling a hideous qualm of uncertainty, and cursing Professor Higgins from the bottom of her heart . . .

This is a common experience of mystery writers. Michael Innes describes it also, in *Hamlet, Revenge!* (1937), when his Giles Gott (a don who writes crime novels pseudonymously) is identified to Professor Malloch: ' "In *Death at the Zoo*, now," ' Professor Malloch observes, "I readily believe that the creature could be trained to fire the fatal shot. But the training of it by means of the series of sugar revolvers to swallow the real revolver? I asked Morgenthaler—you know his Intelligence in the Higher Mammalia?—and he seemed to think . . ." '

As Sayers, Marsh and their colleagues often remarked, scrupulous research is necessary for successful mystery writing.

Of Harriet Vane's characteristics, perhaps the most unusual and attractive to readers in the thirties was her personal self-sufficiency. She felt no modest hesitation about dining alone in a restaurant or going alone on a walking tour. She lived as a successful professional woman ideally should and the housewives and shopgirls who were said to be the typical library subscribers of the period must have been interested if not envious. But most enviable of all was her effect on Peter Wimsey. He fell in love with her at that unpropitious first sight when she was in the dock at the Old Bailey, and like Perseus, like St George, like a knight of the Round Table, rescued her from her peril and sued for her hand in marriage as a reward. Harriet is another part of that legend personified. At the same time she plays the leading female role in a modern replay of a different fairy story, for she is also the Cinderella figure.

Peter Wimsey, who has everything, falls in love with a victim in extremis—a woman who is no longer young, was never rich or beautiful, but despised, imprisoned and rejected. Even when she appears with her freedom restored in later books, she still bears what was a stigma in her day, the reputation of being an unchaste woman, for her unmarried cohabitation with her first lover has been blazoned over every scandal sheet at the time of her trial. She had lived out of wedlock, and not even remained faithful to her lover—and was still considered marriageable by a Duke's brother. The readers of Dorothy L. Sayers' novels could not have known how personally she must have enjoyed inventing that public triumph.

It is, after all, not even as though Harriet is pretty. Clever, undoubtedly, but cleverness in a woman, as Dorothy Sayers must painfully have learnt, is often regarded as ludicrous rather than admirable. Harriet has a sallow skin, which Peter Wimsey thinks is like honey; she has a long throat, with 'a kind of arum lily quality'. As a schoolgirl, Dorothy was nicknamed 'Swanny' on account of her long neck, but later she was once described as having a head apparently joined to her body without the intervention of a neck. Fat had intervened. Harriet's voice was deep and musical—like Dorothy, she sang in the Bach choir. Her hair was dark, and Wimsey tells her to dress in claret colour. The best a man not in love with her can say is that she was 'almost handsome when she was excited'.

And yet the perfect gentleman-hero falls in love with her at first sight, courts her for five years, and once they are married installs her in an eighteenth-century house in Mayfair. Ten servants are engaged without Harriet herself having to bother about it; Peter makes a huge settlement of inalienable wealth upon her, and she is married in cloth of gold and sables. It was every girl's dream.

Part Two

Introduction

W. H. Auden wrote in the foreword to his anthology *A Certain World*:

> Biographies of writers whether written by others or themselves, are always superfluous and usually in bad taste. A writer is a maker, not a man of action. To be sure, some, in a sense all, of his works are transmutations of his personal experience but no knowledge of the raw ingredients will explain the peculiar flavour of the verbal dishes he invites the public to taste: his private life is, or should be, of no concern to anybody except himself, his family and his friends.

Other writers have made similar statements. They are more true, if true at all, when applied to great writers. It really does not matter how little posterity knows of Shakespeare's private life, and there are many writers whose work offers far more pleasure to those who do not know the depressing details of the author's own career; an uncomplicated delight in works of the imagination has often been sullied by discovering how different, and how inferior, an author's behaviour was to his invention. But I think that Auden was wrong about writers whose work is, intentionally or not, second class. Writers who never thought that their work was literature, but who found exactly the right images and tone to appeal to a vast readership which wanted temporary enthralment, seem to have been successful because, with engaging lack of self-consciousness, they put enough of their own fantasies onto the page. It does actually add to the enjoyment of Ian Fleming's thrillers to know something about his own life; it does give an extra dimension to Richard Hannay's adventures to compare them with John Buchan's own remarkable career.

The James Bond Fan Clubs, which existed (perhaps still exist) all over Britain, America and the Commonwealth, were a strange phenomenon. They institutionalised the passion of the type of reader who previously followed The Toff, The Saint, Norman Conquest, Biggles, and other desperadoes too numerous to list. But James Bond was the first also to appeal to more solemn readers, who chose to take him as representative of the Zeitgeist, and who were not ashamed of what they read. Bond has attracted the attention of probably more critics and theorists than any other 'light' fictional character. His influence was considerable; the lists of his belongings and tastes functioned as effective advertisements,even if Fleming simply intended his use of brand names to add verisimilitude. It was even said that Bond had an influence on social and industrial affairs. Security guards used his status as evidence in their demands for a pay rise, and officers in the Salvation Army complained that Bond's promiscuous women and lack of scruples about assassination were a bad influence on the young—not to mention the threat to road safety constituted by his reckless driving. Bond's masochism, his glamorous life style and his self-reliance, at a time when individualism was beginning to seem muffled by states or corporations, were attractive to a vast readership. The life story of Ian Fleming shows that Bond fulfilled his author's fantasy-wishes very closely, at least in his earlier adventures before commercial pressures had altered his original conception. There was no cynical gauging of what the market required in those first books, but the expression of exactly what the author needed to write; his imagination was in step with the reading public's, and his experience such as to fit him to satisfy it. As Dennis Wheatley said, 'Some authors are more fortunate than others. It is not education alone that counts, but also class. Many thriller writers make the most awful boobs about social behaviour. They have never been into a West End Club or stayed for weekends at big country houses. That is why authors like Ian Fleming and John Buchan had an enormous pull.'

John Buchan, too, wrote what he needed to write. The fact that he claimed to be supplying what his readers wanted makes this more, not less, interesting. He provided for the readers' vicarious enjoyment, bloodshed, bravery, action and independence. He gave himself the satisfaction of fantasising a life he never achieved, for he had two distinctly polarised ambitions and could achieve only one, though in that he was much more successful than would have been plausible for a fictional character. He was born the son of a poor Calvinist minister in rural Scotland; he had a public career as lawyer, Member of Parliament, publisher, politician and statesman, and he ended up Lord Tweedsmuir, the Governor General of Canada. His family life was happy and his friends included Heads of State; yet throughout his life he felt 'how thin is the protection of civilisation'. Those words he put into the mind of his character, Sir Edward Leithen, who appears in Buchan's last novel, *Sick Heart River*. It is as though he were Buchan himself towards the end of his life, a powerful public figure, driven by suppressed fears and uncertainties. Buchan's earlier hero, Richard Hannay, is a less complicated man but, like Buchan himself, he is the outsider accepted into ruling inner circles, always aware 'that anything might happen'. The conflict between the insider and the outsider, the dreamer and the practical man, the intellectual and the man of action, in Buchan himself, illumines, and is illumined by, the novels he wrote.

There have been many books in recent years, both scholarly and frivolous, about such adventure stories. Critics are torn between embarrassment at the enduring popularity of what they know should be thought deplorable, and their fascination with works that shaped their own lifelong imaginations. For while it is true, as Buchan himself said, that 'Age is apt to react against what ravished youth', it is also true that our minds are formed by what we have read in our early years.

Why certain fictional characters inhabit a reader's imagination can only be explained subjectively. Where a book is bad by accepted literary standards, the only place to find the reason for its influence is in the personality of the enthusiast. However, where the collective enthusiasm of a large number of readers is aroused, it is fair to deduce that the personality of the writer echoes, and his work expounds, a more than individual passion. It is for this reason that so much has been published about the lives of such writers as Buchan and Fleming, Charteris, Edgar Wallace, Sapper, Dornford Yates and others;

and it is for this reason that it seems interesting now to consider the life stories of women whose more cerebral work appealed to so many people.

The following biographical chapters will show that the five women whose books have been especially lasting had many qualities, of background, life style and even personality, in common. Obviously the events they narrated were not in themselves desirable; there is no wish fulfilment in the action. But I believe that their experiences tended to induce in them similar assumptions: that stability was desirable, and when threatened, should be restored; that reason should prevail over violence; that the customs of a secure and unthreatened class had an intrinsic merit. I think that the ethos they expressed in fictional form was acquired during and from their own lives, and was equally attractive and admirable to readers less able to express it.

5 Agatha Christie

Agatha Christie's first book was published in 1920. Its author was thirty years old, and regarded the concoction of a detective story as on the same moderately creative level as embroidering cushion covers. Her older sister had published some short stories, but in their circle women did not have professions, only hobbies. Even men worked only if they were obliged to do so. Agatha Christie's father had an inherited income and never worked at all.

In Agatha Christie's memory, the years before World War I were full of peace and content. She rarely wrote about children in fiction, but she remembered her own childhood vividly, and in her autobiography depicted an unclouded world in which children bowled hoops, young men 'popped the question' at dances, and girls attended house parties and arranged flowers. It is a charming picture to nostalgic eyes, and probably an accurate one, not of life as it always was, but as Agatha Christie perceived it, unmarred by social or political strife. If her family had been richer, they would have owned an estate in the country, and been aware of, and probably undertaken, the responsibilities of the upper classes to the 'deserving poor'. If they had been less prosperous, the real fears and discomforts of life without a welfare state would have been only too apparent. In Agatha's home, political rumblings, even of the movement for women's suffrage, seem to have been ignored.

Agatha Christie begins her autobiography by remarking that one of the luckiest things in life is to have had a happy childhood, as she had. Agatha Mary Clarissa Miller was born in 1890, the daughter of a devoted couple. Her mother, Clara Boehmer, had been sent as a girl to live with her maternal aunt, with whose American stepson she fell in love when she was eleven. Frederick Alvah Miller was ten years older, and passed some cheerful years in the United States flirting with, among many other girls, Jennie Jerome (later Lady Randolph Churchill). But he returned to marry Clara, and they settled in a house which Agatha was always to think of as home: Ashfield, a villa with slatted shutters and a conservatory on the outskirts of the South Devon resort of Torquay, which Walter Savage Landor had said was 'full of fat, ugly houses, and rich, hot looking people'.

Agatha was the youngest by several years of three children and spent much of her time without other children to play or quarrel with. Her companions were adults—her parents, a devoted old nurse and the servants, who, to a child, were 'the most colourful part of daily life', supplying drama, entertainment and various useful titbits of information. More on her level were the dog and a pet canary, but most pleasing of all to a shy girl who was thought to be the 'slow one' of the family was a large cast of invented playmates, the traditional solace of the solitary child. 'Celia was what is called a "good child",' she wrote in the autobiographical novel called *Unfinished Portrait*, 'meaning that she kept very quiet, was happy playing by herself, and did not importune her elders to amuse her . . . Celia seldom asked questions. Most of her world was inside her head. The outside world did not excite her curiosity.' Agatha's imaginary friends were typical of the breed—kittens, animated rocking horses, dolls, a personalised hoop—and to them Agatha spoke aloud, in the same way that in later years she would rehearse the conversations she was about to write, so that her husband would hear her voice when he came into the house, and wonder who had come to visit them. With other people she was thought to be—and remained—shy and inarticulate.

The Miller's eldest child went to a boarding school in Brighton, later to be called Roedean, where she did very well and was encouraged to go on to Girton College, Cambridge. However, Fred Miller did not want his daughter turned into a bluestocking, and she was 'finished' in Paris instead. The son, Monty, went to Harrow.

By the time that Agatha was born, Clara Miller had completely altered her views both on religion and on education.

Having flirted with other religions she had returned to the Church of England, of which she, and Agatha, remained devout and lifelong members; Clara Miller, and later Agatha also, always slept with *The Imitation of Christ* on their bedside tables. As for education, Agatha's was completely informal.

Mrs Miller had changed from being a passionate advocate of girls' education to being an opponent of it, either on principle, or perhaps because she wanted to keep this youngest child at home with her. Agatha's contemporary, Gwen Raverat, explained in *A Cambridge Childhood*: 'The upper classes did not approve of day schools, though boarding schools for older girls might sometimes be allowed. The Aristocracy however did not even hold with boarding schools . . .'

Years later, Agatha was to write approvingly of the small Arab and Kurdish children she saw driving their cows in the Middle East:

> They are dressed in incredible rags, their teeth gleam white as they smile. I think to myself how happy they look, and what a pleasant life it is; like the fairy stories of old, wandering about over the hills herding the cattle, sometimes sitting and singing. At this time of day, the so-called fortunate children in European lands are setting out for the crowded classroom, going in out of the soft air, sitting on benches or at desks, toiling over letters of the alphabet, listening to a teacher, writing with cramped fingers . . .

Agatha Christie never felt that she had been deprived of an advantage; indeed, she regarded schooling as the cause of so many children's inability to amuse themselves in the holidays. But her own daughter later insisted on being sent to the largest boarding school possible.

Agatha acquired all the accomplishments suitable for a young lady: she read indiscriminately; she did arithmetic with her father and loved it—she was to enjoy anything to do with numbers for the rest of her life; the piano was taught by a German Fräulein; and dancing class took place weekly. French, later to be perfected at finishing school in Paris, was begun early when the Millers were forced to economise; they spent several months at Pau, in south-west France, and returned to Torquay with a French 'bonne' as a companion for

Agatha. It was a peaceful life for a child, leaving plenty of time to stand and stare. Agatha always appreciated the lack of stress and deplored the eagerness of modern women to load themselves with all kinds of work, leaving the male less burdened. Fred and Clara Miller had a staff of efficient and unresentful servants, a house and garden of manageable size, and no estate responsibilities; neither had a profession, and Agatha Christie does not mention any charitable work done by her mother or father. How did they fill in their time?

Agatha Christie remembered her father as a man whose outstanding quality was of being agreeable, something which, as she rightly pointed out, tends to be underrated nowadays. Cleverness, industry and wit would have been superfluous in the life he led. His wife was cleverer than he, with a quick intelligence and, according to her daughter, powers of perception amounting to second sight. They were happy together until Frederick Miller died, when Agatha was eleven. He had been in failing health and his financial affairs were in trouble. He was trying to find some job suitable for an unqualified and inexperienced middle-aged man when he caught double pneumonia, which proved fatal.

After her father's death Agatha learnt to worry. The family did not move away from Ashfield, but Monty was in India with his regiment, and her sister Madge married shortly after her father's death, so that Agatha was left with her mother in the large house, without the person from whom the stability of the home had derived. Clara Miller had what she called 'heart attacks' after Fred died and Agatha used to listen at her mother's door in the night to make sure that she was still breathing. There was no money for entertaining any more, the number of servants was cut down, and the standard of food deteriorated.

Madge, now Mrs Watts, produced a son to whom his young aunt became very attached and for whom she felt responsible, as she did for her mother. They lived a quiet and rather lonely life, with occasional visits to Agatha's grandmother in Ealing and to Madge Watts in Cheshire. In her middle teens, Agatha spent two days a week for four terms at a day school in Torquay, and learnt enough arithmetic and algebra to realise that she would have chosen to be a mathematician if she had been able to finish her formal education. Then, at fifteen, she was parted from her mother for the first time. She attended a *pensionnat* in Paris, and after initial homesickness was very happy there. She was a good pianist, but the very idea of performing in public made her ill. The next year, at a finishing school, she studied singing and piano, but was obliged to accept that she had not the temperament to become a professional musician. She remained shy throughout her long life and always experienced the same incapacitating physical reaction at the prospect of public performance. At the age of seventy-two, when she was a world-famous author, expected to make a speech at the celebrations for the tenth anniversary of her play, *The Mousetrap*, she arrived at the Savoy Hotel saying to herself, 'This is Agatha pretending to be a successful author, having to look as though she is someone, having to make a speech that she can't make, having to be something that she's no good at.' But that was a rare event in a career which had enabled her to work, as she infinitely preferred, in private.

Perhaps the first experience of competition in nursery or classroom came too late, at the age of fourteen, to allow Agatha to acquire that self-confidence which is usually displayed by any family's cherished and indulged baby. For there was evidently no objective reason for her embarrassment: she was clever and musically talented, and she was very pretty, tall, with red hair, grey eyes, regular features and a fair complexion, and a figure which the vagaries of taste had not yet rendered unfashionable. In her twenties she would be described as well-built, and by the time she was middle-aged she was, to her mortification, classed as outsize; but she found good food hard to resist, and her favourite drink, since she never learnt to like any alcohol, was double cream.

The discovery that concert performances were not for her was distressing for a while, but Agatha had the enviable knack of finding pleasure and interest in anything which came her way. She was not, in any case, the sort of girl who expected any career other than marriage, and always believed that a bride should accept as her destiny her husband's place in the world and way of life. This philosophy, shared by most of her contemporaries, made it very exciting to be a girl, whose future would depend on the accident of whom she would marry.

Agatha was not a debutante in London, or, like her sister, in New York. Instead she was taken to spend the winter, and 'come out', in Egypt (then under British rule) where her mother was to convalesce from an undiagnosed illness. Several regiments were stationed in Cairo and Agatha made friends with their subalterns at polo matches, balls and picnics. She was very happy, enjoying the company of young men and the excitement of her first grown-up clothes—and what clothes, all frills and flowers. Agatha did not object to their inconvenience, for conformity came easily to her in everything, but such acceptance was not universal in her generation. Two of her contemporaries later wrote with some bitterness about the wardrobes of their youth: 'I am seized with angry resentment against the conventions which wrapped up my comely adolescent body in woollen combinations, black cashmere stockings, "liberty bodice", dark stockinette knickers, flannelette petticoat, and often, in addition, a long sleeved, high necked, knitted woollen spencer', Vera Brittain said twenty years later; and Gwen Raverat wrote: 'It fairly makes my heart bleed to see photograph after photograph of ourselves as children, playing in the garden in high summer, always in thick black woolly stockings and high boots . . .' and, as a grown-up, she said, 'The thought of the discomfort, restraint and pain which we had to endure from our clothes makes me even angrier now than it did then; for in those days nearly everyone accepted their inconvenience as inevitable.'

Agatha was far too busy flirting to fall in love, although she collected scalps, as it was called, and received several proposals of marriage. Back in England, now that she was 'out', Agatha was invited to dances and weekend parties. Many of her books, written between the wars, are set in houseparties at which there would be a miscellaneous collection of people, invited together for no apparent reason except to fill in their own and their hosts' time. Agatha's accounts of attending such parties herself make it clear that she did not later invent these gruesome festivities: the horseplay, practical jokes, and the hustling hostesses really did exist. 'Hostesses looked after the girls carefully,' Agatha explained. She did not add the Edwardian lady's reason for this kindness: 'Always be polite to unmarried girls; you never know whom they may marry.'

Agatha had many opportunities to marry during the next few years. Several men lost their hearts to her, she lost hers to others. Once she became formally engaged and settled down to wait for her fiancé, an army officer, to be posted home. But while she was waiting she met Archibald Christie. He too was in the army, waiting for his transfer into the Royal Flying Corps. He was brave, adventurous, handsome and self-centred, unlike anyone Agatha had ever known, and in every way unlike herself. He was neither imaginative, nor interested in other peoples' imaginations; he was undemonstrative and hated other people to gush; he shied away from emotional displays, and even from emotion. Becoming engaged to Archie was the first thing Agatha ever did which was not to her mother's liking. Throughout her adolescence she seems to have conformed willingly to everything expected of her, and to have questioned none of society's rules. She was unaffected by, and perhaps even unconscious of, any issues other than those encountered in daily life. Perhaps she was waiting for the space in her thoughts to be filled by the man she married.

The world impinged enough for Agatha and other young ladies of Torquay to attend First Aid and Home Nursing classes in 1913, but to her, and to everybody like her, war, until it was actually declared, was unthinkable.

Writing her memoirs, half a century later, Agatha had little to say about the horror of that war. She mentions in passing young men who died in it, and of course it changed what had been the predictable course of her own life, but she refers to the events of the time with a lack of emotion which is startling when compared with the memories of her contemporaries.

Agatha worked as a ward maid, and then as a nurse, and found that she enjoyed nursing and was good at it. When Archie came on leave for the first Christmas of the war, he and Agatha married, suddenly and privately, and told their families afterwards. He returned to battle; Agatha began to work in the hospital's dispensary; her grandmother came to live at Ashfield. There were food shortages, but in Torquay they seemed to be ignorant of the horrors of war on the other side of the Channel. As Vera Brittain, who had been in France herself, bitterly recounted in *Testament of Youth*: 'From a world in which life or death, victory or defeat, national survival or national extinction, had been the sole issues, I returned to a society where nobody discussed anything but the price of butter, and the incompetence of the latest 'temporary' . . . the triviality of everything drove me to despair.'

It was while Agatha was working in the dispensary at Torquay Hospital that she began to write a detective story. Years before, Madge had bet her that she could not do it. She had by this time written various short stories and many poems, as she was to do throughout her life, and a novel which was sent to a literary agent on the advice of the local literary lion, Eden Phillpotts. The agent had refused to handle it. She also wrote verses with great facility. Her idea in writing was merely to fill the idle moments while she was in the dispensary, and she wrote about what she knew: the country, an upper-middle-class family, a detective, derived from her acquaintance with a group of Belgian refugees living in her parish, a hospital dispensary.

Agatha spent some time playing with her ideas, and wrote her book in longhand and then copied it on Madge's old typewriter. She finished it while she was on holiday on Dartmoor and called it *The Mysterious Affair at Styles*. She sent it to three publishers in succession, who all rejected it, and then to John Lane at the Bodley Head, who sat on it until Agatha virtually forgot its existence. For by that time she was busy thinking about her own life.

Archie had come back to England, unscathed, and was posted to the War Office in London. The Christies established their first home in a flat in St John's Wood. In 1919 their daughter Rosalind was born, Archie was demobilised and found a job in the City, and the family moved to a flat in West Kensington. Setting up home at that time, the young couple had fewer material expectations than they would have had nowadays; they never dreamt of having a car, let alone a house with a garden, but a nurse for the baby and a general servant in residence were considered essential. In these minutiae of everyday life, women's autobiographies are always more informative than men's, and it is clear that in her first novels Agatha was writing about life exactly as it was for people in her station in life. The domestic details which loomed so large in her actual life are the very stuff that detective plots are made of.

While Agatha was preoccupied with choosing flower-patterned wallpapers and animal friezes for the nursery, John Lane offered to publish *The Mysterious Affair at Styles*; he gave a contract which only a new author would have thought adequate, but Agatha and Archie were delighted and celebrated that evening at the Hammersmith Palais de Dance. As she wrote, 'Though I did not know it, Hercule Poirot, my Belgian invention, was hanging round my neck, firmly attached there like the old man of the sea.'

Christie became very bored with Poirot herself but, perhaps because of his impersonality, rather than in spite of it, he became so popular that market forces forbade her to abandon him, much though she regretted the mannerisms she had invented. One of the figures who appears in her later books is Mrs Ariadne Oliver, a crime writer with many of Christie's own traits (she is even described as the author of *The Body in the Library*—a Christie title), including the annoying fact that she was saddled with a tiresome foreign detective. She is asked why her hero, Sven Hjerson, is a vegetarian:

'How do I know?' said Mrs Oliver crossly. 'How do I know why I ever thought of the revolting man? I must have been mad. Why a Finn when I know nothing about Finland? Why all the idiotic mannerisms he's got? These things just happen. You try something —and people seem to like it—and then you go on—and before you know where you are you've got someone like that maddening Sven Hjerson tied to you for life. And people even write and say how fond you must be of him. Fond of him? If I met that bony, gangling, vegetable eating Finn in real life, I'd do a better murder than any I've invented.' (From *Mrs McGinty's Dead*, 1952.)

In *Death in the Clouds*, written as early as 1935, a crime writer says of his detective:

The public have taken very strongly to Wilbraham Rice. He bites his nails and eats a lot of bananas. I don't know why I made him bite his nails to start with—it's really rather disgusting—but there it is. He started by biting his nails and now he has to do it in every single book. So monotonous. The bananas aren't so bad; you get a bit of fun out of them—criminals slipping on the skin. I eat bananas myself—that's what put it in my head. But I don't bite my nails.

Agatha Christie's second book, *The Secret Adversary* (1922), features a pair of detectives, Tommy and Tuppence Beresford, who have slightly more expanded personalities, and were to reappear in middle age and, in 1973, as an elderly couple retired to—where else?—a country village with all the Christie trimmings. They feature in novels which are less routine detection than Poirot's, more action thrillers. The form was not suited to Christie's deductive talents; John Lane published the book, but reluctantly. With her third book Agatha returned to Poirot, and he featured again in thirteen stories written for *The Sketch* in 1933, when Christie was already being described as 'the great detective story writer'. In a series of publicity photographs printed in *The Sketch* at the time Agatha is shown 'with her charming little daughter Rosalind' in her Kensington flat; the pictures show the flowered wallpapers and a collection of ornaments very much of their period, including Tutankhamen cushions and a doll wearing a frilled tutu.

Archie was more sanguine than Agatha about her new money-making potential, and after a trip together round the world while Archie was employed promoting the Empire Exhibition ('One of the most exciting things that ever happened to me', Agatha called it), Archie was offered the type of job he really wanted in the City, and Agatha was offered what was then a very large sum, £500, for her new book, *The Man in the Brown Suit* (1924). On the strength of these professional successes, the Christies bought a house near Sunningdale golf course and a bull-nosed Morris car for Agatha.

Golf exercised a seductive fascination over Archie, as over so many other people then and since. He spent Saturdays and Sundays on the golf course, after being away all week at his office. Agatha intensely resented being a golf widow. Before her second marriage she was to insist that her new husband should promise never to play the game.

In the days before the loneliness of the 'captive housewife' was recognised or pitied, the very fact of marriage and motherhood was supposed to supply a woman's needs; but, isolated from her family and friends (Archie no longer wanted to entertain, because visitors distracted him from the game), Agatha was not happy. She filled in her time with writing, as she had in that Torquay dispensary, and she enjoyed watching Rosalind's development. However, a small child is no substitute for adult companionship, particularly when the mother and child are so different in temperament. Agatha had spent her childhood playing imaginary games with invented playmates; her favourite books had been sagas and fairy tales and stories of fabled heroes. Books which displayed the common details of human nature seemed as boring to her as fairy stories and fantasies do to practical realists. And Agatha's daughter was a practical realist, who disliked make-believe and was full of common sense. All the things which Agatha had loved to do as a child, and would have loved to do again with her daughter, seemed pointless and boring to Rosalind.

Agatha's loneliness was not like the solitary confinement experienced by so many mothers of today. She always had domestic help, and when Rosalind started school, Charlotte Fisher came as a secretary companion; she was to remain a friend for life.

Agatha put her work in the hands of an agent at this time, and he arranged for it to be published by the firm with which she stayed from then onwards, William Collins. The agency, Hughes Massie, took over the financial management which Agatha Christie would have been well able to do herself. She always retained an interest in it and pounced on any small discrepancies in her royalty statements. Some of the office staff describe her as terrifying.

The first book Agatha Christie wrote for Collins was one whose plot had revolved in her mind for a long time, and whose trick ending had been suggested to her independently by her brother-in-law and in a letter from Lord Louis Mountbatten—this book was published as *The Murder of Roger Ackroyd* (1926). It sold well, about five and a half thousand copies, and was already a success when it received another boost because of the sudden publicity about its author.

Now, when everything seemed to be going so well, Agatha's world was shattered. First her mother, with whom her relationship was painfully close and burdened, died at Madge's house, and Agatha felt the traditional guilt for not having arrived there in time to be present at her death (of which she became supernaturally aware from afar). Archie was never sympathetic to other peoples' infirmities (though he expected due consideration for his own delicate digestion) and chose the time when Agatha was still mourning to tell her that he had fallen in love with a girl who worked in his office, whose name was Nancy Neele. At first Agatha refused to divorce him; the laws of the period would not have allowed him to divorce her.

Agatha Christie's reticence about the next few months' events is understandable; she must, in later life, have been deeply embarrassed and ashamed by her behaviour at that time. In her autobiography she describes the symptoms of incipient nervous breakdown. In the novel *Unfinished Portrait* (1934) she is a little more revealing; Sir Max Mallowan wrote that this book was autobiographical, and certainly up to page two hundred it is so similar, sometimes even word for word, to her autobiography that one must be justified in assuming that the remainder of the book is also derived from its author's experience. The heroine, Celia, is in despair at her mother's death; the bottom had fallen out of her world, and her husband appears to funk joining her in a house of mourning. When he arrives (as Archie arrived at Ashfield), having missed the funeral, he is flippant, instead of being sympathetic. Celia weeps over the trunks full of clothes, letters, photographs and juvenilia. She finds letters expressing her father's devotion to her mother, which he had written just before his early death. Celia is told by her doctor that she is heading for a nervous breakdown. Agatha, in her autobiography, wrote that she would cry for no reason, and that she would sometimes even forget her name, and wonder how to sign a cheque. When a name which seemed familiar came into her head, she would realise that it was not hers, but that of some character in a novel which she might not have read for years. Agatha looked forward desperately, as Celia looked forward desperately, to her husband's arrival. But when he came, he was unlike himself, shifty, furtive, a stranger to his wife. It is the enactment of a repetitive dream from her childhood in which an amiable person reveals himself as an ogre—the horror under the surface which must be at the root of all crime novelists' imaginations, which all boil down, presumably, to the fear of good appearances masking evil.

Agatha/Celia was horrified at the idea of her husband being

unfaithful to her, as well as being incredulous both at the deception and at the idea of his being able to contemplate leaving the child. Agatha refused to accept it, and for a while, several months apparently, Archie and she went on living in the same house. In the autobiography, Agatha says, 'after illness came sorrow, despair and heartbreak. There is no need to dwell on it. I stood out for a year, hoping he would change. But he did not. So ended my first married life.' In the novel, Celia's mental health deteriorated. She would lose track of her words and actions, become confused, wake in the night terrified that her husband was trying to murder her, and creep out to hide the garden weedkiller from him. The modern reader has to remember that murder did sometimes seem to be a sensible alternative to divorce in those days. The legal hurdles and social humiliations faced by such couples then would be ludicrous (indeed, *were* ludicrous in A. P. Herbert's farce, *Holy Deadlock*) if they were not pathetic.

Celia walks out at night, forgetting her name, and planning to drown herself in a ditch. When she wanders home, she begs the governess to protect her from her husband.

The real-life facts can hardly be detached either from this fiction, or from those invented by contemporary and subsequent reporters. Unless Agatha Christie's heirs release information which she was determined to conceal, the curious are not likely to be sure what happened to her in December 1926. Her fictional persona tried to end it all by jumping off a bridge into a river. Agatha Christie does not seem to have attempted suicide. The known facts are derived from police and newspaper reports.

On the Friday, 3 December 1926, Archie Christie went straight from his office to Godalming, where he and Nancy Neele were to spend the weekend (as they frequently did) with friends. Agatha Christie went to tea with her mother-in-law, and then went home to dine alone. At 9.45pm she put out two letters, one addressed to her husband, and another asking her secretary, Miss Fisher, to cancel her appointments as she was going to Yorkshire. Also, according to the surviving daughter of the then Deputy Chief Constable of Surrey, she posted a letter saying that she feared for her life and appealing for his help. She then drove away from Styles in her car.

Miss Fisher telephoned Colonel Christie, who left the dinner table in Godalming and drove away alone.

Agatha Christie did not return home that night. The next morning her car was found at a 'beauty spot' called Newlands Corner, not far from Styles. It had been pushed into the chalk pit on the side of the bluff. The car was in working order and its lights were on. On the seat of the car was a fur coat and a suitcase of clothes in which was found an out-of-date driving licence bearing Agatha Christie's name.

Colonel Christie appeared at breakfast in Godalming, and was told by the police that his wife was missing.

That same Saturday morning, Agatha Christie arrived by taxi at the Harrogate Hydropathic Hotel. She had one small suitcase with her and took a room on the first floor. She was wearing the dress and hat in which she had left her home. She signed the register in the name of Mrs Theresa Neele from Cape Town, South Africa.

She attended a dance in the hotel that Saturday evening, wearing the dress in which she had arrived.

On the Monday morning, the national papers printed a message from the Berkshire police:

> Missing from her home, The Styles, Sunningdale, Berkshire, Mrs Agatha Mary Clarissa Christie, aged 35; height 5 feet 7 inches; hair red, shingled, part grey; complexion fair, build slight; dressed in grey stockinette skirt, green jumper, grey and dark green cardigan and small velour hat; wearing a platinum ring with one pearl; no wedding ring; black handbag with purse containing perhaps £5 or £10. Left home at 9.45pm Friday leaving note saying she was going for a drive.

The publicity was voluminous, and hundreds of volunteers joined in the search. The Silent Pool, near Newlands Corner, was dragged. Light aircraft from Brooklands, bloodhounds with their handlers, the Guildford and Shere Beagles, Agatha's own dog, police from four counties, as well as many special constables, all took part in the hunt for the missing woman.

On the Tuesday the *Daily News* offered a £100 reward for information which would 'lead to the discovery, if alive, of Mrs Christie'. The search continued throughout that week, much complicated by the rivalry between the Berkshire and Surrey police, Styles being under the jurisdiction of the one, and Newlands Corner of the other. Colonel Christie was watched by the police, and did not go back to his office until the Thursday.

The following weekend, seven days after the disappearance was announced, there were fifteen thousand people on the Berkshire downs hunting for any trace of Agatha Christie. They were organised into parties of thirty, each with a police officer directing the operations. The publicity was on a similar scale.

During that week 'Mrs Theresa Neele' lived the life of a normal hotel guest in Harrogate; she went to church, played billiards, danced and sang with the hotel band in the evenings and did a great deal of shopping; having arrived with one small case she later appeared in different dresses every day. She read the daily papers and joined in discussions with other guests about the big news story of the week—the disappearance of Agatha Christie. She showed no apparent uncertainty or uneasiness; indeed, her fellow guests thought her composed and serene.

While she was in Harrogate, she posted a letter to Harrods, where she, as Mrs Christie, had left a ring the previous week, and asked them to send it to Mrs Theresa Neele at the Harrogate Hydropathic; she also sent an advertisement for the personal column of *The Times*, which was printed on Saturday, 11 December: 'Friends and relatives of Theresa Neele, late of South Africa, please communicate—Box 702, The Times.'

She spent money freely, using cash; her two bank accounts had been frozen by the police. The other guests found her very agreeable.

Meanwhile Charlotte Fisher stayed at Styles looking after Rosalind, who believed that her mother was away working on a book.

During the course of this week, some of the members of the Hydro's band thought that they recognised Mrs Neele as Agatha Christie. On the Monday morning, the eleventh day after her disappearance, the Harrogate police sent a message to Deputy Chief Constable Kenward that they believed they had found the missing woman. Mr Kenward was still convinced that she had been the victim of a serious crime and that she was still near home. His daughter, years later, is said to have claimed that he had been taking orders from the Home Office on how to conduct the case. But Mr Kenward's colleague, Superintendent Goddard of the neighbouring police force, believed all along that Mrs Christie was alive, and that she had gone away voluntarily.

On Tuesday, 14 December, a reporter from the *Daily News*, Ritchie Calder, had been tipped off that the Harrogate police were watching 'Mrs Neele'. He went up to her in the hotel and addressed her as Mrs Christie. She replied, with great self-possession, that she was suffering from amnesia, and then went up to her room, where she stayed for the rest of the afternoon. That evening, Colonel Christie arrived at the hotel and waited in the lounge concealed behind an open newspaper. When Agatha Christie came down for dinner, he went up to her, and they went in to the dining room together. Mrs Christie told her fellow guests that her brother had arrived. After dinner, the two of them retired to a suite of rooms which Colonel Christie had taken, and later Christie gave out a press statement to the effect that his wife had completely lost her memory; he thanked the police for their help in finding her.

The next morning, Agatha's sister, Madge Watts, arrived with her husband, and all four travelled back together to the Watts' house in Cheshire. Two doctors, a general practitioner and a specialist in nervous disorders, examined Agatha Christie later in the day and announced that she was unquestionably suffering from loss of memory and should be spared all anxiety and excitement.

Those are all the known facts about Agatha Christie's famous disappearance. A variety of suggestions have been put forward in explanation. Was it a publicity stunt? But Agatha Christie was doing well enough with *The Murder of Roger Ackroyd*, her first 'best seller'; in any case, she had always been shy and embarrassed by publicity. In later years she told the novelist Christianna Brand that she preferred people to believe it had been a publicity stunt, to exposing her private life.

Perhaps she really did lose her memory, after the shock of her mother's death and her husband's defection. Certainly she seems to have had some kind of nervous breakdown at Ashfield, a few months earlier. But would a woman who had lost her memory recall that she had left a diamond ring at Harrods the previous week? Would she have seemed so unconcerned and calm? Would she, even though her grandmother had taught her to carry £50 for emergencies, have had so much ready money on her?

Was she acting out one of her own mystery fantasies? Was she showing Archie, who was not at all the sort of man to take her novels seriously, that the sort of events she imagined could really happen? Was she even testing out the practicality of a plot she had invented?

Had she set out to drown herself, like Celia? The Silent Pool, near Newlands Corner, was reputed to be bottomless. Did her resolution fail, and when she found herself unable to start her car—she always needed help to crank it—did she decide to escape from everything? She was used to going to hotels to work on books, and a resort hydropathic would have been a natural refuge for her, just as a similar hotel was the hiding place for an exhausted character in one of Margery Allingham's novels, who 'suddenly got fed up and wanted a quiet place to sleep. That's the kind of thing,' says the heroine, Amanda Fitton, 'I'd do myself.' It was the kind of thing Agatha Christie might do herself as well—and it is surely unlikely that the devoted mother of Rosalind, her pockets full of money, can have meant to commit suicide.

At present the most likely explanation seems to be that Agatha set out to teach Archie a lesson—to make him believe that she was gone and realise that he really wanted her. The storm of publicity must have come as a complete surprise to this modest, obsessed, unhappy woman. What could she then do but sit it out in Harrogate because she had no other idea how to escape from the mess she had got herself into? And in the end, a pretended amnesia must have seemed the only solution. Perhaps she had used the name of Archie's mistress as a clue for him in the frightened and contrite search she expected him to undertake; perhaps she simply used the name nearest the top of her head when handed the register. Perhaps, in the end, she wanted to bring everything down about her ears. It may well be that she hardly knew herself.

All this time, Agatha had felt 'like a fox, hunted, my earths dug up, and yelping hounds following me everywhere'. She escaped to the Canary Islands with Rosalind, and while she was there achieved professional status as a writer by forcing herself to write a book when she did not feel at all like doing so. She was surprised that *The Mystery on the Blue Train* (1928) sold as well as her other books, and always thought it her worst. It is not in fact apparent to the reader that it was written in a different spirit from its predecessors. There can be few writers whose mood is so imperceptible in their work. But she used her formula with unfailing efficiency, presenting puzzles and solutions in a form as lacking in emotion as a comic strip. Her participants are not characters, but collections of characteristics, which require no involvement on the writer's part, and offer the reader an escape without any involvement on his. *The Mystery on the Blue Train* exposes no more of the depression Agatha Christie felt when she was writing it than a series of algebraic equations would. But with hindsight, one can recognise some of her own experience of passionate jealousy and possessive love in those her protagonists pretend to.

On her return from Las Palmas, Agatha moved her belongings into a small flat in Chelsea, and Rosalind was sent to boarding school. Since the child could be visited by Charlotte Fisher and her Aunt Madge, Agatha decided that she would go away for the winter herself. It may be that Agatha was making a conscious decision not to repeat her own pattern of dependent closeness between a lonely mother and a solitary child; perhaps the sensation of failure in her own life—for she felt guilty then and for the rest of her life about consenting to divorce Archie (and she believed that Rosalind blamed her for the loss of her father)—made her wary of bringing up Rosalind as she had been. But it must have been a hard decision; Rosalind was only eight when she started at boarding school, and for the rest of her childhood was away in termtime, often staying with her aunt in Cheshire in the holidays while Agatha was abroad. In a light and amusing form, this life style is echoed in a book published long after Rosalind Christie was married and a mother herself. In *Cat Among the Pigeons* (1959) a schoolgirl's mother, suddenly needed, is travelling around Turkey on local buses. 'Just at the moment, let me tell you, I wish mummy were a good deal nearer and *not* on a bus in

Anatolia,' the girl complains. In the days when her daughter was at school, before flying made world-wide journeys quick, Agatha must sometimes have feared such a summons; once, she arrived back to be handed a stack of telegrams about Rosalind having pneumonia. But the upper middle classes had grown up to assume that children might be at school continents away from their empire-building parents, and Agatha's decision about Rosalind's education was acceptable and usual in its period.

In any case, Agatha Christie felt in some ways that the best thing she could do for her daughter was to give her material things, since Rosalind did not want the emotional offerings her mother made. 'Because I love her, I've left her alone,' says Celia in *Unfinished Portrait*.

For the first term without the child, Agatha had booked a journey to the West Indies, but then she met a couple who spoke enthusiastically about Baghdad, where they had been stationed. All her life Agatha had loved trains, and she longed to travel on the Orient Express; she changed her reservations at the travel agency the next morning. Five days later she set off for the Middle East, travelling alone to a strange land for the first time in her thirty-nine years. The journey was the beginning of what she called her second spring. She fell in love with the desert and its Arab inhabitants, and when she visited the excavations at Ur of the Chaldees she was overcome by the romance of excavation and longed to be an archaeologist herself.

For a girl who had been brought up to be delicate about lavatories—'it was unthinkable,' she wrote of her childhood, 'to be seen entering or leaving, except by an intimate member of the family'—Agatha was commendably undeterred by primitive or non-existent plumbing, and willing to endure the discomforts of indigestion and insect bites. She also displayed heroic coolness about bats, rats, mice and snakes. On this first trip she made friends with the archaeologist Leonard Woolley and his wife Katharine, and she was invited to visit them again the following year. She stayed as their guest in the expedition house, which had a mud roof and plastered walls and a living room decorated in a pale orange, which was the only paint available. The floor was made of burnt bricks, some of them inscribed, and on them were scattered rush mats. Outside the courtyard, armed guards stood. In houses such as these, Agatha was to spend many future months.

On the second visit to Ur, Agatha met Max Mallowan, who was Leonard Woolley's assistant. 'He was a thin dark young man, and very quiet—he seldom spoke, but was perceptive to everything that was required of him.' He appears in the minor role of David Emmott in *Murder in Mesopotamia* (1936), the only book Agatha set at an excavation: 'I had taken rather a fancy to Mr Emmott,' the narrator says. 'His taciturnity was not, I felt sure, unfriendly. There was something about him that seemed very steadfast and reassuring in an atmosphere where one was uncertain what anyone was feeling or thinking.'

Katharine Woolley ordered Max to take Agatha on a trip though the desert, showing her interesting places on the way to Baghdad. Agatha was dismayed at the prospect of inconveniencing a strange young man: Max found her 'a most agreeable person, and the prospect pleasing'.

They inspected ruins together and stopped at a desert lake for Agatha to bathe. On finding that their car was stuck in the sand, Agatha did not fuss, but simply lay down to sleep, and Max decided on the spot that she was a remarkable woman and the ideal wife for him.

Max Mallowan was twenty-six. He was the son of an Austrian immigrant to England who did well enough in business to send his son to Lancing School, and Oxford. Max was taken on as assistant to Leonard Woolley, partly, he explained, because he was not bumptious, and partly on the strength of a good reference from his tutor, Stanley Casson (himself the writer of some good detective stories). Mallowan was a happy man, and a fortunate one, having been just too young to be called up in World War I, and able to enter a profession which at that time had room for few newcomers. In his old age he said that every day of an archaeologist's life is intellectually thrilling, and much of it enjoyable. In Agatha he found a woman who was good tempered, exuberant and unselfish.

Like many newly single women, Agatha had discovered that she had become the target for unexpected attentions from strange men. Max's intentions were honourable. When they were both back in England, he came to stay at Ashfield, made friends with Rosalind and proposed to Agatha.

It is not surprising that she hesitated. She knew, and was reminded by all her friends, of many reasons for refusal: she had intended never to marry again, because she was afraid of being hurt again; Max was a Catholic; she had met him in an unreal, glamorous setting; above all, they were of different generations. Max had been at the university with Agatha's nephew, and was thirteen years younger than she was.

Eventually Agatha was persuaded. They avoided publicity by having the banns called while Agatha was on holiday in the Hebrides, and getting married, on 11 September 1930, in Edinburgh. They falsified the ages on the certificate giving Max's age as thirty-one, not twenty-six, and Agatha's as thirty-seven instead of forty, so that the gap between them seemed to be of only six years. No reporters were present.

Max was still employed by Leonard Woolley, who had been pleased at the idea of this marriage, but Katharine Woolley suggested that it would be good for the young man's character if he had to wait for two years before the wedding. Once she was Mrs Mallowan, and not Mrs Christie, Agatha was no longer welcome at Ur. As Max said, there was room for only one woman there. Agatha described Katharine Woolley as a friend, but she was one of those friends for whom allowances must be made. She appears in unflattering detail in both the autobiographies, and Agatha describes her, in fictional terms, in *Murder in Mesopotamia*. In Hercule Poirot's words:

> . . . her tastes were simple and even on the austere side. She was clearly not a luxurious woman. On the other hand . . . a woman of fastidious and artistic taste. [Katharine Woolley was a talented sculptor.] She had brains and I also fancied that she was essentially an egoist . . . I was convinced that she was a woman who essentially worshipped *herself*, and who enjoyed more than anything the sense of *power*. Wherever she was, she must be the centre of the universe. And everyone around her, man or woman, had got to acknowledge her sway . . . where conquest was too easy, she indulged a more cruel side to her nature . . . it was natural and unthinkable as is the conduct of a cat with a mouse.

Luckily, Mrs Woolley did not recognise this portrait.

In deference to Mrs Woolley's wishes, Agatha and Max separated in Athens after their honeymoon, although this meant that Max had to leave her ill in their hotel, much to the horror of the Greek doctor. She made her way back to England and they did not meet again until the following spring, when she again went east to join Max, and they travelled slowly home together via the Soviet Union, and Persia.

Katharine Woolley's whim was not to separate them again. Max arranged to work with Campbell Thompson at Nineveh. Barbara Campbell Thompson was a kind and unselfish woman to whom both the Mallowans became very attached. They enjoyed their season at Nineveh, although Campbell Thompson was more interested in epigraphy than in the other material evidence of the past. He was notoriously parsimonious, and intensely disapproved of Agatha buying herself a solid table on which to write *Lord Edgware Dies* (1933).

In the following year Max directed his own excavation for the first time. Agatha found no difficulty in co-operating with his work. She had been bred to make a good job of whatever life style she should marry into, and she liked exercising her imagination on the relics of daily domestic life. She was happy to wash and mark pottery, to clean the mud off long-buried ivories, to take photographs and to pay the native workmen.

During the years 1930 to 1938, the Mallowans were in Syria every season. Agatha's nostalgic account of this period, written during the war, *Come, Tell Me How You Live*, gives a delightful picture of a life in which even the discomforts seemed amusing. Agatha found Syria a gentle, fertile country, with simple people who knew how to laugh and enjoy life, who were idle and gay, who had dignity, good manners and a great sense of humour, and to whom death was not terrible. She realised that the life she and Max led there was a good one, busy but not harried, productive and peaceful. Max excavated at successive mounds, and Agatha, in the intervals of helping him, wrote a series of books, though she still regarded writing only as a lucrative sideline. On official forms she put her occupation as 'married woman', not 'writer'. She did not think that she was a 'real' author, perhaps sharing the feeling of intellectual inferiority common to detective novelists. Her mother-in-law would say, 'You write so well, surely you should try something more serious.' (Friends and relations of thriller writers frequently make this remark. As Raymond Chandler wrote to James Sandoe, 'The sort of semi-literate, educated people one meets nowadays . . . are always saying to me, more or less, "You write so well I should think you would do a serious novel." ')

As a matter of fact, Agatha had by then tried her hand at 'straight' novels, using the name of Mary Westmacott. They are not good novels, being as unadorned, and occasionally as ungrammatical in style, as the detective stories, and almost as simplistic about human behaviour, but they do throw the occasional shaft of light on their characters which is illuminating about the types of people Agatha was writing about and about herself also. One feels that sometimes she is writing about people she knows and dislikes, using the deeper feelings which she thought out of place in a detective story, and in at least one, *Unfinished Portrait*, she was writing about herself. In these six 'straight' novels, she was trying to express something of her own view of life. But her mother-in-law thought she should be writing non-fiction.

Non-fiction was all that Max had read when he and Agatha married. He had never voluntarily opened a novel before, though he dutifully learnt to enjoy Agatha's. He wrote his books and articles while Agatha wrote her novels, he in his library, she, until she acquired her first study when they moved to Sheffield Terrace in London, at the dining table, on a marble-topped washstand table, or wherever she could fit her typewriter and shut the door on the outside world. The workroom at Sheffield Terrace was on the top floor and contained a Steinway grand piano, a sofa and a work table. Ariadne Oliver's workroom

> was a good sized room, the walls papered with exotic birds nesting in tropical foliage. Mrs Oliver herself, in a state apparently bordering on insanity, was prowling round the room muttering to herself. She threw me a brief uninterested glance and continued to prowl. Her eyes, unfocussed, swept round the walls, glanced out of the window, and occasionally closed in what appeared to be a spasm of agony . . . picking things off tables unseeingly and putting them down again somewhere else. She fitted with some care her spectacle case into a laquered box which already contained a Chinese fan . . .

No wonder, if this is indeed a picture of Agatha Christie as well as of her fictional *alter ego*, she lost the notebooks in which she jotted down her ideas, only to come across the incomprehensible scribbles much later on. Agatha worked out most of the details of her plots talking aloud to herself, sometimes in the bath, munching apples throughout; she then set the difficult passages down in longhand, and finally typed the book out directly.

Plot, place, people; people, place, plot. Crime novelists are divided into those who invent the events, and then decide on a cast to take part in them, and those who think of their characters first, and then discover, often as they go along with the actual writing, what those people would have done in the given circumstances. The latter type of writer tends to be weak on plot. A perfectly tenoned and morticed plot demands characters whose behaviour must be wrenched to fit it and whose personalities are imprecise enough for them not to protest at what the writer requires of them. Many crime novelists come somewhere in between these two extremes, but Agatha Christie's pleasure and genius lay in the dovetailing of events and the posing of a puzzle. This was the professional aspect of the woman who loved mathematical problems, crossword puzzles and bridge. She had the knack of hiding or altering clues with imperceptible flicks of the pen. When her publisher said one clue was too obvious, she changed the whole emphasis of the book in one hundred words. In fact, working out the plot was by far her favourite part of the work. What followed was hard grind. She tells of complaining with each book to Max that she would never manage to write it. At first he was worried and sympathetic. Several books later, he would hardly raise his eyes from his potsherds to remind her that she had said the same thing last time. (The present writer, who is also married to an archaeologist, has had the identical experience.)

Since the days when she had begged to be given a second doll's house so that she could play at furniture removing, Agatha had loved planning how to convert and decorate houses. She owned several London properties (at one time, she was the owner of eight houses), and the Mallowans moved from one to another until they settled in Sheffield Terrace, in

Kensington. Ashfield was used as a country house, and for weekends they bought Winterbrook House in Wallingford, which is between Oxford and London, and kept it for the rest of their lives.

By 1938 Ashfield was surrounded by houses instead of the green fields Agatha remembered from her childhood; next door was a nursing home for mental cases, and the view of the sea was blocked by a noisy secondary school. It was also dangerously accessible to Agatha's public. The house at Wallingford was protected by a high wall and locked gates. The Mallowans decided to buy a house on the river Dart—Greenway, a late eighteenth-century, white, three-storied cube, standing on a small plateau above the river, flanked by woods which swept down to the water, and with thirty-eight acres planted out with fine trees and shrubs. The Mallowans had the Victorian additions removed, to leave the original Georgian house, and Agatha had the whole thing restored and decorated just in time for the outbreak of World War II.

Agatha's autobiography no longer is informative about servants at this stage in her life, though they played such an important part in her thoughts when she was first setting up home. She had a butler, and presumably a full supporting staff, and mentions that when she was planning how to alter Greenway, it never occurred to her that the time might come when she would have to manage without domestic help. But she seems to have been spared the preoccupations of E. M. Delafield, 'The Provincial Lady', who was living at that time not very far away, and during those inter-war years heard only too often the dread words spoken by cook or parlourmaid, 'Madam, may I have a word with you?', the introduction to complaints and notice. Few archaeologists can have lived as the Mallowans did, even then, when there was not much hope of entering the profession without a private income to live on.

Surely also unusual was the Mallowans' lack of involvement in public affairs. So many of their literary and academic contemporaries were not only aware of international events in the 1930s, but taking some action: some worked with voluntary organisations trying to rescue Jews from Germany. The Mallowans had learnt at the very beginning of the period what was going on in Germany from a conversation with a Nazi archaeologist in Baghdad. It was perfectly understandable to resolve, as the archaeologist O. G. S. Crawford did, that in academic matters he would make no distinction between Communists, Nazis, Fascists, or anyone else, but he was well aware of political pressures and worked with many Jewish refugees in his profession. Neither Max nor Agatha make any mention of recession at home, or persecution abroad. It is true that there is an occasional throw-away, almost absent-minded, anti-Semitic comment or reference in Agatha's novels, which might make one suppose her unsympathetic to the sufferings of the Jews at the time; but it was no more marked than in the writings of many of her contemporaries including Dorothy Sayers, and seems to have been more a verbal mannerism than a conscious belief, similar to those employed by many English people at the time. Other archaeologists were active in, for instance, the Territorial Army. Mortimer Wheeler, who had been an artillery officer in World War I, after Munich, in 1938, savagely hoped for war, as an opportunity to obliterate his country's disgrace. But Agatha wrote that she and Max hoped that Chamberlain's assurance of peace in their time might be the truth.

On the outbreak of war, Greenway became a nursery for evacuees, and was later taken over by the American navy. But during the 'phony war' Max and Agatha were still there, and saw the complete Belgian fishing fleet anchored below their house after Dunkirk. Max was in the Home Guard at that time, and Agatha went back to the dispensary at Torquay Hospital to update and revise her skills.

In 1940 they moved into the first of a series of apartments in London; Max, after working for the Turkish Relief Organisation, managed to get into the intelligence branch of the RAF, in which many archaeologists were deployed using their particular skills to interpret air photographs. Agatha worked at University College Hospital as a dispenser, and when Max went to the Middle East, moved to live in a flat near Hampstead Heath.

Like her mother twenty-six years before, Rosalind Christie married in the first year of the war, but being under-age, had to warn her mother two days beforehand. Matthew Prichard,

Agatha's grandson, was born in 1943; his father was killed in action not long afterwards. Rosalind Prichard was later remarried, to Anthony Hicks.

During these years, while Agatha was working part time at the hospital, she was extraordinarily prolific, finding that writing about domestic death was an escape from a world in which mass death and destruction began to seem almost natural. At this time she wrote her historical detective novel, set in ancient Egypt, *Death Comes as the End* (1944), as well as the book with which she was always the most satisfied, Mary Westmacott's *Absent in the Spring* (1944). Its heroine is temporarily marooned in the desert, and learns for the first time to see herself as others see her. It is well organised technically, with a strong sense of the heroine's growing uneasiness about what she had always thought was a happy and stable life. It seems much more dated now than the crime stories, and gives the impression of being about a type of person, if not an actual person, whom Agatha knew and hated. She wrote the whole book in three days.

The escape from the horrors of war, which Agatha Christie found in writing, her readers derived from reading her books. It had been universally assumed that fictional death would lose its appeal when the real thing in its full horror was all around. Far from it; all over the world, and especially in Britain in the blitz, popular demand was for detective stories. A Mass Observation Report of the time says that many people wanted not thrillers in general, but Agatha Christie's cosy and comforting books in particular. Murder, cosy? Murder, comforting? It is no wonder that those who foretold the genre's abandonment in wartime were surprised. They did not realise that the actuality of death is absent from this type of story. Nobody grieves; nobody bleeds—they are merely surrounded by 'dark stains'. Children never die, and sympathetic characters rarely; the victims are expendable, in brutal terms, but they are set in a well-ordered society where right prevails and the criminal never escapes—so different from the anarchy all around.

Christie was not much interested in the psychology of the criminal; her sympathy and interest were saved for the innocent. But she makes Poirot say quite often that he disapproves of murder: 'I have a bourgeois attitude to murder. I disapprove of it,' he would say. In *Appointment with Death* (1938) he insists that 'the moral character of the victim has nothing to do with it! A human being who has exercised the right of private judgment and has taken the life of another human being is not safe to exist among the community. I tell you that. I, Hercule Poirot!' In Christie's fantasy land, the innocent were always compensated (a consideration which she felt was insufficiently important in our legal system). She offered her readers the chance of devoting their minds to a soluble problem; and she gave them the comfort of an environment where all little local difficulties were susceptible to the attentions of lawyers, doctors, clergymen, or private investigators. Hercule Poirot, or Miss Marple, like the fairy godmother in the pantomime, ensured a happy ending.

Agatha Christie's plays were very popular during the war. She had always enjoyed the theatre herself, and gone to it regularly as a child when staying with the grandmother in Ealing; once she had been whisked off at short notice to Exeter by her mother to catch a performance by the aged Henry Irving. Madge was an amateur actress and also a playwright, and now Agatha, having disliked some dramatisations by others of her books, decided to write her own plays. She assumed that books would always provide her steady income, and working at plays seemed 'entrancing simply because it wasn't my job'. The charm of work which is anything but one's job is only too familiar to most writers, but few are so successful with their surrogates.

Black Coffee was the first play Christie wrote herself; it was produced in London in 1930 while she was away in Mesopotamia. In 1943 her adaptation of *Ten Little Niggers* was produced, and in 1945, that of *Appointment with Death*.

By that time Max was at home, having arrived unexpectedly one night from North Africa. He worked at the Air Ministry (as Archie Christie had done in the last year of World War I). After the end of the war in Europe Greenway was de-requisitioned, undamaged, but tattered and with its grounds a wilderness. In 1947 Max was offered his first teaching job and became Professor of Western Asiatic Archaeology at the Institute of Archaeology. The Institute was then sited in Bute

House, in the middle of Regents Park. It was a beautiful house—Agatha had been invited to it as a child when it was a private home—white stucco, built around a central hall which was surmounted by a great cupola. At that time the Institute was a cheerful, informal establishment; there were few students, all of whom were graduates, and as Sir Max put it, it was 'still possessed of the happy pioneering spirit'. Those who were students then do not recall Agatha as active in the role of professor's wife, though she did occasionally appear in Bute House, a large, grey lady coming to meet her small, stout husband. (Some of the students, unaware that Poirot came into Agatha's life ten years before Max, assumed that she had based her detective on him.) Her husband's professional colleagues found the famous author quiet and shy; but her own literary associates remember an amusing woman with a sharp wit—though, as one publisher said, one had to listen for it.

In the years after the war Agatha became as famous for her plays as for her books. *The Hollow* was produced in 1951, and the first performance of *The Mousetrap* was on 25 November 1952. It is, as all her work is, tightly plotted with a surprise ending, but its dialogue is unlike any colloquial speech and the characters are incredible. Nobody has ever explained the play's longevity. As these words are written, it is still playing to full houses in its twenty-ninth year, and there seems to be no reason why this longest running of all plays should ever end. The play was based on a radio sketch called *Three Blind Mice*—Agatha frequently referred to nursery rhymes in her work—which had been written at the request of Queen Mary. Agatha's own explanation for its success was that it had something for everybody—humour, thriller appeal and good construction; it now has the additional historical attraction of being seen by the children, almost by the grandchildren, of its first admirers. Any member of the audience today must be struck by the positively devotional atmosphere; it is as much like entering a temple as a theatre. The royalties of the play were given to Matthew Prichard, who was aged nine when it opened.

At this time in her life, late middle age, Agatha found that she had a new energy and enthusiasm for the impersonal interests of her youth. She felt that the time for concentrating on personal relationships and emotions was past. Max was enjoying his work, and Agatha relished the post-war life, in which she was free to go to exhibitions, attend the opera, and travel with all her former pleasure.

Max returned to his excavations in 1948, and from that time was to concentrate on Nimrud, where work continued for several years. Agatha worked there as the photographer as well as writing her own books and cleaning and registering the small finds. Many crime novels revealed the corpse in a cutting, but Agatha Christie, whose daily life involved peering into archaeological sites, never wrote a novel in which an excavation trench was opened to reveal a modern victim.

The Mallowans loved their industrious months at Nimrud. Agatha's attitude was in many ways that of the mem-sahib. Her stories of the naive remarks made by her native friends now ring a little uneasily on ears attuned to racial equality, but they seem, just like the occasional anti-Semitic remark, to have been merely part of the vocabulary of a woman with her background. An Iraqi archaeologist worked with the British team at Nimrud, and Max paid convincing tribute to the Iraqi Department of Antiquities.

In the house they built at Nimrud was one room known as 'Beit Agatha'—Agatha's House. Here she wrote her annual novel, and her autobiography, which she finished in England at the age of seventy-five. In it she looked back on a life which had given her many chances to make the most of her innate gift of happiness; she was still happy in old age, even though some great pleasures were denied her: she could, for instance, no longer swim in the sea. But she could still enjoy music and sunshine, silence, the company of dogs, sleeping, eating and dreaming. She had written that there are few things more desirable than to be an accepter and an enjoyer. Agatha was able to enjoy almost anything. This quality, so enviable and fortunate for its possessor and her family, was probably the reason for the failings which scrutineers of her work detect. A person who accepts is unlikely to question. Agatha lived all her life in the stable and comfortable world of the upper middle classes whose values she seems to have epitomised: an Anglican, bridge-playing, garden-loving, family woman. She observed the changes in the society about her with a quick and unerring accuracy, especially the small details of daily life. She wrote about what she knew, but her experience—so wide in geographical terms—was socially restricted and that of a lifelong conformist. To many readers, the novels described all that they found odious; although foreigners apparently believed that the England of large country houses, of expensive hotels and exclusive golf courses, of St Mary Mead, was representative of the country as a whole. It was a country, it seemed, in which no gentleman worked for a living except in one of the older professions, in which those with Oxford accents snub upstarts and policemen favour the aristocracy, and in which—shades of the Victorian novelists—a beard and change of name can render a young man unrecognisable by his relations. This England has its interest all over the world, so that a Chinese politician could denounce her as 'the running dog for the rich and powerful' and an American geriatrician could say 'I put her right up there with Medicare, Medicaid and Social Security in making old age tolerable.' (Quoted by Emma Lathen in her book *Agatha Christie, First Lady of Crime.*)

What Agatha Christie presented was a nostalgic generalisation, incomplete but not, historically, quite false. There were really people like her characters and places like her settings—especially in South Devon and the Thames Valley; but there was more to them than she described, perhaps more than she wanted to notice, and there were vast areas of life and experience which she ignored. Even the places she did describe are more abstract than precise. Robert Barnard, in discussing the secret of Christie's world-wide appeal, concludes that the generality, rather than vividness—which marks her scene painting and characterisation—is her strength, not her weakness; it enables the reader to superimpose the community and human types with which he is familiar onto the broad, anonymous, society she creates; for example, he says, a Norwegian reader 'thinks she is reading about an English village, but what is really in her mind, is an Anglo Norwegian hybrid village, situated on a fjord somewhere near Torquay.' It was unusual for her to write about identifiable places, though she did put Greenway into *Dead Man's Folly* (1956) and the estuary of the River Yealm in *Towards Zero* (1957); Bertram's

Hotel, at which Miss Marple stayed, and voiced her generation's bewilderment about the 1960s, is based on that haven for the provincial gentry, Brown's Hotel. But her fans are unlikely to go place-spotting, as those of D. L. Sayers do.

As for people, it was very rare for her to put real ones into fiction, and she indignantly denied taking characters from real life. 'I invent them, they are *mine*,' she said. 'They've got to be *my* characters, doing what I want them to do, being what I want them to be—coming alive for me, having their own ideas sometimes, but only because I've made them become real.'

There is a gulf here between intention and realisation. Christie's charm lies partly in the fact that her characters do not become real. When the puppet show is over, they are put away in the box. We do not wonder, we do not care, what happens to them next. Many critics do not care what happens to them during the books either. Christie's great popularity was equalled by her inferiority in intellectual eyes. Edmund Wilson said after reading *Death on the Nile* (1937) that the writing 'is of a mawkishness and banality which seems to me literally impossible to read. You cannot read such a book. You run through it to see the problem worked out.'

In her old age, still producing the annual Christie for Christmas, Agatha Christie was loaded with worldly honours, a CBE, and later a DBE, honorary degrees, world-wide acclaim and what was the summit of her own ambition—dinner at Buckingham Palace with the Queen. At the end of her life her health failed and her mind wandered. She had written that she admired the aged Eskimo who, in old age, would walk away across the ice one day and not come back. Thirty years before she had made one of her characters in *Sad Cypress* (1940) say, in reply to the assurance that she might live for years after a stroke, 'I'm not at all anxious to, thank you. I told [the doctor] the other day that in a decently civilised state all there would be to do would be for me to intimate to him that I wished to end it and he'd finish me off painlessly with some nice drug.'

But at the time Agatha was not expressing her own views. She despised the hopeless suicide and agreed with the phrase 'there's always hope'. She was made furiously angry at hearing of the suicide of a French couple when the German army was approaching. She believed, along with her doctor in *Sad Cypress*, that 'one's got an instinct to live. One doesn't live because one's reason assents to living. People who, as we say, would be better dead, don't want to die . . .'Agatha Christie was eventually to believe that the very ease of living made possible by the Welfare State made life more difficult. With nothing to fight for, there was nothing to live for.

Agatha Christie Mallowan died at the age of eighty-five on 12 January 1976. Her husband wrote that death came as a merciful release.

6 Dorothy L. Sayers

In 1975 a plaque affixed to the front of a house in Witham, Essex, was unveiled. It read 'Dorothy L. Sayers, 1893–1957, Novelist, theologian and Dante Scholar, lived here.' The town is the headquarters of The Dorothy L. Sayers Historical and Literary Society which was formed to promote the study of her life and works, to encourage the performance of her plays, and publication of books by and about her, and to propagate knowledge of her achievements. Every available word she wrote is stored there; another archive of material by and about her is kept at Wheaton College, Illinois. She has been much written about, first in the unauthorised *Such a Strange Lady* by Janet Hitchman, and most recently in an official biography written with the co-operation of her family and friends by James Brabazon. There have been volumes of critical essays about her work and thought, theses by research students, numerous pieces of journalism, lectures and articles. Scholars prefer to remember her work as a theologian and translator, but to the general public she became, and remains, famous as a crime novelist, though she gave up writing fiction half way through her career.

Dorothy L. Sayers would have welcomed the attention given to her work, but she suggested that nothing should be written about her life for fifty years after her death, saying that only then would it be possible to tell whether her reputation was to be temporary or lasting; like another reticent writer, Elizabeth Gaskell, she felt that 'the public has no more to do with me than to buy or reject the wares I offer.' It is impossible to tell how genuine such protests by a woman who purposely attracted attention in every way were. The Chairman of the Society believes that 'everything she wrote is brought into focus by appreciation of her unique personality,' and his Society aims to collect memories of her before they fade. There is, consequently, plenty of material on which to draw. The external picture is very clear: a woman who was large, flamboyant, opinionated, entertaining and fluent; with an incisive, trained mind, whose inventions arose more from insight than imagination; someone who perceived her own defects, and, by flaunting them, averted criticism; who created a public personality for herself in order to conceal her private affairs. Many of those who thought they knew her well were astonished to find, after years, that she was married. None knew that she had a son.

The other writers whose contented and industrious lives are related in this book have been described as shy women. They were all embarrassed by public display, and the last thing they wanted to do on the page was reveal themselves. Dorothy Sayers drew largely in her own experience in her novels. She exposed herself. Yet she too has been called shy. She was reticent about some areas of her life, but I doubt that she suffered that inward tremor, that conviction of inadequacy, which afflicts a truly shy person. Sayers had learnt to be self-protective.

When Dorothy Sayers was a child, so many people were passionately interested in her behaviour that she learnt to avoid enquiry when she could even though she had nothing to hide. She grew up in a house full of doting adults who encouraged her to bestow her affections on those in favour. James Brabazon tells a nauseating tale of the four-year-old Dorothy publicly deciding every evening which, out of her parents, a grandmother, a resident aunt, a nurse and a staff of servants, she would love the best.

The family lived during most of Dorothy's childhood in an isolated rectory in the fen country of Lincolnshire, one of the loneliest districts of Britain. Dorothy had been born when her father, the Reverend Henry Sayers, was headmaster of the Christ Church Choir School in Oxford. She would boast in later life of being a native of what was to her a hallowed city. Her mother, Helen Leigh Sayers, was a lively and intelligent woman, but like most of her contemporaries, little educated. She was well suited to the role of parson's wife which became hers when her husband was presented with the rich living of

Bluntisham cum Erith. It was a small community to which the
Sayers family moved, of peasants working land which had been
permanently waterlogged until the fens were drained in the
seventeenth century. This was not the rural England of fiction,
where the gentry enjoyed regular social life. The ordered
society, which Harriet Vane was to remember fondly in
Busman's Honeymoon, had only a notional existence in
Bluntisham: 'In London' [Harriet thinks] 'anybody, at any
moment, might do or become anything. But in a village—no
matter what village—they were all immutably themselves;
parson, organist, sweep, duke's son and doctor's daughter,
moving like chessmen upon their allotted squares.' In
Bluntisham the Sayers family fulfilled the roles of the upper
classes, lending money, giving food, chivvying the feckless,
assisting the helpless. The land was productive but threatened:
the frequent winds could strip the topsoil off ploughed fields,
and in the occasional floods, which even constant vigilance
could not always avert, more than just the arable land would be
overwhelmed. Even if Dorothy had no personal experience of a
great flood, it must have been the most threatening natural
disaster of her childhood. Just as children in the shadow of
Etna would imagine volcanic eruptions, or those in California
another earthquake, so in the Fenland, the memory of the
Great Flood of 1713, and of lesser inundations since, kept the
fear alive. The churches, upon their small eminences, would be
the refuge for all parishioners. In a parish like Bluntisham, as
in the imaginary Fenchurch St Paul of *The Nine Tailors*, the
rector's duty would have been to organise relief.

No doubt Dorothy was brought up to 'good works'. All rich
children were expected to visit the poor and comfort the sick.
The parson in *The Nine Tailors*, like the very similar one in
Busman's Honeymoon, is probably a lifelike portrait of Dorothy's
own father, though by all accounts he was both fussier and
funnier than either. Dorothy's fictional parson's wives are
archetypes too, presumably fair enough pictures of Helen
Sayers.

The education Dorothy received was unconventional, being
far more advanced in arts and linguistic subjects than that of
most boys, and almost entirely lacking in mathematics and
science. Dorothy could read by the time she was four and

started to learn Latin from her father at six. French and German were taught by Mademoiselles and Fräuleins. She was a natural linguist and was later to believe that all children should start Latin very young to take advantage, as she had, of the childish pleasure in chanting and reciting.

There is no suggestion that this only child was lonely. Bluntisham Rectory was full of her relations, some resident, others frequently visiting, and of a large staff of servants who had been so satisfied with their posts that they all voted to accompany the family from urban Oxford to isolated Bluntisham. What Dorothy lacked was the company of contemporaries, and the dilution of the grown-ups' attention. Not surprisingly, in the circumstances, she learnt to show-off at a very early age.

When she was eight Dorothy was joined at her lessons by the daughter of another country parson and the younger brother of one of Henry Sayers' former pupils, but Dorothy was never popular with other children, being both too clever, and too clever-clever. She enjoyed scoring off other people and never learnt to suffer fools.

It is natural that a gifted child in this atmosphere of smothering love, too much cared-for and not enough competed with, should have found her most fulfilling emotions in her imagination. The world of books was more real to her than the actual world.

A certain amount is known about Dorothy's thoughts as a child because she left not only a fragment of autobiography, which she called *An Edwardian Childhood*, but also an unfinished (non-detective) novel called *Cat o'Mary*, based upon it so closely as to allow those who have read them to assume that what she put into fictional form was her own experience. (Neither has been published, nor made available to the present writer. It is amusing to note that there are almost identical sources for the life of Agatha Christie.)

The heroine of *Cat o'Mary*, Katharine, is a spoilt, clever, precocious child who was constantly aware of, and analysing, her own feelings, and who knew from reading what her emotions should be, instead of experiencing them spontaneously. 'What she had read was always a little more real than what she had experienced.' She was always aware of a part of herself watching and mocking her own behaviour. This is not the same thing as introspection. To be unable to be wholehearted, to be continuously conscious of an inner self sardonically watching, is a lifelong, ineradicable characteristic of many people who find the life of the intellect more vivid than that of the emotions. This personality trait can be a source of shame to a young person, especially in an age which values spontaneity and admires people who are overwhelmed by their feelings. By the time they are middle-aged, most human beings learn to accept their own defects. One of the themes of *Gaudy Night* is the conflict between being ruled by the head or the heart, and in that book Dorothy expresses her own rationalisations through Miss de Vine:

> 'Detachment is a rare virtue, and very few people find it lovable either in themselves or in others. If you ever find a person who likes you in spite of it—still more, because of it—that liking has very great value, because it is perfectly sincere, and because, with that person, you will never need to be anything but sincere yourself.'
>
> 'That is probably very true,' said Harriet. 'But what makes you say it?'
>
> 'Not any desire to offend you, believe me. But I imagine you come across a number of people who are disconcerted by the difference between what you do feel, and what they fancy you ought to feel. It is fatal to pay the smallest attention to them.'

Dorothy would probably have liked to be spontaneous, but she was born to be a thinker. It is not surprising that she preferred eventually to write non-fiction, or, when she wrote fiction, to make it the kind which expects its readers to think as much as to feel. Yet Dorothy was drawn towards romance. When she came to specialise academically she chose medieval French, and her fantasy life as a child was concentrated on the personalities, so different from her own, of the Three Musketeers, whose magnificent, grandiloquent behaviour filled her mind when her stout body was planted on fenland soil. Athos, Porthos and Aramis, swashbuckling in their swinging cloaks through a brilliantly coloured landscape, must have represented the unattainable. Even if the life of a plain middle-class girl in the twentieth century were magically rendered glamorous, Dorothy knew that somewhere in herself an imp of irreverence and irony would prevent her from enjoying it. In the scribbled notes for *Cat o'Mary*, she wrote that she got 'strongly the feeling that "inside me I don't REALLY care." '

If such self-observant, self-critical people give way to emotional reactions, they expose themselves to derision. Dorothy was to realise this, like Peter Wimsey, who said, 'When I try to be serious, I make such a bloody fool of myself.' We do not know what events in her childhood taught Dorothy that this was to be her fate; presumably the young woman who fell in love with indifferent men had been through the usual range of schoolgirl pashes, and discovered that a large, bespectacled child mooning after a hopeless target quickly becomes a laughing stock. She evolved a protective technique—she turned herself into a clown, parading her feelings, such as they were, so as to be seen to share in the joke that other people would make of them. At school, where she was sent at the age of fifteen, she played the part of a defiant buffoon.

The Godolphin School in Salisbury gave Dorothy her first experience of proper competition and of being in a large community. Most of the girls there must have been at school from a younger age and have understood the bizarre customs of such places. Dorothy, who had read more about Greyfriars School than Angela Brazil's feminine equivalents, did not settle well into an establishment where she was so unusual—virtually bilingual in French, fluent in German, and infantile in mathematics. She was not popular, for she took little interest in 'the house' or 'the team' and one of the other girls said later that she was neither easy to make friends with nor interesting to know. However, she got on well with the staff, who thought she was brilliant but superficial. She wrote several pieces for the school magazine, acted, played the violin in the school orchestra, and the piano which she learnt from a German teacher with whom she was always to keep in touch, still sending her food parcels after World War II. Dorothy had an excellent singing voice and was obviously talented musically; in the twenties she took up the saxophone.

In the spring of 1911 Dorothy was ill for months with

measles and pneumonia. While she was ill, most of her hair fell out, so that she was forced to wear a wig. She returned to school for a short while, but left again to study at home; she did so to such good effect that she won the Gilchrist Scholarship to Somerville College, Oxford, presumably thus fulfilling her own and her parents' ambitions. School must have seemed to her an interlude among aliens. On the other hand, Oxford in general, and Somerville in particular, were full of people who shared Dorothy's interests and enthusiasms. Here was a place where, in 1912, a clever, educated female was at home, as she could be in few other places. Dorothy loved it. She was by this time a tall, thin girl with sparse dark hair, and noticeably pretty hands. Her voice was beautiful but loud, and her taste in clothes showy.

At Somerville Dorothy made friends of her own contemporaries for the first time in her life. Vera Brittain, who was two years younger, watched with interest the group of 'potentially interesting young women' who were her seniors, and said that Dorothy dominated her group at college, which included Charis Barnett, later Mrs Frankenburg and author of numerous books on birth control and child rearing; Margaret Chubb (Mrs Geoffry Pyke), who became secretary of the National Birth Control Association; Muriel ('Jim') Jaeger, later a novelist; Muriel St Clair Byrne, who was to work in the theatre and teach at the Royal Academy of Dramatic Art, and several others, most of whom remained friends with one another for life. They were all members of what Vera Brittain called 'an eclectic little group known as M.A.S., the Mutual Admiration Society'—self-named, before any hostile outsider could do so. The qualification for membership was the acceptance by the other members of an original piece of writing read aloud at one of their meetings, and membership was much desired. 'They took themselves very seriously,' Vera Brittain recalled in 1933. But she had taken an immediate liking to Dorothy and described her kindly: 'She was affable to freshers and belonged to the "examine-every-atom-of-you" type. A bouncing, exuberant young female, who always seemed to be preparing for tea parties . . .'

Dorothy spent a gregarious three years, chattering, arguing, singing and giggling. She could never imagine, looking back, how she had found the time to do any work, so busy was she with her social life, her singing, with picnics, with rowing, sculling and punting, and presumably, though she nowhere mentions it, with the extra-curricular activities rendered necessary by the war, such as attending Red Cross classes or doing fire drill. Other women who were undergraduates then mention the abnormality of those days when most of the men had disappeared, except for foreigners and medical students, and, after the first months, invalids. Food grew increasingly short, at first from voluntary restriction, and later from rationing; 'sedentary females', as students were classified, were lowest in the rations scale. Coal too was very short, and in the winter much studying was done cocooned in rugs. Other contemporaries have also written of the ever-present 'Belgian problem'—of raising money for the refugees, and visiting them.

Even if the male undergraduates had been in their colleges, instead of dying in Flanders, the young ladies of the women's colleges would rarely have been allowed to see them, for chaperonage remained very strict until well after the war. Vera Brittain remarked on Dorothy's much publicised, and self-publicised, passion for the organist Dr Hugh Allen, who had a reputation for being an enfant-terrible eccentric. He was the conductor of the Bach Choir, of which both Sayers and Brittain were members: 'During the practices of the Verdi Requiem, which we were preparing to sing in the Easter term, she sat among the mezzo contraltos and gazed at him with wide, adoring eyes, as though she were in church adoring her God. But a realistic sense of humour always saved her from becoming ridiculous.' Dorothy was not the only girl to have a crush on Hugh Allen and in a letter she speaks of 'a long procession of little tame cats that have adorned his organ loft in succession.' By guying her own attitudes, Dorothy averted pity; and in the play performed in her last term, Dorothy mocked herself and Allen by acting in a skit on him.

It was in her work that Dorothy was a dark horse. At that time the women's colleges sent reports home to the undergraduate's parents, and Dorothy's referred regularly to her cleverness and critical powers, but also to a shallowness, lack of restraint and want of imagination. In the event, it must have been to the dons' surprise that Dorothy L. Sayers took a first-class honours degree. What surprises later generations is that it was accepted as the end of her academic career. She would have been ideally suited to be a don. Her inclinations, as well as her training, fitted her for research and scholarship, and although she was bad at teaching children, disputation in tutorials with clever students would probably have suited her very well; and she was later to be a skilled and powerful lecturer. Perhaps she was not sufficiently popular with any of the dons for them to have suggested that she should consider returning; of course, by the time that any of them made their extremely guarded comments about her, she had published *Gaudy Night*, which gave great offence to Somerville, not simply because Dorothy assumed that its regulations were unchanged in the twenty years since she had been subject to them, but because her picture of the Senior Common Room was not thought to be flattering. Certainly she makes some of the dons unattractive, but in Muriel St Clair Byrne's memory, they were much more eccentric than Dorothy Sayers made them.

Dorothy's own tutor was Mildred Pope, Tutor in Modern Languages at Somerville since 1894, who appears as the delightful Miss Lydgate in *Gaudy Night*. On her death another pupil, Enid Starkie, wrote, 'A burning desire to redress wrongs struggled in her for supremacy with an unquenchable belief in the native disinterestedness and goodwill of everyone . . . she was incapable of believing that there existed idle or unsatisfactory pupils, but only unhappy or unfortunate ones. She had the humble and disinterested love of learning of a mediaeval monk, whom she resembled in temperament and appearance.' Of her, at least, there is a sympathetic and attractive portrait in *Gaudy Night*. One which was much less kind was that of Doreen Wallace, who appeared as the clever woman wasting her time on the manual labour of farming, 'A Derby winner making shift with a coal cart'. The two women had disagreed violently on the question of tithes, about which Dorothy, the parson's daughter, felt as the parsons in her books did: 'On the question of tithes I am adamant. Adamant.'

Dorothy was never good-looking, and she grew to adulthood at a time when so many young men had been killed and incapacitated that spinsterhood was bound to be the fate of many women. Dorothy wanted to be educated and to work; but she was physically passionate, and as interested in men as the most frivolous social butterfly. Oxford in her time was not the place to meet them, and she knew almost no men before she was about twenty-five.

She returned home to Bluntisham with a first-class degree and without any plans for a career. Unlike other people of her age, she took no active part in war work or service. While one can readily understand that she might have a physical revulsion from nursing and so never became a VAD, it does seem surprising that she did not find some equivalent work—even though the propaganda exhortations merely were to keep the home fires burning and carry on as normal. Those who had no direct contacts with servicemen were kept in the dark about what was going on in France, but Dorothy had cousins serving there, and they came to Bluntisham to recuperate from shell shock and gassing. She spent a few months at home performing the functions expected of a parson's daughter at sewing bees and fund-raising fêtes, and she prepared the poems—bitter little sonnets, mostly—for her first volume of verse. She applied for a teaching post through an agency, and was appointed as Modern Languages teacher at Hull Girls' High School. She taught there for two years, using methods which seemed unorthodox at the time to make sure that her pupils could speak as well as write another language; she formed a school choir, and experienced air raids. Like Somerset Maugham, who discovered as a medical student that pain did not enoble those who suffered it, contrary to accepted belief, Dorothy Sayers found that fear was not the dramatic emotion she had envisaged in her childhood fantasies about chivalry. Fear was 'brutal, bestial and degrading' and it may have been one of the few emotions which Dorothy ever wholeheartedly experienced. Perhaps it was the stripping of the last layer of uninvolved self which made her feel degraded.

Dorothy hated teaching and told her colleagues when she left the school, 'I can stand this sort of thing no longer; I would rather sweep the streets.' Her father moved to another remote rural parish, Christchurch, Cambs., in 1917; in the same year he helped to arrange for Dorothy to go to work as a kind of informal apprentice to Basil Blackwell, the Oxford bookseller,

who was at that time publishing the poetry of new young
writers. He had published Dorothy's own *Opus 1* in 1916, and
in 1919 was to publish her second volume, *Catholic Tales and
Christian Songs* . Both collections display a remarkable virtuosity
of technique without any great originality of thought.
Blackwell's experiment was short lived, for his young authors
abandoned him when they could for publishers who paid them
more, but while Dorothy was with him she learnt a good deal
about publishing and printing, and always remained interested
in it. She would protest, in later years, about such details as
single quotation marks and the choice of type face, and discuss
the layout of her pages with the publisher.

Dorothy moved into lodgings in Oxford and took up her
Oxford life again, making friends with the Somerville girls who
had been freshmen when she was in her last year, and rejoining
the Bach Choir. She had her first experience, now that her own
passion for Hugh Allen was past, of being the object of
somebody else's love. A friend of Basil Blackwell wooed her,
and she hated it. She never enjoyed being cherished, she liked
her relationships to include many bludgeoning arguments, and
she loathed people to worry about her. She spent a certain
amount of time worrying about someone else.

One of the former soldiers who had returned to Oxford was a
young man called Eric Whelpton, who lived in digs near
Dorothy's, and with whom she made friends. He was not yet
recovered from the war and used to faint several times a day;
he felt, he says, far too ill to think of love. Dorothy occasionally
looked after him, and it would not be surprising if the amateur
nurse fell in love with the patient, but if she did, Whelpton was
not aware of it. In his autobiography he wrote of her: 'strictly
speaking she was far from beautiful, but her grey eyes radiated
intelligence, her mobile features vividly expressed her thoughts
and emotions, and her voice, though high-pitched, was a
pleasant one. She usually wore black, but was given to
pendulous earrings and exotic strings of beads.' (Others who
remember Dorothy Sayers usually comment on the depth of
her beautiful voice.) Elsewhere, Eric Whelpton recalled his
Oxford friendship with her—from his own advanced age of
eighty-two—after it had been suggested in the press and in
Janet Hitchman's book that he was the model for Peter

Wimsey: 'our friendship was noble, dignified and a source of inspiration to me. It was intellectual on my side, passionate on hers . . .' The passion came later; Whelpton had no inkling of it in Oxford, and when he took up a post at the French school of Les Roches, he invited her to join him as a secretary and assistant. They were the only two English people there and were thrown very much together, and perhaps then Dorothy did feel more affectionate towards him than he did to her. Whelpton had been impressed by the permissiveness of the young women in wartime and in post-war Oxford, but had not taken advantage of it with Dorothy. When a friend of theirs in France found herself pregnant, Dorothy was deeply upset; however she became very busy first in persuading the girl that abortion was both criminal and sinful, and then in helping her through the arrangements for having the child. She would have been comforting, in an overbearing way, for she was very efficient and liked to be busy. She ran the office at Les Roches admirably, but the work was not time-consuming, and in their ample spare time she and Eric Whelpton read and talked about obscure seventeenth-century poetry and modern French literature. Dorothy filled in a lot of time reading the cheap crime books known as penny dreadfuls, the novels of Maurice le Blanc, and Barbey d'Aurevilliers' *Les Diaboliques*:

> One day, when I teased her for reading such rubbish, she told me that she was part of a team consisting of the Coles, Michael Sadlier and one or two others who were deliberately preparing to create a vogue in detective novels; she suggested that I should join them. I replied rather sourly that I did not imagine for a moment that the public would fall for such rubbish, and that I would have nothing to do with it.

Eric Whelpton never did learn to like 'such rubbish' and never even finished any of Dorothy Sayers' own novels—an admirable lack of vanity, in one who was popularly supposed to be portrayed in them.

Dorothy stayed at Les Roches for less than a year, and when she left, still on good terms with Whelpton, they continued to correspond for some time. Although he shared one or two characteristics with Peter Wimsey, such as an interest in wine and fluency in languages, Dorothy had similar enthusiasms to Wimsey's herself, even when she was too poor to indulge them —a character so clearly derived partly from literary sources and partly from her own personality, needs no model.

In 1920 Dorothy was back in England, in time to be among the first group of women to take their degrees at Oxford; there is an amusing account of them rushing through a quick change of academic hoods in order to take their Bachelor of Arts and Master of Arts degrees almost simultaneously. For the rest of her life Dorothy would enjoy the sonorous phrases by which she had earned the right to be described. Harriet Vane was allowed to derive the same pleasure from them: 'Scholar; Master of Arts; Senior Member of this University; Statutum est quod Juniores Senioribus debitam et congruam reverentiam tum in privato tum in publico exhibeant; a place achieved, inalienable, worthy of reverence.'

Dorothy took a London flat, in Mecklenburgh Square, Bloomsbury, and worked at a series of teaching jobs, between bouts of unemployment. She was still, at the age of twenty-nine, being supported by her father, but the plan for money-making she had proposed to Eric Whelpton was now put into action. She wrote *Whose Body?* (1923), the initial idea for which—the naked, unidentified body in a bath—had come to her when she and her friends at Somerville were playing a game in which each player added a new dramatic incident to a story. 'I've written a silly book, but I don't suppose any publisher will take it,' she told her parents, and for some time no publisher did. Eventually it was bought by Fisher and Unwin (later Ernest Benn) and she stayed with Benn for her first three books, then moving to Gollancz (and embarrassing Victor Gollancz by trying to entice other Benn authors to defect with her). *Whose Body?* was sold in America also, and Dorothy was able to write to her parents that she could now support herself and stay on in London. 'I haven't the least confidence in the stuff,' she said about her book, but added that it was a pity, because she enjoyed turning it out.

When her career was established, Dorothy claimed that her aim had not been to create a vogue for shockers, but to write a book which was as much a novel of manners as a crossword-puzzle type of detective story. *Whose Body?* is original in plot, excellently worked out, and written in a literate style which marked it out on its publication in 1925 as a notable first book. But it is not a novel of manners. Peter Wimsey is too much a caricature of an aristocratic dilettante, Bunter of a superlatively efficient manservant. They are almost indistinguishable from Wooster and Jeeves. Sayers herself did not know anybody who lived the life of a rich nobleman, and derived her characters from an amalgamation of her wide reading.

By the time that *Whose Body?* was published, Dorothy had been working for some time as a copywriter at Benson's Advertising Agency and had moved to a new flat in Great James Street. The work may not have seemed important to a woman with a first-class degree in medieval French but it paid her a good salary and was ideally suited to someone with her facility for word-games and verse making. She was prodigal with ideas; *Murder Must Advertise*, the novel she set in Benson's, uses a good many which could have been put to commercial use. The novel gives an accurate description of life in this old established firm, and the spiral staircase down which the murder victim falls now has attached to it a plaque which records its place in fiction. Dorothy made no effort to disguise the organisation; some of their personnel appear in the novel as to such events as Benson's Annual Cricket Match against Virol Ltd. Dorothy did not spare herself either; she is the sardonic Miss Meteyard, the plain, unmarried, Oxford graduate, amusing on any subject, facile with witty copy, never without an apt quotation, and able to cover any subject except 'women's goods'. In the Whiffling campaign, Dorothy gives an amusing account of the development of 'The Mustard Club' which was an advertising sensation in its day.

Dorothy enjoyed the work at Benson's, and was easily able to satisfy any conscientious scruples she might have had. In 1940, she puts these words into the mouth of an advertising executive, in a propaganda article: 'As a matter of fact I don't much mind—never have minded—the sort of direct lying we put out. It's labelled "advertisement" and if the public believe everything we tell them, they have been warned.'

Dorothy stayed at Benson's for ten years, during which period her private life was full of excitement. Some time in 1921 she had become involved with a writer and journalist called John Cournos. She was twenty-eight and longed to be married and have children. She thought that a woman was disgraced by barrenness and virginity. Many years later, writing about medieval Italy, she was to say,

> the denial of a physical desire was not then looked upon as a solecism, nor had the achievement of happiness been erected into a moral obligation. The lover who had set his heart on the unattainable suffered, no doubt, the usual bodily frustrations, but he was not haunted by a guilty sense of personal failure and social inadequacy. He was not despised as an escapist; nobody told him that he was maladjusted, or hinted that there was something seriously wrong with him if he was not uproariously releasing his repressions at every turn.

At the age of twenty-eight she felt obliged to release her own repressions.

The description of John Cournos makes him seem an extraordinarily perverse choice for Dorothy. He had been born in Kiev in 1881, in an orthodox Jewish home. With his family he emigrated to Philadelphia as a refugee from persecution. In 1912 he came to live in England. He spent the war decoding and translating Russian wireless messages, and worked in the Russian department of the Foreign Office between 1917 and 1920, when he resigned to concentrate on writing. He often stayed in Dorothy's flat.

She was too old, by modern standards, for rebellion, but it really looks as though her attachment to Cournos was just that. A proud woman, a practising Christian, a Conservative by conviction, could never have found anything in common with an emigré Jew who wanted no responsibility, and was, moreover, a man full of self-importance and self-pity; and Dorothy's critical faculties must have been offended by Cournos's deplorable style of writing.

In their circle of friends, free love and open marriage were much discussed, and no doubt Dorothy was as dogmatic about them as everything else. Two of her friends were active in the Birth Control movement, but Dorothy disapproved of it. She thought contraceptives were unnatural, and refused to sleep with Cournos, who did not want children, 'with the taint of the rubber shop'.

In October 1922 Cournos went back to America. By the time she was middle-aged, Dorothy had convinced herself that there was an inherent incompatibility between Jews and the indigenous populations of their 'host nations'. She wrote that there was a difference in Jews, traceable back to the life of Christ, which was the division between their history and that of the Christian nations. Perhaps her own indefensible supposition is traceable to her life with Cournos who, Jewish or not, was certainly different from Dorothy L. Sayers. (She remained on excellent terms with her flamboyantly Jewish publisher all her life, however.)

Her next relationship was with a man as unlike Cournos as possible, a cycle and motor mechanic, 'a poor devil whom I chummed up with one weekend, finding him left lonely.' He was a practical man, not given to agonising over moral choices. Whether Dorothy endured 'the taint of the rubber shop' or not, is not known, but within a few months she was pregnant. If contraception was unnatural, then how much more so was abortion, though, in her London circle, easy to arrange. Dorothy must have remembered the arguments about sin and crime she used to her pregnant friend in France; she must have been reminded of her harangues to John Cournos about the wholesomeness of procreation. Perhaps indeed she assumed the child's father would marry her and became pregnant on purpose.

Dorothy managed to avoid her family for a few months, telling them that she would be busy with her second book; she arranged to bear the child at a private nursing home near Bournemouth. It was even easy to find a foster mother: a cousin, the greatest, closest, best-loved friend of her childhood, Ivy Shrimpton, who with her mother was already fostering three other orphans. John Anthony was born on 3 January 1924, and registered in his mother's real name. At the end of the month Dorothy delivered him to Ivy Shrimpton in Oxfordshire, and only then, by letter, told Ivy that the child was her own, and begged her to keep this secret. Ivy did so throughout the years of bringing the boy up, not even telling the truth to her aunt Helen Sayers, the child's grandmother, on her visits to Oxfordshire.

Dorothy was only away from Benson's for eight weeks, and

it is said that none of her colleagues there, beside whom she worked until the end of the eighth month of pregnancy, noticed her condition. She was in any case growing fatter. By the time of her death she was an extremely large woman, impeded by her own girth. In the April of that year her lover finally disappeared from her life. She was very depressed, and the cause was not only hormonal, for a year after the child's birth.

During all this time Dorothy was trying to write her second novel. She needed the money for Anthony, whose sole financial support she would be. *Clouds of Witness* (1926) was always associated in her mind with the humiliations and miseries she endured while she was writing it. The book depicts a man's hopeless love for a beautiful woman—so bitterly different from Dorothy's own situation; and in part of the plot Wimsey's pretty sister is yearned for by his friend the police inspector. The Duke of Denver, Wimsey's brother, is accused of murder, and is acquitted at a full-scale, fully robed trial by his peers in the House of Lords. Part of Wimsey's rescue involves a trans-Atlantic flight in a storm—'My Lords, the barometer is falling'—a year before Lindbergh did it. The French style on which the Oxford examiners had congratulated Dorothy is given full rein in letters from the dead man. There is a witty and catty description of The Soviet Club (to which Dorothy had no doubt been introduced by Cournos) where the prosperous bourgeoisie discuss the abolition of capitalism. 'I'm afraid we shall never get it put right without a bloody revolution, you know. It's very terrible, of course, but salutary and inevitable.'

For two years Dorothy had been writing to Cournos that she was looking for a husband. She wanted a practical man about whom she would not have to lie to her family. In 1926 she found one: Captain Oswald Arthur Fleming, who called himself Major Oswold Atherton Fleming and was always addressed as 'Mac'. He was the same age as Cournos, twelve years older than Dorothy. His family was Scottish, and he had been married before the war to another parson's daughter by whom he had two daughters. He fought in the Boer War, and from 1915 to 1919 served in a Royal Artillery regiment. Between these two episodes, he had become a successful Fleet Street journalist. He did not return to his wife after the war, or see his children again. He was divorced in 1925. Though this was evidently not on Dorothy's account, she began at some time to make regular payments to the first Mrs Fleming, and carried them on after Mac's death. However, Mac's daughters always blamed Dorothy for separating them and for keeping them apart from their father, with whom they had no further contact at all.

Mac was an attractive, entertaining man when Dorothy met him, much interested in painting, photography, and food; he published a cookery book, though apparently did not cook. He worked as a correspondent for the *News of the World*, specialising in motoring and crime. He and Dorothy had fun together. (One of their outings was to visit the Silent Pool and Newlands Corner in Berkshire, when everyone was hunting for Agatha Christie.)

With only two days warning to Dorothy's parents, Mac and Dorothy were married in a register office. Mac, a divorced man, could not be married in church. They presently took the flat above the one Dorothy already rented. When Dorothy's father died in 1928, they bought a house in the main street of Witham for Mrs Sayers and Aunt Maud. Mrs Sayers herself died a few months after moving there and the house became the Flemings' home, and the London flat a pied à terre.

Dorothy may have hoped that Fleming would welcome Anthony, but no adoption took place. Anthony did take the name of Fleming, and at some stage in his childhood 'cousin Dorothy' began to sign her letters to him 'mother', but he did not find out that she was more than an informally adoptive parent until after the war when he needed to see his birth certificate to get a passport. Anthony corresponded with Dorothy, and she went to see him, but their relationship was not close. Those who had heard of him in Witham supposed him to be the son of Mac's first marriage, Dorothy's stepson. Anthony's home remained with Ivy Shrimpton. He was educated at a boarding prep school, at Malvern, and at Balliol College, Oxford (Peter Wimsey's college). He then went to work in the petroleum business and now lives abroad. Neither of Dorothy's parents, nor any of her friends, knew that she had borne a child. In her will, she refers to him as her adopted son.

Her husband too was something of a mystery to many of her

friends. He was ill, on and off, almost from the time they were married, and drank too much. Their relationship was one which others have tried to analyse, but it remains enigmatic. It has been asserted that they had a happy sexual relationship; that they enjoyed eating together, for he was a gourmet and she both gourmet and gourmande; that they shared an enthusiasm for real ale. Mac painted and sketched and had numerous undemanding hobbies. He was fond of Dorothy's Aunt Maud who lived with them in Witham. However, Dorothy rarely mentioned Mac to her London friends, and such references as there are to him in her letters are unaffectionate. Neighbours describe the two as leading separate lives, one in the front, the other in the back half of their house in Witham. They felt that Mac was overshadowed by his wife; and he took offence if he was introduced as Dorothy Sayers' husband. He was that figure from stock, the bar-propping major, 'a wonderful entertainer in the Red Lion', a teller of tall stories. Mac ceased to work as a journalist soon after their marriage, possibly because his health was poor. He led a leisurely life, and a neighbour thought that 'he lived in a half world between reality and fantasy'.

Janet Hitchman pointed out, unkindly but probably rightly, the resemblance between Mac and the husband who is the victim in *The Documents in the Case* (1930). This novel is a little bit dull, but it is technically flawless, being told in the form of letters in which the writer's acute ear and talent for pastiche have full scope. Wimsey does not appear. The book was written with the help of that same Robert Eustace (a Dr Barton) who had earlier collaborated with L. T. Meade. The plot consists of a wife's affair with an artist, and her husband's death from poisonous fungi. The husband, Harrison, is like Mac in several ways: he publishes a cookery book; he draws in pastels and crayons; he is sincere, unimaginative and irritable; he is considerably older than his wife, and has been married before. They even have an 'Aunt Maud' figure living in their house to perform the Greek chorus role. Hitchman interprets the book as a warning from Dorothy to Mac that his attitude was poisoning their lives, but she doubted that 'Fleming's shallow mind could take in the lesson she was trying to instil'. He may not even have read her books.

The question has been asked, why did Dorothy stick to Mac? It would be more remarkable if she had left him. Emotional women may flounce off in a fury, unconventional ones may prefer loneliness to irritation. A worldly and sensible woman of Dorothy's time would have preferred to retain the status of a married woman—so important to one of her background; and she would have reminded herself that even register office promises are binding. The two probably developed a perfectly satisfactory modus vivendi, and they did live together until Mac's death in 1950, though of course Dorothy was only at Witham at weekends, except during the war.

The life the Flemings led in Witham was not typical either for a daughter of the parsonage or for a small town. Dorothy caused some resentment by taking little part in local affairs. When the Flemings came to live in Witham, it was, her secretary said, 'a nine days wonder'. Apparently her appearance startled the natives as much as anything. Her usual clothes were a mannish suit, with an expandable, wrap around skirt, a shirt and a tie, topped by a wide felt hat. This, combined with her size and her jangling jewellery, would certainly have made her stand out from the crowd. In those days, and still to a certain extent today, people who lived in a small community were expected to contribute their time and interest to its doings. Dorothy must have known this perfectly well. If, understandably, she wanted no part of it, why did she choose to live there? She hated the country and never went for walks; nor did she enjoy gardening. Surely she would have been much happier in the urban anonymity of London.

Mac, however, fitted into Witham well, and was a popular figure there; he even presented a cup to the bowling club. Most people in the place evidently liked him very much the better of the two. In a volume entitled *Talking of Dorothy L. Sayers* (privately published by the society set up in her honour), which would probably have infuriated its subject as much as it would have amused her, several shopkeepers and neighbours remember her queue jumping, shopping, picking the brains of craftsmen and tradesmen and attending eight o'clock church services. Some speak of Mac and Dorothy calling each other 'old boy' and 'old girl', others say that Dorothy shouted and Mac slunk away. All mention her lack of interest in domesticity. She kept cats, whose food made the house smell, the timbers were riddled with woodworm, the pipes were carelessly allowed to freeze and burst, her own blocked gutters caused a flood in the house next door. It is all very trivial, but no doubt one would devour such details about Shakespeare or Milton. Everything seems to add up to a woman who had learnt not to care what other people thought of her, and who was not particularly interested in what she thought of them. It is not surprising that the life at Witham is the only part of her experience which is not in some way transmuted into fiction. The closest she comes to it is Great Pagford in the background of *Busman's Honeymoon*.

Dorothy Sayers published a remarkable quantity of work between 1923 and 1938, the fifteen years in which she was writing detective novels. Considering that each book is long, densely written, elaborately planned and characterised, and that for ten of those years the author was working full time in another profession which also demanded her creative energy, her output is prodigious. There were altogether twelve full-length novels, some memorable criticism of crime fiction, including a regular review column in the *Sunday Times*, two masterly potted histories written as prefaces to columns which she edited, and several volumes of her short stories. These stories are lively and original, some very macabre. She put less of herself into them than into the novels. In addition, in 1929 Ernest Benn published Dorothy's translation of *Tristan in Brittany*, a medieval verse drama, parts of which had appeared in the journal *Modern Languages*. She also collected material for a projected biography of Wilkie Collins, but did not finish it.

Each of her novels draws to some extent on Dorothy's own experience. She used the settings which she knew, that of her childhood in *The Nine Tailors* (1934), of her university for *Gaudy Night* (1936), and of her work at Benson's for *Murder Must Advertise*, which she finished just after her ten years' stint there. *The Unpleasantness at the Bellona Club* (1928) and *Strong Poison* (1938) use her experience of 'Bohemian' life in post-war London; there is an interesting contrast, echoed by Dorothy and Mac's own lives, between the attitude expressed by Mary Wimsey in *Clouds of Witness*—'We believe in men and women being equal. Why should the one always be the breadwinner more than the other?'—and that of the unhappy shell-shocked George Fentiman in *The Unpleasantness at the Bellona Club*, deeply resentful of the working women who, he thinks, have taken the jobs he cannot get, including the wife who supports him. 'I *know* you don't want to work. I know it's only because of the damned rotten position I'm in. You needn't keep on about it. I know I'm a failure. Thank your stars, Wimsey, that when you marry you'll be able to support your wife.'

For their honeymoon and subsequent holidays, Mac and Dorothy went to Kirkcudbright, in south-western Scotland, where Mac could go out with his easel or fishing rod, while Dorothy presumably visited her own elderly relations who lived there, and got on with her handwork and writing. She was a great craftswoman; she did knitting, embroidery, lino-cuts and carpentry, and after her introduction to the theatre in 1936 she built herself a model theatre and set the stage with hand-made puppets. The *Five Red Herrings* (1930) is set in Kirkcudbright; Dorothy said it was the only book which she wrote around a place. The year after it was published visitors to Kirkcudbright were to be seen identifying the scenes in the story. Unfortunately, a book which is written around a place, rather than around people or a plot, is liable to be dull, as this one is.

Have His Carcase (1932) takes place in a south-coast resort. Presumably Dorothy had visited more than one such town, but the distaste with which she describes the place she calls Wilvercombe makes it seem likely that Bournemouth, where she spent four weeks when her son was born, was in her mind. 'One is always vulgar at watering places,' Wimsey remarks in *Gaudy Night*. *Have his Carcase* marks Harriet Vane's second appearance. *Strong Poison*, in which Wimsey falls in love with her and proves her innocent of a murder charge, was the first. *Strong Poison* includes some outstandingly good scenes and characters as well as some memorable vignettes of the kind of life Dorothy had led in her own bachelor days; it also contains a conversation which might well be from life in which Harriet Vane's detective stories are unfavourably compared with her dead lover's novels.

Murder Must Advertise was written to fulfil Dorothy's contractual obligation, for her agent, David Higham, had arranged for her publisher to pay her a regular income, rather than advances for individual books. Dorothy was stuck with the book she had intended to write, and did finish afterwards, *The Nine Tailors*, and wrote *Murder Must Advertise* in a hurry. In many peoples' opinion it is her best book, which makes it one of the best detective novels of all, and it is interesting that it should have been the one she dashed off, as it were, from the top of her head. It is the perfect example to illustrate her own belief that a detective story's success depends very much on an accurate and well-written background. 'Readers seem to like books which tell them how other people live—any people, advertisers, bell ringers, women dons, butchers, bakers or candlestick makers—so long as the detail is full and accurate, and the object of the work is not overt propaganda.'

Looking back over her novels, Dorothy Sayers said that each successive book worked gradually nearer to returning the detective novel form to what it had been in the hands of Collins and Le Fanu, and that *Murder Must Advertise* was her first real attempt to fuse the novel of manners and the crossword-puzzle type of story. In it, she wrote in 1937:

> for the first time the criticism of life was not relegated to incidental observations and character sketches, but was actually part of the plot, as it ought to be. It was not quite successful; the idea of symbolically opposing two cardboard worlds—that of the advertiser and the drug taker—was all right; and it was suitable that Peter, who stands for reality, should never appear in either except disguised; but the working out was a little too melodramatic and the handling rather uneven . . .

Actually what readers remember is not something metaphysical about cardboard worlds, but the vivid description of a busy advertising agency.

The Nine Tailors, Dorothy said in the same article, was a shot at 'combining detection with poetic romance'. Again, it is for something else that the book is memorable. The plot, though sound, is very much less interesting than the setting and the information about campanology. That is the major example in her fiction, among numerous others, of Dorothy's delight in precise, specialised knowledge. She liked to be informed about other peoples' 'shop'. Writing this book was a labour of love, she told Victor Gollancz, but the book has a faint odour of the tutorial about it. Edmund Wilson, that jaundiced commentator on crime fiction, said that it was one of the dullest books he had ever encountered in any field.

Dr Trevor Hall points out a marked likeness between details of this book and John Meade Faulkner's *The Nebuly Coat*—another example of the way in which Dorothy Sayers' style was influenced as much by literature as by life.

By the time that she had written *The Nine Tailors*, Dorothy was playing with the idea of writing a 'straight' novel. Peter was no longer the puppet she had invented for *Whose Body?* and there seemed to be no way in which she could either marry him and Harriet off, or part them, without doing violence to her idea of them. In any case, Dorothy wanted to impart a message about intellectual integrity. She planned a self-evidently autobiographical novel 'about an Oxford woman graduate who found, in middle life . . . that her real vocation and full emotional fulfilment were to be found in the creative life of the intellect.'

This impulse is fascinating. It is as though Dorothy at the age of forty, having once been embarrassed by her own intellectualism and emotional caution, had now come to accept her own personality. The girl who had been a 'brain' had probably learnt from society that girls should be something quite different—emotional, loving, impulsive and physical. She had spent years forcing herself into the romantic mould. In *Gaudy Night* it is as though she were answering all the tacit or spoken criticism over the years, both of her 'coldness' and of her work in a field which so many people think inferior. Harriet Vane answers this point also:

> For one thing, writers can't pick and choose until they've made money. If you've made your name for one kind of book and then switch over to another, your sales are apt to go down, and that's the brutal fact . . . I know what you're thinking—that anyone with proper sensitive feeling would rather scrub floors for a living. But I should scrub floors very badly, and I write detective stories rather well. I don't see why proper feelings should prevent me from doing my proper job.

Dorothy ardently believed in a doctrine of 'the proper job'. When she was no longer interested in writing fiction, she referred to it often. She believed that each individual has some work which is properly his, and that he betrays himself by not doing it. 'The writer's duty to God is his duty to his work . . . the writer is about his Father's business.' She respected craftsmanship and thought of herself as a craftsman. She said:

> there is not only a trick but a 'craft' of writing mystery stories. It does give just that curious satisfaction which the exercise of cunning craftsmanship always give to the worker. It is almost as satisfying as working with one's hands. It is rather like laying a mosaic—putting in each piece—apparently meaningless and detached—into its place, until one suddenly sees the thing as a consistent picture.

Dorothy believed that the work is more important than the worker, and put her conviction into words in a religious play, *The Zeal of Thy House*:

> Death gnaw upon me, purge my bones with fire
> But let my work, all that was good in me,
> All that was God, stand up and live and grow.
> The work is sound, oh Lord, no rottenness there—
> Only in me.

By the time that she wrote these words, Dorothy Sayers no longer believed that writing novels was her proper job. One can sense a valedictory air in *Gaudy Night*, as though she regarded it as her final fictional statement.

The idea of using her existing characters to express the message she had wished to make the theme of her straight novel came to Dorothy when she was considering her speech for a dinner at Somerville:

> I discovered that in Oxford I had the solution to all my three problems at once. On the intellectual platform, alone of all others, Harriet could stand free and equal with Peter, since in that sphere she had never been false to her own standards. By choosing a plot that should exhibit intellectual integrity as the one great permanent value in an emotionally unstable world, I should be saying the thing that, in a confused way, I had been wanting to say all my life . . .

The crime was to be the result of emotion uncontrolled by intellect. The reconciliation between Peter and Harriet was to come through their common realisation that

> she must come to him as a free agent, if she came at all, and must realise that she was independent of him, before she could bring her dependence as a willing gift. At all costs, and even at the risk of losing her altogether, he must prevent her from committing
> The greatest treason
> To do the right thing for the wrong reason.

Critical reaction to *Gaudy Night* has been mixed. Dorothy herself was even more dubious about her manuscript than usual—she always feared that they were 'rotten' or 'disagreeable' or 'not altogether satisfactory'. The book was very successful on its first publication, especially in America. To some people, it is Dorothy's worst book, full of high falutin' pretentiousness. It was felt that a detective novel was not the place for a lesson on the eternal verities. Julian Symons' cool judgement is that it is 'essentially a "woman's novel" full of the most tedious pseudo-serious chat between the characters', and he sees a breathtaking gap between Dorothy Sayers' intention and achievement. Barzun and Taylor, on the other hand, thought it 'a remarkable achievement'. Mary McCarthy said, 'Her venture into the novelist's field is exactly as regrettable . . . as the stage debut of a drawing room mimic,' in an article called 'Highbrow Shockers'. Q. D. Leavis, not surprisingly, was the most acid of all. She said that Sayers 'performed the function of giving the impression of intellectual exercise to readers who would very much dislike that kind of exercise if it was actually presented to them.' This may be true; but there is no doubt that generations of schoolgirls have been inspired to try for a place at one of the Oxford or Cambridge women's colleges because of reading *Gaudy Night* at an impressionable age; one such, myself, is unchanged in her admiration for the book.

Dorothy Sayers' last crime novel was an afterthought. By the time it appeared as a book, she had been bitten by the theatre bug to which women novelists seem so susceptible. Her friend Muriel St Clair Byrne had persuaded her to try writing a play around Lord Peter, and the two women collaborated on one during 1935. The initial idea came from a comical chimney sweep who had amused Dorothy in Witham. Dorothy absolutely refused to allow Gollancz to publish the book before the play was produced, in late 1936. *Busman's Honeymoon* was successful on the stage, with Dennis Arundel playing Peter Wimsey to Dorothy's great satisfaction. She was always to feel, and show, unrestrained loyalty to individual actors and producers. The famous middle-aged lady was the same person who had given way to adolescent crushes.

Dorothy padded the play out into a book, 'a love story with detective interruptions'. The love story part is a little embarrassing, and the detection slight, but Dorothy's gusto and verbal energy carried her through even that, and some of the minor characters, particularly the 'comics' are very well done.

Although one should believe Dorothy's regular denials that she used real-life models for her hero and heroine (apart, of course, from herself—aspects of both are autobiographical), she was certainly producing portraits in many, if not most, of her minor ones. The clergymen are all so similarly holy and so like the descriptions others have left of the Reverend Henry Sayers, it is as though she could not imagine any other kind of vicar; their wives are all so hardworking and self-sacrificing, the charwomen so pawky and cockney, the spinsters all so very spinsterish, that if so many of them were not so vividly memorable, one would suppose them all to be drawn from some novelists' central casting. But we know that the characters in *Murder Must Advertise*, at least, are identifiable, and it does seem likely that this is true of many of the others. They are all people whom Dorothy had seen or met, and, especially, heard. She was more of a reporter than an inventor.

Dorothy Sayers always said that she had only written detective stories because she needed the money, and that she was glad to be able to stop. 'It's surely not unreasonable that after making a sufficiency of money for a modest existence, I should feel inclined to return to the sort of literary activity for which I originally trained.' There were to be no more Wimsey books, only a few perfunctory short stories and some letters from various members of the hero's circle, written as a kind of

social propaganda or commentary for *The Spectator* in the first
months of the war. They are full of wit and observation, but
their tone is patronising, and after a few months they ceased to
appear.

It is probably true that Dorothy was glad to escape the
bondage of a freelance fiction writer as soon as she could afford
to; few who have not experienced it can understand to what
extent home can become a prison and freedom illusory in that
chancy profession. The attractions of alternative employment
must have been great, particularly since Dorothy had by then
experienced the exciting 'togetherness' of rehearsing a play,
and , as Muriel St Clair Byrne said, 'become stage struck with
all the new people she met after the success of *Busman's
Honeymoon*, and was drawn out from her reclusiveness'. In the
theatre she found what she would like to find in her Church,
she told an audience to which she lectured after the war:
comradeship, charity, a common cause and co-operation.

What is much less easy to understand is that the impulse to
create fiction disappeared so completely. Why did Dorothy
decide that it was no longer her proper work? She did at some
stage write about a third of another Wimsey novel called
Thrones Dominations, which was, according to James Brabazon
who has been permitted to read it, intended to contrast the
marriage of Peter and Harriet with that of another, more
selfish, mutually exploitative couple. The notes include an
elaborate diagram of the development of the relationships, and
the word 'murder' in capitals, but this exposition of her beliefs
about marriage was never finished.

I suggest, with no other evidence than intuition, that the real
reason Dorothy gave up writing fiction was that she had used
up all her experience, described all the places she knew well,
presented all the characters, said all she had to say on subjects
other than religion. By the time she had new material, she had
thrown herself into other enthusiasms and occupations, and
there was no going back to fiction. She remained an interested
critic of crime novels, indeed one of the best critics the form has
ever had, for she applied her scholar's mind and personal
experience to the task. She carried on as a member, and later
as President, of the Detection Club, assiduously attending its
meetings and dinners, and partaking with gusto in the rituals

which less histrionic members found rather embarrassing. But her career as a detective novelist was over by 1942, when her last short story, *Tallboys*, appeared. Less than five years before she had said, 'I can now see no end to Peter Wimsey this side the grave.'

Forty years on, Dorothy Sayers' novels are still read, and have been introduced to new enthusiasts by broadcast radio and television dramatisations. The offence caused to her contemporaries by her snobbery is blurred now that her books are period pieces; the social judgements, the assumption that right-thinking people are Conservative Anglicans, the general atmosphere of 'the rich man in his castle, the poor man at his gate' are more readily ignored by readers who think that since the days when God made men high or lowly and ordered their estate we have changed all that. However deplorable some of the sentiments explicitly or implicitly expressed in the novels, however irritating some of the irrelevant intrusions, Dorothy Sayers' novels so far remain supreme in that nebulous area where a detective novel has pretensions to be read for more than its plot.

They also remain the perfect examples of part of my thesis: that the popularity of such books is very largely due to their authors sharing, and thus providing, the ingrained fantasies of their readers. In her early life, Dorothy Sayers did rebel against the rules she had been brought up to obey; but by the time she was married she was unconventional only in such superficialities as her clothes and her 'look-at-me' behaviour. Her principles were profoundly conservative.

Dorothy became, or began to show that she was, immensely patriotic on John Bullish lines, especially after the outbreak of war. She would pronounce on the characteristics of The English whenever she had the chance, in that peculiarly English manner in which even criticism is really inverted praise. Her politics were high Tory, and she had settled into High Anglo-Catholicism. She loved expounding her views, and was a regular lecturer and broadcaster. She was said to be excellent as both, the hatred of teaching children which she had felt in Hull having been changed into an eagerness to enlighten adults. During the 1930s she had given many radio broadcasts, sometimes participating with other novelists in serial stories, sometimes pontificating on programmes like *Any Questions*. She had written two verse plays for performance at Canterbury, *The Zeal of Thy House* in 1937, which was a blank verse drama centring around the sin of pride, and in 1939, a version of the Faust legend called *The Devil To Pay*.

In 1938, Dorothy wrote a nativity play for the BBC called *He that Should Come*, and also began to contribute to a series of religious talks. In 1940, she began work on a series of plays under the title *The Man Born to be King*, which were originally intended for broadcasting on Children's Hour. Their production was complicated by the kind of adverse publicity which is the best possible advertisement. Dorothy had read some of the work aloud at a Press Conference, which resulted in such headlines as 'Life of Christ In Slang', and 'Broadcasting House—The Temple of Blasphemy'. The Lord's Day Observance Society protested, a knight from the shires asked questions in the House of Commons, and a rousing quarrel was enjoyed by all, not least Dorothy. Eventually the works were broadcast and enthusiastically received, even by Mac. There were dramas within the studios as well as outside, for Dorothy resented any suggestions for change, and quarrelled with some of the BBC staff. James Brabazon, who is a professional television producer and in a good position to judge her behaviour, says that she behaved like a spoilt and hysterical amateur.

Through these broadcast plays, and other lectures and articles, Dorothy became famous as a theologian. To many people she seemed a potent apologist for the Christian Church. I am incompetent to judge this aspect of her work; but James Brabazon says that her only really original book was *The Mind of the Maker*, in which 'she managed, without any intellectual cheating, to bring God and Man closer together'. He added that she offered 'something remarkable and marvellous: a sense that there were some real intellectual grounds for perceiving a connection between God and Man.' In religion, as in everything else, she was a traditionalist. She believed in the accepted dogma of Anglicanism.

Dorothy, by the time she was middle-aged, did not want to change her own life, or the state of society. She would innovate in details—as she had tried to change the crime novel into a

novel of manners, and as she used new methods to describe the
life of Christ—but her message was a traditional one. Even in
her poetry she continued to use formal metres and rhyme
patterns; late in life some of her verse became more free, but by
then, free verse was a convention too.

Dorothy did attend church at Witham, but the centre of her
religious life was St Anne's House, Soho, an Anglo-Catholic
mission centre originally intended for 'thinking pagans'.
Dorothy lectured there herself, and spent much of her time
there. It gave her many opportunities for advocacy and
argument as the premises were threatened with redevelopment
and the church hierarchy queried the value of the work done in
them.

A continuing theological discussion was offered by a
protracted correspondence with other lay theologians who were
members of an Oxford-based group calling itself 'The
Inklings', because they had an inkling of the meaning of God.
Charles Williams in particular had become a regular
correspondent, and when Dorothy read his *The Figure of Beatrice*
she was inspired to go on to the works of Dante.

Dorothy had never read Dante before because she did not
know Italian, although Wimsey had already been collecting
Dante folios in *Whose Body?* (presumably Dorothy never read
the Russians in her life, if she only read in original languages).
However, Italian was easy for her to learn, since she was at
home in Latin and French, and she began to read what she
expected to be poetry—no less, but no more. She was stunned
by the excitement of the story, by the humour and horror of its
style, and above all by the personality of the poet. In Dante she
found the supreme love of her life, her 'soul mate and master'.
For years she was to wake and sleep with Dante, and soon she
had arranged to make a new translation for the Penguin
Classics series, which was edited by E. V. Rieu.

It made Dorothy furiously angry if the right of a detective
novelist to translate *The Divine Comedy* was questioned. She had
after all published a translation of *Tristan in Brittany* in 1930
and, as she pointed out, her education had amply qualified her
to interpret medieval romance languages. Translation was a
work which exactly suited her talents. She had always loved
playing with words, as a writer, as a solver and setter of

crossword puzzles, as a linguist; she welcomed the difficulties imposed by her decision to use the same rhyme scheme as the original, instead of prose or blank verse. She had always been fascinated by the period in which Dante wrote. Above all she found that *The Divine Comedy* offered exactly what she had always wanted: a poet whose times were as troubled as her own, in whom 'passionate flesh and passionate intellect [were] fused together in such a furnace of the passionate spirit . . . we need not forget that Dante is sublime, intellectual and, on occasion, grim; but we must also be prepared to find him simple, homely, humorous, tender, and bubbling over with ecstacy . . .'

No wonder Dorothy fell for Dante and that, having discovered him, she was finished with her own fictions, whether detective stories or religious plays. An education in literature is a danger for any potential novelist; their own fiction always seems so inadequate in comparison with what they have read and studied. In this, I believe, lies another reason for Dorothy's initial choice to write 'genre' fiction—her unwillingness to complete a straight novel. She did not want to be compared with unattainable models. She knew that her own insight and imagination were incapable of producing great fiction. She did not want to enter an unwinnable competition.

But I think that this decision to write a second-class type of imaginative work was one she was ashamed of in later years. When she was talking or writing to people who admired her work she was possessive; she took it at their estimation and was willing to write about her motives and meanings. In the second half of her life, the people she admired—and here one should bear in mind her capacity for hero worship—were those who rather despised the type of fiction she wrote and would not read it themselves; Tolkien, for instance, forced his way through a few of her books an increasingly disliked both Wimsey and Harriet. The silence of such correspondents as Tolkien, Williams and C. S. Lewis on the subject of the books which had initially made her well known, must have been its own message—and that not an unexpected one, for the academic education she had herself received must have taught her, even before the first word of *Whose Body?* was written, that scholars despise such books. Dorothy Sayers cared for approval and the opinions of others whom she respected were important to her. I believe it was, perhaps subconsciously, to appease them, that she spoke in later years of her work having been no more than a money spinner.

It was during the war that Dorothy found Dante, and—apart from a translation of *The Chanson de Roland*, which she published in 1957, just before her death—she concentrated on Dante for the rest of her life.

The account of Dorothy Sayers' work on Dante is interesting; less so, to the present writer, is her involvement in religious controversy, and in proselytising. Neither, however, is relevant to her development as a crime novelist, except in so far as medieval romance on the one hand, and an acceptance of orthodox ethics on the other, reveal something of the lifelong proclivities of a writer who has managed to enthral so many readers. Both these aspects of her later career have been amply discussed by other commentators.

Dorothy Sayers spent World War II at Witham, with Mac, Aunt Maud, and, for two years, a boy evacuee. She kept a series of pigs, which came in and out of her house like dogs; she knitted socks for seamen, cherished her collection of cactus plants, gave lectures and broadcasts and wrote industriously. Even when she was not working on specific projects, she expressed herself with her pen. C. S. Lewis said that she was 'one of the great English letter writers'; she wrote poetry; she thought onto the page. Her methods were incomprehensible to outsiders, and unexpected in a person with such a tidy mind, for her house was messy and her desk disorganised. She used to clear herself a space in the mess of papers to write in, and she hoarded old papers in the attic, which was so damp that after her death some had to be scraped off the floorboards.

Most writers offered to work for the Ministry of Information when war broke out, but Dorothy was not taken on. The file in the Public Record office shows that scribbled beside her name on the list of writers who had offered help are the words, 'very loquacious and difficult'. After the war she began again to spend much of her time in London, working almost always at Dante, on whom she had started in 1944. She wrote two more religious plays and several theological pamphlets.

The translation of *The Inferno*, which Dorothy insisted should simply be called *Hell*, appeared in 1949, and *Purgatory* in 1955. Dorothy was a little over half way through *Paradise* when she died.

After the war Dorothy began to lecture about Dante, and in 1946 she met Barbara Reynolds (Mrs Lewis Thorpe) whose friendship became very important to her, and to whom she felt, it seems, more maternal, and showed more affection, than she ever had to anyone else. She became Barbara Reynolds' godmother at an adult baptism. She kept her many other friendships in good repair also. Mac, on the other hand, was rarely mentioned, and some friends who thought themselves close to her were surprised to hear of his existence. After the war he was in and out of Guy's Hospital; he resumed contact with his brother for the first time since his second marriage, but did not meet his daughters. Mac died in 1950 and Dorothy arranged that a friend should scatter his ashes near Kirkcudbright.

Dorothy was invested with an honorary doctorate by the University of Durham and was proud to call herself D.Litt., but when she was offered an honorary Lambeth D.D., she refused to accept it, even after a correspondence with the Archbishop of Canterbury himself. Brabazon was not permitted to read the correspondence, but he believes that she thought herself unworthy because she was still in a state of sin. That sad conviction was the only aspect of religious truth which she knew from personal experience, she once said. All other dogmas were accepted only through the intellect. But there was also a more practical reason to hesitate. If Anthony Fleming's true parentage were ever publicised, Dorothy might cause the Lambeth honour to be made a mockery. She would undoubtedly have wished to avoid that.

Dorothy was busy with her translation, her lecturing, her friends, and always with the vehement arguments, in public and in private, which she so much enjoyed. She had grown mountainously large, and was a chain smoker. Though she never mentioned her health, she must have had some twinges of discomfort if not illness. But her death, on 17 December 1957, was sudden; she had spent a day buying Christmas presents, and returned home because the cats had to be fed. The next morning her body was found at the foot of her stairs.

She had gone up to take off her hat and coat and was on the way to the kitchen when a coronary thrombosis struck her down.

Since her childhood, Dorothy had longed to stand out from the crowd, and she had enjoyed fame. She claimed to disapprove of the personality cult, but she exposed herself in fiction; she was scholarly and vulgar; secretive and boastful. She said that she hated personal enquiries; but she would have been glad that people wanted to know. The paradox of her life has been best expressed by Professor Peter Green; in a review (in the *Times Literary Supplement*) of Janet Hitchman's book he gives an account of the fairies in attendance at her cradle in 1893:

> The Good Fairy, a romantic creature, got there first. She bestowed on Dorothy fame, wealth, creativity, first class brains, a gift for languages and music, an artistic scholar's temperament, the soul of a great lover, and a lifelong involvement with God. The Bad Fairy arrived late, nursing a hangover. Like the Greek Gods, she could not countermand gifts already issued; but she could, and did, do everything in her power to neutralise them by endowing the baby with other less desirable traits. She made Dorothy large, awkward, ugly, gauche and intense, with a loud unattractive voice, a weakness for rhetoric, and a self destructive naivety in affairs of the heart. She ensured that the writer's wealth would be won in a way that effectively prevented scholars from taking her seriously, and wasted her marvellous lingustic gifts until it was almost—but not quite—too late. She made the polemicist's public persona aggressive, pernickety and a trifle ridiculous. Then she went home, sourly confident in the abortive effect of her actions, yet still with a lurking (and as things turned out, justified) suspicion that God and the imagination would yet frustrate her plans at the eleventh hour.

7 Margery Allingham

Margery Allingham was unusual as a writer, in that she came to the profession with forethought. Indeed, she was trained for it, as in some families the children are trained to skate or swim. Her father taught her the tricks of the trade at an early age, with technical advice about such things as the layout of typescripts and the retention of copyrights.

Margery's great-grandfather, who was born in 1800, left £10,000 and the injunction to his family that no gentleman ever works; his son was the editor of the *Christian Globe* and had eight children, of whom Margery's father, Herbert John Allingham, was the oldest, and was brought up to believe that it would be his duty always to look after the younger members of the family. He followed his father as the editor of the *Christian Globe* for a while, and also edited the *London Journal*.

Herbert Allingham married his first cousin, Emily Jane Hughes, who was a milliner. They lived at first in west London, but later moved to Essex where she became a prolific journalist. Both the Allinghams contributed to many weekly and monthly magazines. They kept a flat in London, but their home was the converted rectory at Layer Breton, on the Essex salt marshes, where they were visited every weekend by friends who were writers, journalists, and newspaper people of all kinds.

Margery was born in 1904. Her earliest memories were of long, quiet days playing by herself in the garden, when the only sound seemed to be the scratching of pens and the murmur of bees, occasionally interrupted by the soft drone of voices when the writers read their own work aloud to themselves, or to anyone else who would listen. 'My father wrote, my mother wrote, all the weekend visitors wrote, and as soon as I could master the appallingly difficult business of making the initial marks, so did I.' She had been taught to read by her grandmother. Later she was to say that in her family writing was regarded as the only reasonable way of passing the time, let alone of making a living. The life style must have seemed peculiar to the natives of that unsophisticated place. Once a new housemaid was so exasperated by her employers' behaviour that she snatched the notebook from the small Margery's hand, exclaiming, 'Master, Missus and three strangers all sitting in different rooms writing down LIES, and now you are starting!' Margery's Albert Campion was later to say that 'all young persons who voluntarily shut themselves up half their lives alone, scribbling down lies in the pathetic hope of entertaining their fellows, must necessarily be the victims of some sort of phobia.'

Herbert Allingham gave up his editing job when he was in his late thirties to devote himself to pouring out melodramatic stories for magazines, in at least two instalments of five thousand words a week; he also wrote numerous boys' school stories. He was a peaceful, logical man with a low threshold of boredom, but he believed strongly in being tolerant, which was his interpretation of loving his neighbour. In politics he was an unemphatic Fabian. His son-in-law remembered him as 'a handsome, scholarly man whose appearance suggested an eminent theologian rather than a Grub Street hack' who wrote his serials and fairy tales with donnish precision.

Margery's mother was much younger than her husband. She was a startlingly quick and efficient worker, and ran the large house, brought up her three children, and produced her many articles, with unique speed and apparent ease. Her son Philip and daughter Joyce were born respectively two and nine years after Margery, but for some reason Margery was to recall her childhood as a lonely one, with all the adults in the house preoccupied: 'All the interesting people in the world appeared to be on the other side of the glass.'

When she was seven, Margery's father gave her a pencil, paper and plot, to enable her to make a professional start, and her first publication appeared in that year, in her grandfather's *Christian Globe*. He took her out for a cream tea to celebrate. The story was published exactly as it had been submitted, and the printed version began, 'Once Apon a time . . .' The first earnings from this predetermined profession came at the age of eight, seven shillings and sixpence for a story printed in a journal edited by her aunt Maud Hughes.

At seven, Margery was sent to boarding school, the Misses Dobson's Academy for Young Ladies, in Colchester. They taught such accomplishments as seemed useful for young ladies in 1911: to read aloud with expression, to embroider satin flowers onto black cushion covers, and to enter a drawing room gracefully. For book-learning, she was free to read—and did. But in her teens, Margery went to the Perse School, in Cambridge, where a proper academic education was provided.

Throughout her childhood, Margery assumed that she would be a writer, like everybody else in the family. She often talked about the profession with visitors at home. One of them was the novelist William McFee, who wrote much of *Consuls of the Sea* while he was staying with the Allinghams, and dedicated *Aliens* to Margery. He warned her how hard a writer had to work for success; but she must have observed that already.

Another frequent visitor was the Irish writer George Richard Mant Hearne, who came from Cork, and was 'witty and gentle and poetical, and quite different from ourselves, who were second generation London Irish and packed with intellectual savagery and a curious delight in self-derision.' Hearne earned his living by writing weekly instalments of the adventures of Sexton Blake and Robin Hood, but he amused himself by writing fairy stories. He discussed his work with the teenaged Margery; when he talked about the hack work he used to say that the author of simple action stories has unexpected artistic freedom. 'They never mind you putting all you've got into this sort of stuff. They never pay you any more for it, but they don't stop you.'

Towards the end of 1917, Herbert and Emily Allingham abandoned the financial struggle to keep up the house in Esssex, and moved to a flat in central London; they hired a holiday house in Essex, on Mersea Island, for short breaks. Margery found it agonising, at thirteen, to be jerked out of one life style into another. In London, the whole family felt like 'pigeons in a sealed dovecot'. But Margery was not there in term time, of course; for eight months of the year she was at the Perse School, where she was not particularly happy or successful, and she left it before she was sixteen. By that time she had been through the poetic phase, like most literate adolescents; she used to get up at dawn to find time for writing long blank-verse plays, which the other girls then performed.

It was at this time that Margery had a mystical experience which led to her first published book. One of the girls had brought back to school some kind of ouija board. All devices of this kind, which purported to put the living in contact with the dead, were much in vogue in this last year of the war. This particular method involved twenty-six slips of paper, marked with the letters of the alphabet and set round the edge of a table, an upturned tumbler in the middle of which the participants rested their fingers, and a series of questions, to which the answer was supposed to be spelled out by the glass moving from letter to letter. The results at school were inexplicably convincing. The Allinghams tried it out at home; for ten nights running, with different people at the table each time, the glass gave answers to a series of questions. By the end of the period a complete story had been related from the different points of view of eight or nine witnesses, whose evidence sometimes tallied and sometimes had been tailored to conceal their own delinquencies. 'It was like cross examining in a murder trial,' Margery recalled, 'but by a series of long distance telephone conversations.'

It was clear that the adolescent Margery was the medium, and her father saw in it a startling and original way of getting first-class copy. Margery, however, after some more weeks of experiment, was nervous and exhausted and decided to leave the whole thing strictly alone in future. She never experimented with spiritualism again, but that first experience had given her a story which she longed to write and believed to be true. It is a story of smuggling and murder in Mersea Island in the Essex marshes during the seventeenth century, and it was published when Margery was seventeen as *Blackerchief Dick* (1921). Margery's father wrote a preface explaining the origin of the story for the English edition, and William McFee did the same for the American one. The young author received a good deal of publicity as well as a full-scale publisher's party – a much less frequent event than those outside the literary world suppose. But Margery found herself shy and tongue-tied when she was confronted by curious outsiders; she had 'no conversation and a stammer', and she soon felt that she had tasted some of the Dead Sea Fruit of authorship. The picture for the dust jacket was designed by Philip Youngman Carter, the son of family friends; his uncle and Margery's father had been close friends since they were at Cambridge together in the 1880s, and Philip's mother and Herbert Allingham were once romantically involved with each other.

Margery Allingham came to believe that any girl of fifteen or sixteen had some similar mediumistic gift, but that it should not be developed. The receipt of a story by spiritual means is not unknown. Rudyard Kipling's sister Alice Fleming had the power of automatic writing for which she became celebrated, and was investigated by the Society for Psychical Research. Margery's contemporary, Angela Thirkell, had a similar experience when she was middle-aged. She intended to write some stories along the lines of Grimm's Fairy Tales, based on woodcuts by Ludwig Richter: she looked at the pictures, the pencil moved in her hand across the page, and the stories were written. When she came to read her own writing, she could only suppose that she had been in some kind of trance. But like Margery Allingham, Angela Thirkell decided not to try to do it again.

After writing *Blackerchief Dick*, and before it appeared, Margery became a drama student at the Regent Street Polytechnic. She hoped that she had some talent, and knew that she had a passion for the theatre. Her father simply wanted her to be cured of stammering and snobbery. While she was there she wrote an ambitious poetic drama about Dido and Aeneas and persuaded fifty of her fellow students to perform it; the work received kind reviews from several London critics. Not long after that success, *Blackerchief Dick* came out. Margery was not yet eighteen, and her family believed that she was a prodigy.

On Pip Youngman Carter's advice, she left Drama School in 1921; he said that neither her face nor her figure were up to the competition in the theatre. She then spent eighteen months working a forty-eight-hour week, and produced a massive psychological novel about desperate teenagers, or 'The Bright Young People'. Her father, by whom she was always much influenced, had told her to try writing 'a factual account of the inmost thoughts, aspirations and actions of the young as you know them'. The book, *Green Corn*, was unpublishable and, as she later realised, 'the most weary stuff imaginable'. It completely put her off the idea of Art for Art's sake.

Margery Allingham divided her own work into 'left-handed' and 'right-handed' writing. 'Right-hand writing is the story one tells spontaneously at a party, left-hand writing is the one which one is made to tell by somebody else.' Right-hand writing was between Margery and her audience, and she could 'coax the life out of herself onto the dead paper in any private way one pleases'. In left-hand writing, she was constrained by rules, by professional editors, and above all, by perishable fashion. It was this latter on which she had been living for two years, churning out stories for the tuppenny magazines. She now decided to concentrate on them instead of on Art, and left home to live in her own studio flat and, she hoped, grow up a little. She was very conscious of belonging to a generation which had to learn to live by trial and error: 'We were given doorkeys and the freedom of a shambles.' For her parents' generation, having lost their younger brothers or elder sons in the war, through some unidentifiable fault of their own, had nothing they dared to tell their children. The most elementary morals and maxims seemed dubious:

> Those of us who were in our teens when the war ended came out early into a disillusioned world wherein everything, including God, was highly suspect. To most of our elders—and they were considerably our elders—this was a passing phase . . . to those of us who were green, and rather frightened, as all people are at that age, there was nothing but broken planks wherever we trod. . . . Every formula for behaviour whose use was not instantly apparent had been thrown overboard. Our parents, schoolteachers and clergy, sickened by a catastrophe which everybody said was the direct outcome of a world in which most of them had lived happily and innocently, turned from any thought of instructing us with weary self disgust.

The hand which Margery held through these uncertainties was that of Pip Youngman Carter. Having heard of each other for years, mainly through a shared relation who told each that the other was a prodigy, they met in 1921 expecting to hate each other on sight. But they became friends, and while Margery was at the Polytechnic, Pip was at Art School in London. They went together to every play in London and became secretly engaged in 1922. During the next few years they both enjoyed 'educational romances' elsewhere, but married in 1927. Pip was a painter and etcher, and at the time of his marriage was a flourishing commercial artist. At various times, he became features editor of the *Daily Express*, editor of *The Tatler*, and an illustrator and designer of book jackets. The first years of their married lives, they lived just a few yards from Holborn Bar, on the boundary of the old City of London, in a tiny flat hidden in a courtyard, near one of the busiest throroughfares of the town.

Margery earned a good living turning the stories of silent films into five-thousand-word stories for magazines, usually for one of her aunt's papers, *The Girls' Cinema*; she also produced short stories and serials of her own, with such titles as *The Adventures of the Society Millgirl* and *The Seven Wicked Millionaires*. With her 'right-hand' she decided to try those simple action stories which George Hearne had told her about when she was a child. She had decided that straight novels were too solemn for her; but what most attracted her, after the disastrous experience of trying to express her thoughts about the Bright Young People, was 'the protective covering offered to the author':

> Nobody blamed the mystery writer for being no better than himself. If he got his facts wrong, the readers wrote and abused him, but no one, not even in the literary columns, ever wrote to analyse his twisted ego or to sneer at his unformed philosophy. Nobody cared what the Mystery Writer thought, as long as he did his work and told his story. It suited me. The only definite thing I had to tell the world was that I liked it, even if nobody else did.

In retrospect, Margery Allingham realised that she was typical of a generation which was disillusioned by discredited philosophies, and preferred not to believe in anything. She felt that there was nothing left for the novel of human relationships to discuss but sex; romance had disappeared in the mud of Flanders. The mystery novel, in which the author could introduce her knight errant in modern guise, was the only possible form for a person with a romantic and picaresque imagination who would have liked to write comedy. The rules of the mystery story in the 1920s were very strict, but 'their restraint was negligible compared with the dreadful straitjacket of keeping bitterly serious when one was not that way inclined.'

In middle age, Allingham was to comment on the change she had seen in the emotional climate. 'Nowadays young novelists, who are neither furious nor particularly depressed, need not hide any more.'

Her first mystery novel, *The White Cottage Mystery*, was published in 1927. Margery Allingham was not proud of it, and later excluded it from the lists of her published work. It first appeared as a newspaper serial and was a conventional detective tale about the murder of a recluse, and its investigation by a Police Inspector and his son—who falls in love, of course, with one of the suspects. The solution, though not unguessable, is original for the period.

Albert Campion was introduced in *The Crime at Black Dudley* (1929). When she first invented him, Allingham had no idea how important the character of Albert Campion would be to her readers or to herself. In *The Crime at Black Dudley* he was actually a minor crook. But in *Mystery Mile* Margery needed a recognisable sleuth whom the reader could follow without too much trouble, and she promoted him:

> He appealed to me because he was the private joke figure of the youngsters of that period. The zany, or goon, laughing inanely at danger . . . was in those days considered a very unhealthy and esoteric phenomenon. He was misunderstood, and regarded with misgiving by all but the enlightened few, and the idea of making him a detective in a light hearted mystery story was absurd and rather fun.

In *The Crime at Black Dudley*, *Mystery Mile*, and her third Campion book, *Look to the Lady* (called *The Gyrth Chalice* in the USA), Margery Allingham worked on the 'plum pudding principle' of putting in as many incidents, jokes and ingenuities as she possible could. The result is a trio of perhaps excessively frivolous books, not intended to be taken seriously. In *Mystery Mile* comes the invention, later copied by other writers, of a gang leader who has inherited his position as though it were a peerage. Those who knew the period should recognise many contemporary jokes, some of them delicate references to sayings unpublishable at the time; one example is 'sweet Fanny Adams'.

Allingham herself was to divide her work in threes: after those three frolics she tried to write some 'straight murder mysteries' and technically *Police at the Funeral* and the two books which followed it conform to the pattern. But her imagination could not be confined to mechanisms. All her books have a personal, whimsical originality. However, if her reputation had rested only on the early work, it would have been slight. Her first remarkable novel appeared in 1934—*Death of a Ghost*. Purists do not consider it one of her best works, but those who read her less for straight detection, and more to enter the worlds she described, will particularly enjoy this impression of the 'art' world: the studio of a famous dead painter, his hangers on, his rivals, his widow. The ménage of Augustus John must have given her the idea for the book, but as Pip was an artist she was in a good position to describe the world from the inside, and the dead Lafcadio himself was a cross between Sargeant and Whistler. She intended *Death of a Ghost* to have more attractive characters than she had put into *Police at the Funeral*, and a more romantic atmosphere. It was planned as a story in which the unpremeditated murder is contrasted with one which was carefully planned.

Flowers for the Judge takes us inside a London publisher's office and was dedicated to Allingham's own publishing house. One of the fictional partners says at an early stage, 'I've had a most extraordinary letter from Mrs Carter. I wish Paul would learn not to enthuse to authors. It goes to their heads and then they get spiteful if a book doesn't sell.' Mrs Pip Youngman Carter was much more professional than her namesake. When *Police at the Funeral* did badly in the United States, she was hurt that she had not been told so earlier. 'Why will people take it for granted that I am sensitive about my work? I only want to send them what they can sell.'

She was making a good living by this time, and at last felt able to do what she and other members of the family had longed for during all her adult life—return to Essex. In 1929, the Carters rented a house there, and in 1934 they bought their own home. This was just before the 'left-hand' job of telling movie stories folded. Somehow they managed to stave off financial disaster, and they lived in D'Arcy House for the rest of their lives; Miss Joyce Allingham, Margery's sister, lives there still.

D'Arcy House fronts onto the centre of the attractive village of Tolleshunt D'Arcy on the river Blackwater. Across the road is a maypole, and next door the village pub. The house was built in the days when the most rustic builders could hardly avoid creating a pleasant and satisfying piece of architecture. The front dates from the reign of William and Mary, the back is older still; it is a long, low, brick-built house of extreme charm. It had been the home of 'the old doctor', a well-known local figure who is still remembered. Dr Salter had planned to become a surgeon, but he injured one eye, and was forced to turn to general practice. He ruled the roost in his part of East Anglia throughout a long career.

In only one of her books did Margery Allingham leave out the usual disclaimer; in *More Work for the Undertaker* she wrote, 'Every character in this book is a careful portrait of a living person, each one of whom has expressed himself delighted not only with the accuracy but with the charity of the delineation. Any resemblance to any unconsulted person is therefore accidental.' Her usual practice was to derive her settings and her characters from a mixture of experience and invention, but the doctor who appears in *Dancers in Mourning* (1937), Dr Bouverie, must surely be a portrait of Dr Salter. Dr Bouverie, like Dr Salter, was omnipotent in his district, and is described with a loving detail which is not necessary for the plot. He grows roses, which he protects against the night air with little white canvas hoods on stakes, and to which he says 'Goodnight, my little dear'. Campion, we read, never forgot his first glimpse of Dr Bouverie: 'His first impression was of an enormous girth in a white lounge suit. Then he saw an old, pugnacious face with drooping chaps and a wise eye peering out from under the peak of a large tweed cap. Its whole expression was arrogant, honest, and startlingly reminiscent of a bulldog, with perhaps a dash of bloodhound.' Campion identified him as a 'Georgian tough'.

Dr Salter, a real-life Georgian tough, was a famous sportsman, shot, and gardener. He had brought the children of Herbert and Emily Allingham into the world, and they had known his house all their lives, as it was only a mile or so from their own home. It was panelled inside, with carved cornices and many antique details which are apparently typical of that Dutch-influenced corner of the eastern seaboard. The Carters furnished the house with comfortable and suitable treasures collected locally and abroad. A journalist writing about Margery Allingham for a woman's magazine gushed, 'Her house is the loveliest, homely house. Everything in it is extremely comfortable. It is the kind of home where all the chairs are heaven, and there are numerous footstools and heaps of flowers and lots of ashtrays and really soft cushions that you can plump to fit your head. Anyone who looks less like a criminologist I have yet to find.'

The layout of the old doctor's garden was simplified by enlarging the lawns and planting rows of fruit trees. Margery Allingham used to have garden parties there, and lend it for fêtes and flower shows, under the ancient trees. She was much interested in planning what should grow in the garden and conservatory, though she preferred to have a gardener carry out her ideas. The gardener they inherited from the old doctor won medals and prizes with their flowers and vegetables.

The Carters retained a flat in London, but they regarded the house in Tolleshunt D'Arcy as home, and played an active part in village life; the small pub-style bar is hung with photographs of village cricket teams (of which Pip was a member) and summer festivities, and the day-long party described in *The Beckoning Lady* was exactly the sort of event which Margery enjoyed organising herself. In the bar are many photographs of Margery herself, looking happy and humorous and not unlike what she said about one of her own characters, Campion's sister Valentine (in *The Fashion in Shrouds*, 1938):

Like most of those whose personality has to be consciously expressed in the things they create, she was a little more of a person, a little more clear in outline than is usual. She had no suggestion of over-emphasis, but she was a sharp, vivid entity, and when one first saw her the immediate thing one realised was that it had not happened before . . . her yellow hair, folding softly into the nape of her neck at the back, and combed into a ridiculous roll in front, could have belonged to no-one else . . . unexpectedly warm grey eyes saved her whole appearance from affectation.

Unlike Val, however, Margery was a big-boned, heavy woman.

The Beckoning Lady, which came out in 1955, was badly reviewed, and its pastoral note does strike a little false, perhaps even sentimental, especially as it followed immediately on the sinister *Tiger in the Smoke*, but the book was Margery's own favourite. In it she expressed her affection for the place and the kind of life she lived at Tolleshunt D'Arcy; it is evidently a deeply felt emotion on her part. It was an agreeable, peaceful way of life. Like Margery's parents in an earlier generation, the Carters filled their house with a gang of friends, mostly their colleagues from journalism, writing and painting, who came to stay, looked in for meals, and generally enjoyed themselves together. Two friends, who were unrelated to one another or to the Carters, lived with them at D'Arcy House, and Pip scandalised the village by going riding unchaperoned with the girl. Margery had chosen not to have children. She felt that an arduous profession and a time-consuming husband were enough to manage; in any case, she considered that cooking was her only domestic gift.

The profession was indeed arduous, and she never found writing easy. Even when the film work came to an end, she kept up a high output of short stories, which were published in *The Strand*, *John Bull* and many American magazines. Some of these stories were later reprinted in *Mr. Campion and Others*, and were regarded by their author as 'left-hand writing' having been heavily edited by the remarkable Reeves Shaw, one of the last of the 'superb tyrants of the great fiction magazines'. 'Reevo' was an exacting employer, who taught Margery a great deal, and incidentally, put her off violence in fiction for life. She had written about a thug who kicked his opponent. 'Fighting with feet is the beginning of sadism,' Reeves told her. 'Sadism means *impotence*, and I won't have it in my paper. Tear that thing up, I don't want any part of it. Now go home and write something *clean*.'

The advice was interesting, and surely good. The threat, and the implicit violence, in *Tiger in the Smoke*, are much more frightening than any descriptions of brutality would have been.

Margery wrote a play, called *Water in the Sieve*, which was published by French's in 1924, and occasional book reviews. There was a lot of business work, as rights for reprints, translations and dramatisations were discussed. Margery worked very hard, and her 'right-hand books' became the money-spinners. In the early part of her career, she worked with Pip. They would discuss the plots, and then she would dictate the words which he wrote down in longhand, arguing about every word. Later she herself wrote in longhand, but taught herself to type in 1940. The manuscripts received by her publisher were those 'of a complete professional—they came in typed and seemingly written without undue strain.' But the writing of books, which the blurbs consistently described as light-hearted, was not as easy as it seemed. She took a year to conceive her plots and characters, and write the synopsis, another year to get them down on paper, and a third to recover. 'I write every paragraph four times', she told her American publisher, 'once to get my memory down, once to put in anything I have left out, once to take out anything that seems unnecessary, and once to make the whole thing sound as if I have only just thought of it.' She then dictated it quickly, to make sure it was all acceptably colloquial. Apparent spontaneity is one of the most difficult literary achievements.

After she became famous, reporters from glossy magazines and television programmes frequently came to visit Margery Allingham. She found broadcasting a terrifying ordeal, but co-operated because, like all professional writers, she knew the cash value of self-advertisement. Reporters would be shown the dining room with its gigantic carved Flemish sideboard, which had originally been made for St Osyth's Priory; the garden room, where she often wrote with a pad on her knees; the study which was her official work room; and the former stables, converted into a studio for Pip, with a gallery in which Margery could write while he painted. The studio appears in *The Beckoning Lady*. It was an attractive place in which to live an agreeable life, but not long after they were settled into Tolleshunt D'Arcy World War II broke out.

When England awaited the Nazi invasion, Essex was in the
Front Line. It was on the flight path to London, and the area
was often a target for bombs. At the outbreak of war, evacuees
from the East End of London had been billeted on the village,
and as Billeting Officer Margery was busy dealing with them;
later in the war she became First Aid Commandant for the
Area, worked in the ARP, and was designated—suitably, for
the inventor of Albert Campion—underground liaison and
resistance agent, in case of invasion. When Essex was declared
a Defence Area, the evacuees were sent away, and a company
of soldiers arrived to protect the area. Five officers were put up
in the house and a couple of hundred men camped in the
cricket meadow. Margery recalled having been through this
before, at the age of ten: 'The Old Doctor, who was an
important person locally at that time and allowed to wear a
uniform and a brass hat occasionally, had called to see the
grown-ups, and there had been a hasty conference in my
father's study . . . I gathered that the threatened invasion,
which had been talked about for months, was actually upon us
. . .I was confronted by the same question: would I honestly die
rather than give in?'

Twenty-five years later she came to the same answer: mental
and moral slavery was worse than death. In the climate of a
Britain that has not been at war for a third of a century, the
question is almost embarrassing, but it was of desperate and
immediate importance twice in Margery's lifetime, and the
awareness of it shaped all her thinking. After World War I,
which eventually seemed to have been so disastrously aimless,
she and her friends hardly believed in the possibility of ideals.
After World War II, evil was revealed as a reality to the
generation which had laughed solemnity off. Margery became
aware of evil, and its opposite, and of a moral dimension to her
own life.

Margery Allingham referred to herself as middle Church of
England, but she became very interested in religion in middle
age; she wrote some unpublished paragraphs about her own
beliefs, but did not, as her mother had at the same age, toy with
other religions. Emily Allingham, like Agatha Christie's
mother, had run through the Church of England, Christian
Science, Mary Baker Eddy, Madame Blavatsky, and the

Vibrate-to-Colour School. Margery merely studied sorcery and witchcraft, with an outsider's interest, excited, probably, by living in the part of England where the traditions of witchcraft survived the longest.

At the end of what Margery called the long armistice between the wars, there seemed to be no place for frothy books or their silly-ass hero. She finished *Black Plumes*, and wrote *Traitor's Purse*, which is an ingenious thriller about the amnesiac Campion foiling a plot to engineer Britain's downfall by means of an artificial inflation. At the end of the book, he gets his girl. The plot was treated as implausible in 1941, but it was less peculiar than the actual Nazi plan, very similar in detail, which was revealed after the war.

In 1939 and 1940, Margery wrote a book-length letter to friends in America which was published as *The Oaken Heart*. It sold well all over the world. It is a personal picture of how the phoney war and the beginning of the blitz struck very typical upper-middle-class people and their village neighbours. It reads now, like Jan Struther's *Mrs. Miniver*, and Alice Duer Miller's *The White Cliffs*, as a historical document; people were gallant, ironic and determined, in those frightening days, and for women like Margery Allingham it was almost comforting to be able to leave the moral quandaries of peacetime for the simple certainties of the Front Line. In 1943 she published *The Dance of the Years* (in the USA, *The Galantrys*) which is heavy going and probably her least successful book, though she intended it to be her bid for recognition as a serious novelist. It is the history of a family very like the author's own, from Essex, during the eighteenth and nineteenth centuries, and is as close to a moral tract as Margery Allingham could force her ironic talent; its message is that what is eternal in humanity will go to God the Father, but that Mother Earth will take what is mortal, cleanse and restore it, and that the Father will then breathe spirit into the human again: ' "Be not afraid of dying," the kind earth said.' It was an important principle in 1943.

Margery returned to fiction when it became clear that Britain would not lose the war, and that her own family was safe. Joyce had been in the WRNS, Philip Allingham had worked for ENSA, before volunteering for the army, having, before the war, followed an occasional family tradition of joining a travelling fair. Pip Youngman Carter had served in the Western Desert and Iraq, and was safe; and the house still stood. Margery wrote *Coroner's Pidgin* in 1944. Campion had returned from three years' war service:

> The sun had bleached his fair hair to whiteness, lending him a physical distinction he had never before possessed. There were new lines in his over-thin face, and with their appearance some of his own misleading vacancy of expression had vanished. But nothing had altered the upward drift of his thin mouth, nor the engaging astonishment which so often and so falsely appeared in his pale eyes.

Margery had realised that if she could change and mature, then so could Campion: 'The difference between a real character and a paper one was life, which changes all the time. As the only life I had to give anyone was my own, we grew very close as time went on.' There is a distinct dividing line in Campion's career; the post-war books are for adults.

Coroner's Pidgin has a particularly attractive ending. Campion eventually solves the case and arrives home, where Amanda has spent the war years. 'There was a person not yet three on the path. He was white haired and wearing sunglasses.' Amanda comes out of the house. Margery Allingham finishes the book with the words: 'Hullo,' said Amanda, 'Meet my war-work.'

Amanda is a recurring character in the books, and her child Rupert also appears at various stages in his youth. Allingham was good at creating brilliant and unusual women, quite apart from Amanda herself who is a professional aircraft designer. Some of the most successful characters Allingham created are the women in *The Fashion in Shrouds*, Marthe Papendeik, the couturier, Georgia Wells, the actress, and Campion's sister Valentine, a dress designer who married Amanda's boss.

But the most completely rounded character in all Allingham's work is her post-war police detective, Charles Luke. He first appears in *More Work for the Undertaker*, and the vividness of his personality overshadows Campion's intentionally unobtrusive vagueness. Erik Routley, in *The Puritan Pleasures of the Detective Story*, says that in Luke he found, at last, the one thing that detective literature is always short of—human passion of the relevant sort.

Luke is a large, vivid, powerful man who radiates nervous energy and intelligence. His most engaging peculiarity is that 'he amplified all his stories with a remarkable pantomimic sideshow which he gave all the time he was talking. He drew diagrams in the air with his long hands and made portraits of his characters with his own face.'

Luke gives pictorially graphic descriptions of people and places; on their first encounter he shows Campion, through a spy-hole, a suspect who is talking to 'Price Williams of the Signal'. ' "Pricey hasn't got anything. He's bored. Look at him scratching," the D.D.I. said softly. It was the voice of the fisherman, experienced, patient, passionately interested . . . Campion recognised it immediately . . . Charlie Luke was going to be one of the great detectives.'

It was with the introduction of Charlie Luke, and the more serious, less fantastic cases which he investigates with Campion, that Margery Allingham changed from being a writer of good, but sometimes dating thrillers, to a writer of novels which thrill. She herself, by this time, made no distinction between the novel and the thriller. 'If you have an intelligent mind, and you like to read and you need to escape, then you require an intelligent literature of escape.' But we see a difference between Allingham's pre- and post-war literature of escape: her early books were novels of *event*; the characters who partake in the events are drawn deftly, lightly, in impressionistic representation, so that they are as real, but no more real than, for instance, Little Red Riding Hood, or Cinderella. By the late 1940s, Allingham was a novelist about characters and the behaviour resulting from their predicaments. *Tiger in the Smoke* (1952) is thought by many critics (including myself) to be one of the best crime novels ever written. It is about a hunted man, who calls himself Jack Havoc, and his hunters, and it gives us a chilling picture of the moral collision between a good man and an evil one.

In Canon Avril (Campion's Uncle Hubert) Allingham created a uniquely convincing clergyman who is at once instructed in worldliness and unaffected by it. When he meets Charlie Luke he says:

'Good evening Chief Inspector. I'm afraid we are giving you a lot of trouble.'

The greeting stopped Charlie Luke, who had come swinging into the room behind Campion, filling the room to bursting point by the mere size of his personality, short in his tracks. Suspicion leapt in his bright eyes. He always suspected people wanting to save him trouble. One good stare at the old man appeared to re-assure him, and without being in any way discourteous he soon managed to convey that he had seen faces like Uncle Hubert's 'befuddled old kisser' before. He smiled with a secret quirk of sheer street-boy naughtiness in his twisted lips, only to receive a considerable shock as he found it not only remarked and recognised but also forgiven by the old priest. It was the most complete introduction taking place within a few seconds which Mr. Campion had ever witnessed.

Avril's prayer is 'deliver us, take us away, hide us from evil.' He encounters Havoc, who believes in the Science of Luck; to Avril, that is the pursuit of death, the choice 'Evil, be thou my God.' But Avril tells Havoc, 'Our Gods are within us. We chose our own compulsions. Our souls are our own.'

Havoc (whose appearance was based on that of a travelling brush salesman) is a genuinely frightening character, thrown up by the chaos of the only world he has known, and Avril an admirable one even for an atheist reader. On a less spiritual plane, the book is surely the best twentieth-century evocation of a fog-bound London, and some of the secret people who use its 'concealment':

Crumb Street, never a place of beauty, that afternoon was at its worst. The fog slopped over its low houses like a bucketful of cold soup over a row of dirty stoves. The shops had been mean when they had been built and were designed for small and occasional trade, but since the days of victory, when a million demobilised men had passed through the terminus, each one armed with a parcel of Government-presented garments of varying usefulness, half the establishments had been taken over by opportunists specialising in the purchase and sale of second hand clothes. Every other window was darkened with festoons of semi-respectable rags based by bundles of grey household linen . . . The impatient traffic was moving a little, and they were held up for a moment or so on a street island. As they waited, Mr. Campion reflected that the evil smell of fog is a smell of ashes grown cold under hoses and he heard afresh the distinctive noise of the irritable, half blinded city, the scream of brakes, the abuse of drivers, the fierce hiss of tyres on the wet road. Just above it, like an appropriate theme song, sounded the thumping of the street band. There was nothing of the dispirited drone there. It triumphed in the thick air, an almighty affront of a noise, important and vigorous.

The whole book gives a vividly convincing picture of London as it was in the days of post-war austerity. In fact, Margery Allingham had a strong sense of place in all her writing; each one of her books is set in either East Anglia or London—none in the places she went to for holidays, none abroad. The lonely part of Essex which was her home seems familiar to a first-time visitor who has read her novels, with its wide flat fields and sky, the low-towered churches, the flint and brick houses, the marshy Thames estuary, and the undeniably secretive atmosphere. She uses the local names in all her books—'Totham School', Anscomb, and other names which are painted on modern shopfronts and signposts. Her pictures of the tenacious districts of East London, surviving in spite of bombing and redevelopment, also have a powerful conviction. The Carters kept on the London flat during and after the war, and Margery enjoyed going there, though she was always glad to get back to the country. Her house, her garden and her friends were her chief concerns. She would hanker for people and for excitement, but in fact she preferred entertaining to going out, and once said that writers and riotous living do not mix. She longed to meet people and know what made them tick, but quoted Chesterton, who had pointed out that Jane Austen and Elizabeth Barrett Browning, both acute interpreters of human nature, had led quiet and restricted lives.

So Margery lived the conventional life of a prosperous lady, and invented, perhaps because her life did not involve them, contemporary horrors. *Hide My Eyes*, the 1958 book, and *The China Governess* (1963) both make pointed social comments about post-war villains. *The Beckoning Lady*, which she wrote between her two most serious books, in 1955, seems to represent an attempt to return to her more frivolous vein. Erik Routley found it unreadable. He felt that it left the reader with the feeling of being shut up with a great crowd of people all of whom were talking at once. He also objected to Inspector Luke being made to fall in love with 'a terrible stick of a woman'. It is sad to have to agree that the book is not a success, for it includes many attractive episodes and characters, and the atmosphere of happy summer in rural East Anglia is pleasantly pervasive. The book is dedicated to Margery's 'Old Friends and their Merry Wives' and the expansive hospitality depicted in it is reminiscent of the Carters' own, and the character Minnie, of Margery herself. The unspeakable pressure to keep up with the retrospective demands of the Inland Revenue on the self-employed earner must have been painfully familiar to both Margery and Pip, though one hopes that they had a better accountant than the victim in this book.

Several of these later books were badly received by the reviewers. They seemed to feel that Margery Allingham was wrong to introduce portentous seriousness when her talent was for charming trifles. I do not believe that the earlier books would have survived without the interest aroused by the later ones. In any case, Margery Allingham herself had changed. The experience of World War II affected her far more deeply than, for instance, Agatha Christie, perhaps because before it she lived among friends who treated everything with determined amusement, and the war and its aftermaths were experiences which could not be laughed off. She saw bombing, and the results of bombing; she and her family were in danger. Things could not be the same again.

It is interesting to compare the effect of the war with a brief experience she had as a girl, which should have been traumatic, but involved her no more than a stage play would. Margery was staying in her aunts' London flat, to the east of Gray's Inn Road, in a high building which looked down onto a courtyard which was in a small Italian colony. She was standing at the window watching some kind of festival which was going on below. She glanced at the window in the house opposite, where a man was standing on a window sill to watch the proceedings. Margery saw a hand come towards his back, and push him down to his death. But this macabre experience left her, she said, unaffected. It was not that which inclined her imagination to crime. Margery Allingham wrote mysteries to entertain, mainly; and also because she was attracted by the conventional shape, the need for a plot, and a beginning, middle and end. She found the discipline beneficial. At the same time, she believed that the unimportance attributed to the mystery story gave it freedom. The shape, like a sonnet's shape, was set; the content, like any poem's could be free. 'We have the privileges of court fools,' she wrote. 'There is very little we dare not say in any company in any land.'

Margery Allingham died on 30 June 1966. Her sister, Joyce, had moved to live with her and Pip ten years before, and had helped with the business side of her work and with running the house, but Margery grew tired very easily in the last years of her life. She would sleep a lot, and have little time or energy for anything but her work. She thought her weariness was due to overwork and 'her time of life', but when it was too late, her illness was identified as cancer.

Pip survived her by three years. He completed the unfinished *Cargo of Eagles*, and wrote *Mr. Campion's Farthing*, and *Mr. Campion's Falcon*. In 1959, Margery had written to a friend, 'the old art and fiction factory looks as if it's going to come into being again after all these years. Pip and I are both working on the synopsis of the new book, and we haven't done that since 1939.' But without her, he wrote quite commendable pastiche.

Margery Allingham's books have not, at the time of writing, been made into television plays, and apart from a bad version of *Tiger in the Smoke* in 1956, have not been filmed. But all her novels are constantly reprinted and sold to new readers all over the world, as well as to those who found, as the publishers' blurbs say, that Albert Campion and the other recurring characters have 'gradually become the close personal friends of their generation.' Perhaps the reason lies finally in Margery Allingham's own explanation for the popularity of the mystery form:

> When the moralists cite the modern murder mystery as evidence of an unnatural love of violence in a decadent age, I wonder if it is nothing of the sort, but rather a sign of a popular instinct for order and form in a period of sudden and chaotic change. . . . There is something deeply healthy in the implication that to deprive a human being of his life is not only the most dreadful thing one can do to him, but also that it matters to the rest of us.

8 Josephine Tey

Josephine Tey was a respectable Scottish, not English, woman, whose best books were about other crimes than murder. She did not produce a large volume of work upon which to build a reputation, but of her eight crime novels, five at least were so good that they have remained in print, and popular, since their publication. She herself regarded them as of very inferior importance to her other work. To her, the crime novels represented 'my yearly knitting', as she described them to the actor, Sir John Gielgud. What she cared for were the plays which she published under the name of Gordon Daviot. Her real name was Elizabeth MacKintosh. She was born, the eldest of three daughters, in Inverness, on 25 June 1896. Her father, Colin MacKintosh, was a native Gaelic speaker from Wester Ross, who had grown up in a community of farmers and fishermen and only learnt the English language at school. He became a greengrocer when he moved to Inverness, and married, at the age of twenty-nine, Josephine Horne, who was then twenty-three. She was the daughter of a joiner, who belonged to a severe religious sect not unlike the Plymouth Brethren. Her maternal grandfather had introduced what seems to have been the only non-Scottish blood into the MacKintosh line; he was called Robert Ellis, and came from Suffolk to work as a forester in Perthshire. Josephine Horne had been a tomboy as a child, and a teacher before her marriage; her children grew to think of her more as a friend than a mother. She seems to have been a woman unsuited to the restrictions of her time. She was happiest when she could help her husband in the shop, or walk on the hills with her daughters, but she used her strong sense of duty to force herself through domestic chores.

The daughters were Elizabeth, Jean and Mary. They went

to a day school in Inverness, the Inverness Academy, at a time when Scottish education was world famous for its universality and excellence; they spent their holidays not far from home, at first near a village called Daviot, and later at Rosemarkie.

When she left school, Elizabeth went to the Anstey Physical Training College in Erdington, Birmingham, having been rejected by a college in Dunfermline because she wore spectacles. She started in Birmingham in 1914, and during her two and a half years there, experienced Zeppelin raids and blackouts, and taught 'keep fit classes' at Cadbury's factory. During the vacations she worked at a convalescent home in Inverness as a VAD.

The training for teachers of physical education was arduous, and taken very seriously. It included far more than athletics and gymnastics. A quarter of a century after she had experienced it herself, Josephine Tey drew a detailed picture of such a college in *Miss Pym Disposes*. The curriculum included sports and gymnastics, ballet and folk dancing, psychology, physiotherapy, pathology, anatomy, first aid and public health, as well as training in how to teach these subjects. It was a daunting, strenuous course, punctuated by a long series of minor accidents like bruises and sprains, and it was evidently quite exhausting. However, it qualified its graduates for a variety of jobs, and Elizabeth MacKintosh's first was in a private physiotherapy clinic in Leeds. She then taught in schools, first in Nottinghamshire, then in Oban at a co-educational school where she was injured when some boys allowed the boom in the gymnasium to fall on her face. In *Miss Pym Disposes* that is the way in which the victim is killed.

From Oban she went to teach at a girls' boarding school in Eastbourne, and then at Tunbridge Wells, whence, in 1923, she was summoned home to nurse her mother. Josephine MacKintosh died of cancer on the day before Elizabeth's twenty-seventh birthday. Elizabeth had been away from home, studying and teaching for less than ten years. She was never to leave it again, except for holidays, for after her mother's death she stayed in Inverness with her father. Both her sisters were married.

Elizabeth MacKintosh began her career as a published writer with verse, the first of which was published in the

Westminster Gazette in 1925. She used the name Gordon Daviot, which she presumably chose in memory of happy childhood holidays in the village of that name. Like most new authors, she intended to keep her identity a secret, and Gordon Daviot's real name was not locally known until about four years later.

She continued to publish verse, as well as short stories, in the *Westminster Review*, the *Glasgow Herald* and the *Literary Review*. Her first novel, *Kif: An Unvarnished History*, appeared in 1929. It is the story of a boy who cares for horses and goes through the Great War; it includes crooks and crime, and the climax is murder, but it is not a mystery story, and though it was extremely successful for a first novel, with good reviews, an American sale, and a mention in *The Observer*'s list of Books of the Week, it now seems remarkable only for the style in which it is written.

Three months after *Kif* was published by Benn, Methuen's published Gordon Daviot's first mystery story, *The Man in the Queue*, which appeared in May 1929. It was the winner of a competition for thriller writers which Methuen ran, and two months later, when it appeared in America, it was awarded the 'Dutton Mystery Prize'. Elizabeth MacKintosh wrote it in less than three weeks. She had disagreed with a friend who remarked on the horror of dying in a solitary place, and her victim dies in a crowd so tightly packed together that his body is carried along with it unobserved. It depends on the premise that the stabbed man would not have been aware of what happened, or cried out, until his death minutes later. The book introduces Inspector Alan Grant, a determined bachelor, an enthusiastic fisherman (like Elizabeth's father, who must have taught her to regard it as something between a sport and a religion), the subject of his sergeant's hero-worship, and the possessor of a private income sufficient to allow him to retire if he wishes. Grant, though acute, elegant and witty, is in fact a slightly unamiable character in his professional detachment from life's untidy emotionalism, but he does conform to much of the set pattern for a detective hero. For instance, like Marsh's Alleyn, he does not look the part. In this first book, a woman he is to interview found 'the sight of the police officer in reality so astonishing that she looked again at his card quite involuntarily.' And we are repeatedly told of his dapperness, of the fact that he looks more like a civil servant or soldier than a policeman. But even in this first book, it becomes clear that the author is not going to produce formula detective stories. She says of Grant, 'Murder bored him stiff. What interested him was the possible play of mind on mind, of emotion on emotion.' In private, Elizabeth MacKintosh admitted that her own sense or reality and her common sense, made her unable to produce a real 'shocker'. She could not help finding the machinations of a traditional villain funny.

Elizabeth MacKintosh was not to write another crime novel for some years. She told a friend that the almost mathematical structure they demanded involved the writer in something too much like hard work, and did not give enough scope for the imagination. Instead, she wrote a play, which was rejected; she then turned it into a novel which was published by Benn in 1931 as *The Expensive Halo*. It had been inspired by summer evenings spent listening to an orchestra with a particularly good cellist on the Ness Islands near Inverness, and is about two pairs of brothers and sisters, one aristocratic, the other working class. It seems badly 'dated' now, and as close to being sentimental as this author ever was.

Elizabeth MacKintosh's real ambition was to have a play of hers running in the West End of London. In 1932, she achieved this aim when *Richard of Bordeaux* was produced at the New Theatre. She had written it after being deeply moved, on a visit to London, by John Gielgud's Hamlet, and by the Royal Tournament at Earl's Court. She was always overcome by the sight and sound of marching men, and had a remarkable knowledge of military tactics. In *Richard of Bordeaux*, her main theme was the conflict between veteran warriors, who concentrated on international power politics and on martial arts, and the younger generation, which cared more for beauty and culture. It was a timely theme and in its colloquial modern English the play was, and remained, immensely popular. In 1934, two more of her plays, *The Laughing Woman*, and *Queen of Scots*, were produced at the New Theatre.

With her second crime story Elizabeth MacKintosh assumed her second pseudonym—Josephine Tey; presumably Gordon Daviot was by then too well known as a successful playwright for his name to be attached to a 'shocker'. *A Shilling for Candles* appeared in 1936. It is a competently written and plotted book, good by the standards of its own or a later time, but not yet fully representative of its author's originality. It repeats some themes which first appeared in *The Man in the Queue*, particularly details about the stage and its hangers-on; the sensible, horsy girl, Erica, is very like the later sensible, horsy girls of *Brat Farrar*. Inspector Grant reappears and, as in the previous book, his chief suspect, whom he cannot help liking, is proved innocent in the end.

In the next year, Elizabeth MacKintosh produced her only non-fiction book, a biography of John Graham of Claverhouse, Viscount Dundee. It was written in vindication of someone whom Elizabeth MacKintosh regarded as a libelled hero. She said: 'It is strange that a man whose life was so simple in pattern and so forthright in spirit should have become a peg for every legend, bloody or brave, that belonged to his time.' Her intention was to nail the lies. It is a biography written with care, accuracy and an unexpected expertise about military campaigning, but it is too partisan for excellence. In all her fiction, this writer found it impossible to resist making digs against the Scottish character and she dissected all that she thought its worst aspects in this biography; her particular hatred was reserved for the Kirk. As she put it in a footnote to *Claverhouse*, 'Even today in Scotland in 1937, the churches, powerless and dying and of no consequence in the life of the people, hate each other as they hate nothing else.' Tey, whose only non-Scottish blood was derived from her English great-grandfather, and who lived nearly all her life in the Highlands, found it all too easy to see the worst in her compatriots: the Scot from the West Coast is 'lazy and tells lies, and has much charm that is all of it quite synthetic . . .' (*Miss Pym Disposes*); 'The highlander's usual desire to say the thing he thinks will be acceptable to his hearer . . .' (*The Man in the Queue*) and so on. The countryside is described with knowledgeable affection, particularly in *The Singing Sands*, but not with the same passion that the soft English south evoked. 'The neat green English world' of *Brat Farrar* seems to have been what its author really loved. According to her obituary in the *Inverness Courier*, she spent a good part of each year in the south, and she bequeathed her valuable copyrights to the National Trust not for Scotland, but for England. Certainly Scottish local affairs had no interest for her. That same obituary tartly complains, 'While living in Inverness, Gordon Daviot took little or no interest in the life of the town.' Her spare time was thought to be taken up by writing.

After the end of World War II, Josephine Tey published six crime novels. The best, and the one on which her reputation rests, is *The Franchise Affair* (1948). It is a modern reconstruction of a case which has fascinated criminologists since the eighteenth century, the disappearance of Elizabeth Canning. Tey's explanation is less memorable than the exposure of the characters in the story and the convincing detail of the setting in a small English town. This was her first mystery without murder, and it is the better for it. Tey is one of the few writers who can make other crimes equally interesting. *To Love and Be Wise* is about transvestism and revenge, and *Brat Farrar* about impersonation. Although the plotting of these stories is good and the characterisation of a very much higher standard than that found in other contemporary mystery novels, the chief charm, and what lingers longest in the reader's memory, is the style in which Josephine Tey wrote. It is not always perfectly grammatical—she over-used the short, verbless, dramatic sentence—but her wry wit has a very personal flavour, and the acid clarity, almost cattiness, with which she dissects some of her characters and their pretensions may not appeal at all to some readers, but it is attractive to others. Several times she strips the pretensions from actresses, not only in *The Man in the Queue*, which was written before she could have met many, but also in *A Shilling for Candles* and *To Love and Be Wise*, which were both written after her experiences as a successful playwright and give the impression that she knew what she was talking about. She also took an unenthusiastic view of reporters and of the sentimental viciousness of cheap scandal rags. In *To Love and Be Wise* she exposed the pretensions of the arty and the crafty, and especially of the arty writer. The author's own voice is very audible in these novels. She always felt as a writer that her characters' emotions, whether virtuous or malign, were projections of her own complicated self.

Josephine Tey reveals not only her contempts, but also her

enthusiasms. Apart from her love for the English countryside, she had a knowledgeable passion for horses, horse racing and bloodlines. She knew what she was talking about when she wrote in *Brat Farrar*, 'So this was what riding a good English horse was like, he thought. This communion. This being one half of a whole. This effortlessness. This magic. The close, fine turf slipped by under them . . . England, England, England, said the shoes as they struck. A soft drum on the English turf.' *Brat Farrar* is full of informative details about the genus *Equus*, and how to find the way round stud books.

But the best of Josephine Tey's work has a historical slant, either based on some past mystery, like *The Franchise Affair*, or set in the past, like many of the plays, and like her last book, a fictionalised reconstruction of the life of the buccaneer Henry Morgan, *The Privateer*. That was published in the year of her death, 1952, as was *The Singing Sands*, which appeared posthumously. In the previous year she had published her most famous book, *The Daughter of Time*. It is in the form of an investigation by modern deductive method into the death of the Princes in the Tower, and like Claverhouse, it is a vindication. Inspector Grant, turning to history from boredom when he is in a hospital bed, shows to his own satisfaction that Richard III was a good king, whose memory was besmirched to justify the behaviour of his wicked successor, Henry VII, who was himself the instigator of the double murder. To some commentators the book is 'a masterly piece of historical detection' (Routley), while to Julian Symons the book seems 'a freakish performance' remarkable for Inspector Grant's almost total ignorance of history and for its dullness. The verdict must be a question of taste. To the present writer, the book seems interesting, well written and acceptably scholarly. The fact that the thesis it propounds was already well known at the time of its publication becomes clear towards the end. But to members of Richard III's supporters' club, their cause is well served by a book which achieved a far wider audience than any non-fictional history could.

In *The Daughter of Time* Josephine Tey defined a belief which had already appeared *obiter dicta* in all her earlier work: that the face is the mirror of the soul. Inspector Grant always uses his reading of features as a potent clue. In *The Singing Sands*, a brief

glimpse of the dead man's 'reckless eyebrows' convinces Grant
that the face could not have been that of a French criminal. Not
for Tey the remark which Ngaio Marsh puts into the mouth of
one of her characters in *False Scent*: 'People talk about eyes and
mouths as if they had something to do with the way other
people think and behave. Only bits of the body, aren't they?
Like navels and knees and toenails. Arrangements.'

To Tey, these arrangements of the body were of paramount
importance. 'Faces are my business,' Inspector Grant says.
'Long before he had entered the Force, he had taken a delight
in faces, and in his years at the Yard that interest had proved
both a private entertainment and a professional advantage . . .
It became a conscious study. A matter of case records and
comparisons.' The quest in *The Daughter of Time* arises because
Grant, looking at the anonymous portrait of Richard III, sees a
conscientious and perfectionist magnate rather than a
murderer. In *The Franchise Affair* the colour of eyes is a clue.
The girl who claims to have been kidnapped is called
oversexed: 'I have never known anyone, man or woman, with
that colour of eyes, who wasn't. That opaque dark blue, like a
very faded navy, it's infallible,' says the accused woman, who
is later to be proved right. Her views are shared by the local
policeman, who also judges people by the colour of their eyes.
'Believe me, there's a particular shade of baby blue that
condemns a man, as far as I'm concerned, before he has
opened his mouth. Plausible liars, every one of them.' And he
goes on to explain how he recognises murderers by the
asymmetrical setting of their eyes.

Elizabeth MacKintosh, that sharp observer of physiognomy,
with her trenchant wit and ready tongue, may well have been
an alarming, though as her obituary said, an interesting
companion. She was reserved; but was thought to long for
friendship. She died, two years after her father, in 1952 while
she was on holiday in England. Her contribution to literature
had not been large, but lasting.

9 Ngaio Marsh

Ngaio Marsh celebrated her eightieth birthday in 1979. That same year she published her thirtieth thriller. Her first novel appeared in 1934. Whether her books have the lasting quality which will make them popular when the author is no longer around to benefit from them time will show, but she is always regarded by those who write about the genre as one of the 'big four'.

Henry Edmund Marsh, Ngaio's father, was an Englishman, one of ten children brought up by a widowed mother in relative poverty. The family were tea-brokers, like Galsworthy's Forsytes. They liked to believe that they were descended from the de Mariscos, in title Lords of Lundy (which is a tiny island in the Bristol Channel) but pirates in practice. More certainly related was a Marsh who as Governer of the Tower of London persuaded Charles II to be merciful to Fox the Quaker. The men of the family served the Crown, or followed the few professions acceptable for a gentleman. Ngaio's father was to be a banker in Hong Kong, and learnt Chinese at London University. However, he became tubercular, and though he recovered, he needed a milder climate, and was therefore sent to New Zealand, where he spent his whole working career as a clerk in the Bank of New Zealand. His daughter describes him as a principled, humorous and kind man.

Ngaio's mother was a second generation New Zealander whose father had come to the country as a young man and as one of the first wave of white settlers. He eventually became the superintendent of a mental asylum; his hobbies were mesmeric therapy and amateur theatricals. Rose Seager, Ngaio's mother, was an outstandingly talented amateur actress, but she refused all offers to become a professional.

Henry and Rose Marsh had only one child. She was born in

Christchurch in 1899 and given a Maori name, which is variously translated as meaning 'Light on the Water', the name of a flowering tree, or simply, 'clever'. Ngaio Marsh was to point out that New Zealand is the only country where white parents give their children native names.

Although some of her books are 'more English than the English', Ngaio Marsh has always regarded New Zealand as her home, and the descriptions of it in the few books she set there, and in her autobiographical volume, are more evocative and enticing than any of those set in the England of which she is so fond. In these, as in all her work, we are very aware of the scenery. Marsh's training was in painting, and her main interest is in the theatre; it is very evident that the strongest of her senses is the visual one. Even her descriptions of childhood are of what she saw rather than what she felt. She grew up happily, loved and cherished as the only child of a united couple. They lived at first in a suburban house, and later in a house designed by an architect cousin and built out of local timber, in what was then the open countryside of the Port Hills overlooking Christchurch. It is now surrounded by the residential suburb of Cashmere; there is a garden descending in a series of terraces, and a view for miles over the roofs and spires of the city, across the Canterbury plains, to the snow-peaked Kaikoura Mountains.

Ngaio was educated first at a little nursery school, then by a governess, and later at a school called St Margaret's which was run by an order of Anglo-Catholic sisters. The Marsh parents could ill afford it, and neither subscribed to its doctrines. Her father was a vehement rationalist who deplored the disastrous influence of religion on world affairs; her mother was interested neither in Christianity, nor in the second sight which she occasionally experienced.

At St Margaret's, an inspired teacher of English taught Ngaio to love Shakespeare, and while she was there she wrote a play which was performed by the other girls (as Margery Allingham and Dorothy L. Sayers also did). Home life was punctuated by rehearsals of plays in which Rose Marsh was appearing, and by frequent visits to the theatre. Many of the family friends were on the stage.

After school, Ngaio went to Canterbury University College

School of Art. World War I was taking all the young men
away, and there were, Ngaio said, no entirely fit young men in
New Zealand. Her partners at school dances, and the male
friends of her childhood, all vanished one after another. Few
were to return. Ngaio's mother worked for the Red Cross; her
father trained with the Civil Defence Corps.

Ngaio Marsh must have been a promising artist; she went all
through college on scholarships, and had a good academic
training, learning to see everything in terms of line, mass and
colour, and to be brutally self-critical. During the vacations she
travelled to the West Coast—an adventurous trip, at that time,
and one which introduced her to more beauties of the country
to whose landscape she was already highly responsive. After
one of these holidays she sold an article about it to *The Sun*. It
was her first published work. Soon she became a regular
contributor to its pages.

Her next effort was a play, called *The Medallion*, which she
sent to an English actor manager who had been touring New
Zealand with a Shakespearian repertoire. *The Medallion* was a
Regency romance, complete with insult and duels. The actor
manager, Allan Wilkie, and his wife, who was the leading
actress in his company, read the play and commented kindly.
Later they invited Ngaio to join their company for a winter
tour as a salaried actress; this showed Ngaio what she most
wanted to do with her life.

It was a curious introduction to the world of the stage.
Surely, even then, just after the end of the war, there must
have been far more stage-struck girls than parts available for
them; yet Ngaio, untrained and inexperienced, was offered a
part for which she had not applied. She must have impressed
the Wilkies very much when they discussed her play with her,
perhaps because of her notably deep and well-modulated voice.
Ngaio was encouraged by her mother—who had thought the
life too Bohemian for herself twenty-five years before—to join
the Wilkie's company. Ngaio suggests that her mother may
have been relieved to get her away from the memory of an
unsuccessful love affair. 'I've had quite a number of affairs of
the heart,' she told a journalist on the *Sunday Express* fifty years
later. Indeed, she was once engaged, but her fiancé died. 'But
if he'd lived, and we'd married, it's quite possible that I

wouldn't have liked it very much. I think I'm one of those solitary creatures that aren't the marrying kind.' No more information than that is available about Ngaio Marsh's emotional life. She exemplifies in its most extreme form the reticence of the crime novelist.

The winter of 1920 was spent touring with the Wilkie Company. A visit to the North Island was Ngaio Marsh's first voyage away from the South Island in her life. She saw a drunk for the first time. She had a blameless romance with a member of the company. She painted and drew and learnt about the techniques of the theatre, laying down 'a little cellar of experiences which would one day be served up as the table wines of detective cookery'. In the autobiography, the company's travels by train through New Zealand are reminiscent of the fictionalised journey described thirty years earlier in *Vintage Murder* (1937). This novel, in which the Carolyn Dacres English Comedy Company tours in New Zealand, is dedicated to Allan Wilkie. 'There was something about these people that gave them a united front. Their very manner in this night train, rattling and roaring through a strange country, was different from the manner of other travellers. Dozing a little, [Alleyn] saw them in more antiquated trains, in stage coaches, in wagons, afoot, wearing strange garments, carrying bundles, but always together.'

At the end of that winter tour, Ngaio returned home to paint, and to do some freelance writing; later she had another touring engagement with an English comedy company which survived for three months before folding up. The next performing tour was with some friends of Ngaio's own, and with her mother. They offered a play written by Ngaio herself, called *Little Housebound*, and some recitations by a friend who had attended the Royal Academy of Dramatic Art. After that, Ngaio was invited to produce plays for several amateur societies in Christchurch.

It was at this time that Ngaio made friends with a family which was to have a considerable influence on her life, and which she described in her novel *Surfeit of Lampreys* (known as *Death of a Peer* in the USA) written in 1941.

Barzun regards this book as an 'intolerable tale'. Erik Routley puts it in his short list of the very best. It probably

depends on whether one likes or loathes the family, whose
description is really the whole point of the book. It consists of
an earl's heir, his wife and their six children. They dazzle the
herione of the novel, a young New Zealand girl; they enchant
many readers and they clearly both dazzled and enchanted
Ngaio Marsh. They are meant to be funny though not witty,
unmusical but capable of entertaining an audience, kind but
selfish, broke but not poor. Life with them was exciting, and
Ngaio fell in love with the whole family; like Roberta in the
novel, 'with appalling simplicity, she gave her heart to the
Lampreys.' When Alleyn is confronted with this family, he
feels after only twenty minutes 'as though they were handfuls
of wet sand which, as fast as he grasped them were dragged
through his fingers by the action of some mysterious
undertow.' At various stages in the book they are called
elusive, vague, flippant, scatter-brained, unstable and
reprehensible. But for the fact that they are united in affection
for one another and possess that elusive quality, charm, the
novel would not seem to be a very flattering portrait of people
to whom its author was devoted; in the autobiography she says
that they are sweet of disposition, generous, Christian, and
nothing if not Irish.

The 'Lampreys' had moved to New Zealand in the hope of
living more cheaply than in London, but they moved back to
England to educate their children there and soon Ngaio
decided to fulfil one of her long-standing ambitions and go
'home' to visit them, and England. She arrived there in 1928
and the visit lasted five years. She was full of romantic longing
to see places whose names had been familiar all her life.

The England she encountered was that described in
exaggerated form by Evelyn Waugh and Nancy Mitford. The
Lampreys taught Ngaio their jargon ('too too shymaking',
'Heaven', 'divine'), and took her to theatres, to night clubs
where she saw the Prince of Wales, Lord Alfred Douglas and
Michael Arlen, to the midnight floor show at the Savoy, and to
Saturday-to-Monday house-parties. At Monte Carlo they tried
out a system at the roulette tables, and Ngaio rather oddly
refers to this as her first experience of 'abroad'. Then they
opened a shop to sell the hand-made trifles they had originally
begun producing for a jumble sale. This was a great success,

and the Marsh and Lamprey shop was moved into first one and then another, larger, house in Beauchamp Place; they started to offer interior decoration and to provide specially made furniture. The Lampreys moved from their manor house in the Chilterns to a large flat in London; Ngaio's mother arrived from New Zealand and they moved into a flat together, and the shop struggled on until the year of the Depression.

Marsh does not mention journalism during these London years. She had started, and abandoned, an attempt at writing 'the great New Zealand novel'. She was not a great reader and rarely read crime novels, though she had loved *Sherlock Holmes* as a child. However, one wet Sunday when her mother and her friends were away, she borrowed a detective story from a lending library in a stationer's shop and spent the day reading it. It made so little impression that later she could never recall whether it had been a Christie or a Sayers. In any case, she decided that she could do as well, went back to the stationer's to buy some pencils and sixpenny exercise books, and sat down to start writing. Her story was based on the 'Murder Game'. It was set at a house-party, and was complete with the obligatory butler and footmen, the silly young ass, the pretty ingenue, Russian conspirators and a glamorous detective. She worked at it in the evenings and was surprised when her mother said it was good enough to publish. Its eventual title was *A Man Lay Dead*, and though it now seems too humdrum to be worth reading, it presaged the qualities which made its successors popular.

Marsh decided that she must have a detective quite different from the eccentrics like Poirot, Holmes and Fortune. She felt that his 'chance lay in comparative normality'. She decided not to tie mannerisms round his neck like labels, and hoped to create an attractive civilised man whose background resembled that of her English friends. So she made him the younger son of a landed family in the Chilterns, who was educated at Eton, was briefly in the Foreign Office, and whose mother bred Alsatian dogs. He was named after the Alleyn who had founded Dulwich College, where Henry Marsh had been to school, and his first name was chosen after a visit to Scotland where Roderick is a popular name.

A friend gave Ngaio an introduction to the agents Hughes

Massie, and they agreed to try to place her book. Meanwhile, she was summoned home. Her mother was ill, and died a few weeks after Ngaio's return to New Zealand. Her death, Ngaio said later, marked the moment of her own coming to maturity. She was thirty-four years old.

Ngaio settled down to live with her father, and paint and write. Bles accepted *A Man Lay Dead*, and brought it out in 1934; the contract was for Ngaio's next three novels also. Her second one was set in a London theatre, and the third, after she had been ill and undergone a series of major operations, was written in collaboration with a doctor and set in a nursing home. Marsh was from that time onwards to publish steadily and regularly. She had found her length, as it were, and stuck to it. Her talent was for light, glancing characterisations, excellently realised settings, precise plotting, and for conversation as good as might be expected from a writer whose true love was the theatre.

It is perhaps because Marsh regarded writing as of very secondary importance to her dramatic work that she was able to repeat the same type of book again and again. She never tried to change the kind of novel she wrote as the years went by; never grew irritated with her hero; never wrote anything which touched her emotions more deeply, although she apparently continued to hope until quite recently that she would one day be able to write a serious novel about the early settlers in New Zealand. As well as the odd play, she has written a book about New Zealand for American schools, but otherwise she sticks to detective stories. 'They are most exacting things to write,' she told a journalist. Certainly she works very hard at the research on her novels, partly because she believes that the majority of her readers are professional men, 'the very people who can catch you out.' Consequently she is very careful to be accurate about weapons and wounds, although her books are rarely explicit about gory details. 'I often envy the straight novelist,' she said in 1978. 'A detective story has to be disciplined. It must have a beginning, middle and end. A lot of novel writing at the moment tends to be formless. Also straight writers don't have to do anything like the same amount of grilling homework. You can't afford to make mistakes.'

This disciplined framework on which Marsh constructs her novels is either their merit or their drawback, depending on taste. Those who prefer the puzzle novel enjoy Marsh's stories precisely because they do set out their clues and problems in such a structured way. As reviewers always write, 'Dame Ngaio plays fair'.

To other critics, this very rigidity is a fault. One has the feeling that the novels all begin as a perceptive exposure of certain people and places, but that at the stage when the initial layout is ready to be exploited, the author takes fright. This is a failing of other crime novelists too. Raymond Chandler said in 1952: 'it has been clearer to me for some time that what is largely boring about many mystery stories, at least on a literate plane, is that the characters get lost about a third of the way through. Often the opening, the mise-en-scène, the establishment of the background is very good. The plot thickens and the people become mere names . . .'

Ngaio Marsh herself has not said much about her approach to crime writing; but she has written that her books attempt to treat of 'people in the round'. She begins every time with two or three people that she wishes to write about, and often starts to write before developing the plot and its denouement. She recognises the difficulties that this intention creates. 'The more deeply and honestly [the crime writer] examines his characters, the more disquieting becomes the skulduggery that he is obliged to practice in respect to the guilty party.' Her aim is, it seems, to create rounded characters of all but the villain, but in nearly every book one feels that she withdraws from the dangerous process of dissecting her character's emotions, and retreats into discussion of those physical details which will result in the traditional resolution of crime in an ordered society. Her books avoid social judgements and do not question the political basis of society. Alleyn has no doubt about his duty.

All this is evidence of that extreme desire for privacy, that mask, which is typical of novelists who choose to write mysteries. Marsh invents, or describes, characters which are of interest to her, and potentially to her reader, but seems to be unable to force herself into the self-exposure which revealing more about them would entail. In some of the books which adhere too mechanically to the recipe it does not matter; they make excellent puzzle novels. In others, it is a disappointment. The Lampreys, for instance, are potentially as interesting to the reader as to their affectionate chronicler, but we see them too much from the outside. *Opening Night* (1951) (called *Death at the Vulcan* in the USA) presents a varied group of theatre people, portrayed with perception through the eyes of a young New Zealand girl newly arrived in London. But once the police investigators join the cast the characters lose a dimension. It is not that Marsh is incapable of greater subtlety, merely that she is evidently determined to reserve for herself, or for her work in the theatre, her deeper insights and understanding.

So we are left with a corpus of work which is pleasant and entertaining but not entirely satisfying. One feels that Allingham put all she could into her work, that Sayers put in far more than she intended, that Christie used as much as was appropriate for characters who were not intended to inspire more interest than a puzzle-plot required. But in Marsh's work one senses withdrawal.

The locales of her books, on the other hand, are vivid and evocative. Naturally, many of them are set in theatres, and several in New Zealand. Others derive from her experiences in hospital (*The Nursing Home Murders*, 1936), or on holidays—she has set stories in the Channel Islands, on a canal hotel-barge, in Cornwall and in the South of France—or in the theatre. But the predominant impression of her surroundings is of the same village England as Agatha Christie's, with such characters as squires, spinsters who worship God and the vicar, the retired colonel, district nurse and tweedy doctor. The heroines have names like Rose Cartarette, Nicola Maitland-Mayne and Camilla Campion. The locals are yokels and use words like 'thikky' meaning 'that', 'dussn't' meaning 'dare not', and such phrases as 'wonderful queer to think of, hearts' (*Off With His Head*, 1957). In this use of dialect, as in her picture of upper-class life, Marsh is 'more English than the English'. Perhaps it is because her view of England is inevitably one of a visitor, however devoted, that she retains this idealised view of life in the Northern hemisphere.

No writer can avoid giving away some information about herself. Marsh's passionate affection for English ways and life is merely one example of attributes she cannot conceal from the reader. We learn a good deal about her interests not only in the theatre, but also in art. Alleyn loves, and eventually marries, a world-famous painter called Agatha Troy and, as detective-hero's girlfriends tend to be, Troy is a bit of a give-away about her creator. There was certainly more of Sayers in Harriet Vane than she would have cared to admit, and the likeness between Troy and Marsh has been noticed by several commentators. Troy is regularly described as thin, nervous, tall and dark, with 'an air of spare gallantry about her' and continuously pushing long fingers through her short hair. A journalist writing in the *New Zealand Vogue* remarked on the physical likeness between the two women and said that Marsh herself was tall and slender, and like Troy, had 'style, an air of well-bred distinction, good bones, and long, capable, expressive hands'. Marsh herself has said that anything of herself appears in Alleyn, not his wife:

> He . . . had no begetter apart from his author. He came in without introduction, and if, for this reason, there is an element of unreality about him, I can only say that for me, at least, he was and is very real indeed . . . I have grown to like him as an old friend. I even dare to think he has developed third dimensionally in my company. We have travelled widely . . .

It is therefore presumably Marsh herself who feels that an artist's work is more important than a detective's. 'Look here, Brer Fox,' Alleyn says, 'I've done my bloody best to keep my job out of sight of my wife, and by the large I've made a hash of it. But I'll tell you what: if ever my job looks like coming between one dab of her brush and the surface of her canvas, I'll chuck it . . .' (*Black As He's Painted*, 1974).

Alleyn fell in love with Troy on a sea voyage; he had brought himself to her notice by being able to remind her of a detail in a scene she was painting from memory. Throughout the books her paintings are described in detail. Several murders, and several books later, they marry, apparently much to the dismay of Marsh's publishers and agent. The one Alleyn child, Ricky, appears occasionally in the novels until in *Last Ditch* (1977) he takes over as detective. Ngaio Marsh is not the only inventor of a series detective who has tried to pass the interest along to the next generation; Michael Innes had introduced Appleby's son Bobby in the same role. In neither case is the device very successful, and both authors returned to their old friends and contemporaries in subsequent books. Alleyn is addressed by his son as 'The Cid' but this, like other similarly whimsical touches—Brer Fox, for Alleyn's subordinate, for example—can grate on the reader.

The whole assumption behind Ngaio Marsh's novels is of an agnostic conservatism, and an acceptance of the value of stability; but the only political point to be made in any detail is about racial discrimination.

It is evident from her autobiography, and from the novels also, that Ngaio Marsh is proud of the way in which New Zealand has adopted the principle of integration from the very beginning—'the intention of our forefathers: that the Maori and the Pakeha shall be as one people.'

She does not deny that friction exists, but regards it as springing from differences in behaviour, and not from past injuries. 'We are a picture in miniature of what happens when the dominant race adopts a civilised attitude, and, inevitably, blunders from time to time in the effort to realise its ideals.' This interest in the relationship between members of different races appears again and again in her novels. *Colour Scheme* (1943) is a fascinating picture of the contacts between the European and the aborigine in New Zealand; of the young English woman, Barbara, who talks to her contemporary Huia and thinks 'I shall never understand them'; of her father, an Anglo-Indian Colonel, who 'by his very simplicity has fluked his way into a sort of understanding of native peoples,' and her mother, who treated the Maori community as though they were English villagers, nursed them when they were ill and taught their children Christianity in Sunday Schools. 'He and his wife expressed neither extreme liking nor antipathy for the Maori people, who nevertheless found something recognisable and admirable in both of them.' The Maoris are described by Marsh with a quite unsentimental affection, and she is particularly successful with her portrait of the tribal leader, Rua, who has been a warrior, an editor of a native newspaper, and a Member of Parliament. He is an extremely old man whose father had set his mark to the Treaty of Waitangi; his grandfather, a chieftain and a cannibal, was a Neolithic man. His descent was from the Polynesian sea rovers. He says: 'Our people stand between two worlds. In a century, we have had to swallow the progress of nineteen hundred years. Do you wonder that we suffer a little from evolutionary dyspepsia?'

The respect she has always felt for the Maoris has made Marsh sensitive to the infamies of colour prejudice. On her first trip to Europe her ship called at Durban, where she was horrified to see rickshaws drawn by Zulus: 'I came from a country where it would be beyond the limits of anyone's imagination to envisage a member of one race running between shafts like a horse for the convenience of a member of the other.' As Marsh herself comments, a fleeting impression indicates more about the observer than about what is observed, but she does tell of the dismay with which she watched the Afrikaners' treatment of the Africans, and her dislike of what she took to be arrogance and coarseness. In later books she writes again about colour prejudice, though her comment is incidental, for her novels are never propaganda tracts. In *Clutch of Constables* (1968) a black doctor is a fellow guest on a hotel barge with Troy; he is well dressed at 'High Establishment' level, and is almost too cultured, refined and civilised. Those who, like Alleyn and Troy, like him immensely, still think of him as strange. Marsh, like Troy, sees the doctor in visual terms, and there are several descriptions of the light falling on his skin, 'warmly dark, with grape coloured shadows', his 'exquisite bone structure', his 'long fingers that looked as if they had been imperfectly treated with black cork.'

Black As He's Painted (1974) features an African president who had been at school with Alleyn. 'The steel wool mat of hair was grey now and stood up high on his head like a toque. The huge frame was richly endowed with flesh and the eyes were very slightly bloodshot, but, as if in double exposure, Alleyn saw beyond this figure to that of an ebony youth eating anchovy toast by a coal fire and saying "you are my friend: I had none here, until now." ' Troy Alleyn naturally has to paint this president, as she did Doctor Natouche, and Marsh has the opportunity again to use her pen as a brush—'those reflected lights in the hollow of temple and cheek' and a chance

also to express the feelings which she has about the European-
isation of other races. The President sees a ravine between his
own assumptions and those of his old school friend: 'Justice has
been done in accordance with our need, our grass roots, our
absolute selves. With time we shall evolve a change and adapt
and gradually such elements may die out in us. At present you
must think of us . . . as an unfinished portrait.' A liberal,
agnostic, tolerant supporter of the status quo: in that at least
Ngaio Marsh has revealed herself.

After recovering from the shock of her mother's death and
from her own long illness, Marsh's life took up an alternating
rhythm: some years in New Zealand and then some in
England, half the year writing, and half in the theatre. She is
widely credited with having been almost solely responsible for
the revival of live theatre in New Zealand. Before World War
II, she produced many amateur companies, but later her
greatest successes came with productions of Shakespeare plays
performed by students at Canterbury University. The
University now has a permanent theatre which is named after
her, and she was made a Dame of the British Empire in 1966
for her services to the theatre. It is about that side of her life
that she writes in the autobiography, *Black Beech and Honeydew*,
and about her happy childhood; but she tells us little about her
writing. Her happiest moments have been during her work on
plays, especially on those by Shakespeare, for whom she has an
overpowering devotion. Like many other fictional detectives,
Rory Alleyn quotes Shakespeare often and at length—and his
wife can cap his quotations. One of the novels, *Death at the
Dolphin*, is peppered with bard worship. The hero (who has the
typically modish name of Peregrine Jay) is a theatrical director
who is passionate and knowledgeable about Shakespeare's life,
and moved to a positively religious rapture by an authentic
relic of 'The Bard'.

As clearly as her passion for those plays, is evident Marsh's
love for acting and actors, and for the theatrical life itself. This
is understandable to many readers; one only needs to listen to a
representative week's offering of broadcasting on any of
Britain's radio channels to realise what an emphasis there is on
programmes about 'show business'; presumably the listeners
are offered what market research shows they wish to hear. It

should therefore not be surprising that many popular writers share this public enthusiasm. Marsh and Tey, Christie and Sayers all knew some of their happiest moments during productions of their own plays, and Allingham went to drama college. It may well be that this eye for the dramatic and for the presentation of a scene is what makes their books live for the readers. Alternatively, one might guess that readers of crime novels have a particular interest in what is presented to an audience, as opposed to what is going on inside the heads of the cast.

During World War II, Ngaio Marsh became a Red Cross Transport Driver, doing fortnightly duties on a hospital bus, and chauffeuring wounded soldiers on their return from the war. It is necessary to remember that New Zealand expected to be invaded as certainly as Britain did. After the fall of Singapore, the Japanese were expected to arrive, as the Germans were expected in England after Dunkirk, and in the same invading boats or aeroplanes, or dangling from parachutes disguised as nuns. By that time, the entire population of fighting men had been emptied out of the islands, as they had been during the previous world war, to join their allies in Europe. A policeman in the novel *Colour Scheme*, set in New Zealand and published in 1943, says, 'We'd got into the way of thinking these things don't reach us down here. The boys go away, reinforcement after reinforcement, and then it gets a bit closer and we begin building up our home forces, but we don't somehow think in terms of fifth columnists . . .' It took the English policeman seconded out to New Zealand to do that.

After the invasion of Singapore, New Zealand felt itself as threatened as its European allies. People erected air raid shelters—'my father dug a funk-hole in the garden', Marsh wrote—and a total blackout was imposed.

Ngaio Marsh's father died soon after the war; they had lived together in harmony and she missed him deeply. (She has continued to live in the house he built when she was a child.) By this time, she had a resident secretary, and kept up her steady flow of novels. She still wrote them by hand, but now had them typed for her; and she continued to be published initially in Britain by Collins Crime Club. The system was highly organised, with numbered pages of typescript or

alterations sent to various recipients thousands of miles away.
Marsh was said to accept criticism unresentfully, and to alter
passages willingly. She was diffident and lacking in confidence
about her work, worrying about it until assured by agent and
publisher that it was acceptable. Then she was surprised that
anyone—let alone so many people—should wish to read it.

After the war, Ngaio Marsh returned to England and her
Lamprey friends. Her novels continued to reflect her
experiences: *Swing Brother Swing* deals with another family of
eccentric aristocrats in austere post-war London; *Spinsters in
Jeopardy*, which like the pre-war *Death in Ecstacy* uses the
peculiarities of a lunatic and vicious religious sect as the peg for
its plot, is set in a converted Saracen stronghold carved into the
cliff face in the South of France—the Lampreys and Ngaio
Marsh had spent a holiday in just such a castle above Monte
Carlo. From this theme, as from others, Marsh retreats from
full exploration; she is amused and sardonic, even a little
disgusted, but not really interested, and the irrational urges of
the devotees, the corrupt motives of those who batten on them,
are seen wholly through a policeman's eye. It is interesting to
compare this treatment with Margaret Millar's of a similar sect
in *How Like an Angel* (1962). Millar makes events arise from the
necessities of the cult and its dogma, rather than using it as
merely a setting.

In Britain, Marsh had become a well-known and popular
writer. At home in New Zealand she was better known for her
theatre work. In Britain she was surprised, she wrote, to find
herself taken seriously as a writer, and justified her work, as
her colleagues Sayers and Allingham had also done, by saying
that the mould into which a detective novel was forced was no
more contemptible than that of any other conventional form of
writing—for instance, the diamonds, hearts and triangles into
which the metaphysical poets fitted their verse. 'The mechanics
in a detective novel may be shamelessly contrived, but the
writing need not be so, nor, with one exception, need the
characterisation. About the guilty person, of course, endless
deception is practised.'

While in London on one of these post-war visits, Ngaio
Marsh saw the performance of *Surfeit of Lampreys* at the

Embassy Theatre in Hampstead, but found the production unsuccessful and lugubrious.

Her life continued to consist of theatre work in the antipodes, including tours of Australia, and the writing of a series of reliably entertaining detective novels. She travelled all over the world, from Hong Kong to Spain, from the Crimea to the United States. She lived in the family house in Christchurch and in a little cottage in South Kensington. She spent her time with the friends of her youth, or with the Lampreys. Throughout her life she has retained that quality of privacy which pervades her fiction. As she wrote at the end of the autobiography, 'I find I have withdrawn from writing about experiences which have most closely concerned and disturbed me. What I have written turns out to be a straying recollection of places and people; I have been deflected by my own reticence.'

In the same way, the author's reticence has diminished the life of her novels. It is this, more than anything, which may determine whether they survive.

10 Conclusion

The best modern detective novels, while technically in the same form as the work of the five women whose lives are described in the preceding chapters, present an essentially different view of the world. The difference is between optimism and pessimism, almost, in some cases between hope and despair. This may seem an excessive meaning to read into books which are written to entertain; but they are of more serious purpose than their predecessors.

Detective stories form only a sub-division of the crime novel, though with the lessening of interest in the decipherment of clues, and the increasing concentration on human motive, the distinction is increasingly blurred. But novels of suspense, as publishers weakly describe them (for what good is any novel without suspense?) are the antithesis, romantic rather than classical, the excitement dependent on a succession of dramatic or violent episodes. A sub-division is the crime novel which follows the progress of a criminal, rather than of his identification. In an age of do-it-yourself psychology, the dissection of deviant motive has become more and more popular.

Frances Iles was one of the first to say that the detective story was changing from a puzzle of time, place, motive and opportunity, to a puzzle of character, and he published several books which showed events through the criminals' eyes as early as the 1930s: *The Second Shot* (under the name A. B. Cox) and, perhaps the most influential of his books, *Malice Afterthought*, which was the account of a doctor's murder of his wife based on the Armstrong murder case. The distinction between such books and 'mystery' novels is less and less easy to make, now that even writers who set puzzles believe that characterisation is as important as the clues. Today the questions 'How?' and

'Who?' are scrupulously answered, but few people care for ingenious or inventive murder methods any more, and the real interest lies in the answer to the question 'Why?'.

This progress of the crime novel leads one to ask why writers should choose to discuss crime, if they do not care for the minutiae which originally filled the crime story. One of the reasons most often suggested as an explanation for the excellence of the women writers in this genre is that women are thought to be especially observant of the small details which may provide clues. If this is an especially feminine characteristic, it is curious that there have been so few, if any, outstanding female investigators of crime in real life. In any case, the finer points of human behaviour are important in spheres other than the criminal, so that the question remains as to why women should choose to direct their attention to this limited area of human life. In Rebecca West's words, 'There is this curious flight that so many intelligent women make into detective writing.'

The implied question includes another: what are they fleeing from? The serious novel of the twentieth century has moved away from the tale which entertains. 'Feminine' literature has been deformed by a straitjacket of wincing sensitivity; general fiction has become the laboratory bench of experimenters with methods, states of mind, symbolism, and even with the random arrangement of pages of text. An exciting new development of the 'straight' novel must be due, and perhaps an intelligent woman will be the important innovator; but writers whose work is objectively important, whose books do more than simply entertain, are few, and it is surely quite respectable to be a craftsman, rather than an artist. A great writer may show others the way forward from the currently accepted forms of the novel, but there is no reason to despise those who are content to go along already-explored paths. If writers choose to work within established bounds, and do not wish to follow the modern novel's erratic course, then, as Julian Symons pointed out in 1972, the crime novel 'could attract writers who twenty years ago would have written novels, readers who would have read them.' Nearly ten years later, the state of the 'non-genre' novel is even more parlous. The 'women's novel' concentrates on the sufferings of women who are oppressed by society, biology and other people, and strip the layers of their sensibilities like onion skins. Other writers have moved even further in the direction of symbolism and unreality. Those who persevere with traditional stories of event and human relationships are dangerously underrated. One example is Nina Bawden, who began her career with two crime stories in the 1950s. In the preface to the reissued first one, *The Odd Flamingo*, she says:

> I was attracted to the detective story because it seemed to provide a frame within which I could comment on things that interested me: the difference between what people say and what they actually mean (the difference, if you like, between appearance and reality) and the way a violent event, murder or some other catastrophe, will shock them into showing who they really are.

These are reasons obviously shared by other writers of detective novels; Nina Bawden herself turned to writing books without crime because 'I found that I was more interested in social comedy, in the ambiguities and oddities of human behaviour, than I was in the strict attention to plot that was necessary for a detective story.' It may also be that Nina Bawden was more willing to expose her own feelings in fiction; certainly some of the experiences she describes in her later books give the impression of having sprung from her own.

Crime novelists, on the other hand, as we have seen, are particularly reticent about their own personal lives. They wish to write about things which are outside themselves, and recoil from exposing their own personalities to public view. I also suggested above that crime novelists exorcise their own fears in fiction. Now that stability and protection seem uncertain, this is perhaps even more true.

What *has* changed, apart from the psychological emphasis of the books, since the earlier period, is the general message of the crime novel. The importance of preserving the existing state of society is no longer implicit in them.

Widely regarded as one of the major figures of the contemporary crime novel, and in Julian Symons' view, the most important of all, is the American Patricia Highsmith. Her books are the opposite of the conventional mystery. Colin

Watson called them a 'welcome emetic after the sickly moralities of the Golden Age'. Highsmith writes about anarchy. She believes that the only free spirits of the twentieth century are those who are not imprisoned by laws or rules: the criminals. Thus she finds the criminal of major dramatic importance, and her books usually follow his actions, without any overt moral comment. Other crime writers are concerned with the effect of the criminal upon the people around him; it is the effect of other people on *him* that really interests Highsmith.

The earlier detective novelists did consider the effect of crime on their invented communities but the implication was usually that, after the solution, everything would return to square one. In contemporary fiction, blood is no longer ketchup, and grief is lasting. The attitude towards fictional violence has changed. To Christie and her colleagues, the corpse was the spur to curiosity. Even when it is quite vividly described, as for instance some of Ngaio Marsh's are, the reader is unlikely to feel horror, shock or disgust. The immediate emotion is intellectual stimulation. Contemporary writers aim to excite horror, to evoke some of the reactions which a murdered body would produce in real life.

In her autobiography, Agatha Christie wrote of her disapproval of the amoral Raffles, and she went on:

> But Raffles was a light-hearted exception. No-one could have dreamt then that there would come a time when crime books would be read for their love of violence, the taking of sadistic pleasure in brutality for its own sake. One would have thought the community would rise up in horror against such things; but now cruelty seems almost everyday bread and butter.

It is not everyday bread and butter to modern detective novelists, other than the least admirable and memorable of them, but nor is it unreal, as it was to Christie herself. P. D. James, for example, makes death genuinely horrific. In *Shroud for a Nightingale*, a student nurse has swallowed an oesophageal tube, to demonstrate, with what should have been warm milk, the method of intra-gastral feeding:

There was a squeal, high pitched, horribly inhuman, and Nurse Pearce precipitated herself from the bed as if propelled by an irresistable force. One second she was lying immobile, propped against her mound of pillows, the next she was out of bed, teetering forward on arched feet in a parody of a ballet dancer and clutching ineffectually at the air as if in frantic search of the tubing. And all the time she screamed, perpetually screamed, like a stuck whistle. Miss Beale, aghast, had hardly time to register the contorted face, with foaming lips, before the girl thudded to the floor and writhed there, doubled like a hoop, her forehead touching the ground, her whole body twitching in agony.

This is a far cry from the neat, round hole through a forehead, seen in the library by the butler, or from the apparently sleeping corpse to whom the housemaid brings early tea. This death is not one which the other participants can shrug off so easily. Yet in form this book is a traditional detective novel. There are clues, there is a mystery and a solution. The detective, Inspector Adam Dalgleish, a cultured and sensitive widower, is too faintly drawn for hero-worship. Like Josephine Tey's Grant, he casts an ironic eye on his subjects, and is distantly attracted to several of the female characters in his various cases. He is a well-known poet, summoned to one case from a party given by his publisher, but none of the critics who so deplored Sayers' social and intellectual snobbery has objected to Dalgleish's extra-curricular accomplishments.

Highsmith's world is that in which she lives herself, the world of American expatriates in Europe. James sets her books in a society familiar to her, that of contemporary, professional England; her characters are doctors (like her late husband), nurses, pathologists, professors, writers, and civil servants (as she was herself for many years). She writes about places she loves—Cambridge, the East Anglian coast, London. In her own opinion women write well about crime because in them 'aggression is more subtle, less overt, than it is in men, and writing such books is one way in which a woman sublimates it'. Her view of society is conventional, and she accepts its shibboleths, while viewing them with an acute clarity. All her books are densely written, long, literary, and full of very observant detail about often disagreeable aspects of life.

Kingsley Amis commented once that an interest in realism turns up when a genre is past its first youth. 'Stories about daily Martian life and routine came along after decades of alien monsters; Chief Inspector Barlow of *Z Cars* and *Softly Softly* replaces Lord Peter Wimsey (not before time); John le Carré and Len Deighton start off with some apparent concern to tell the truth about the Secret Service.' Similarly, respectable women crime novelists tell us now about crime which is so plausible, in such precisely described settings, with such clearly exposed participants, that they might as well be writing about 'true life' crime. It is the difference between writing to amuse and writing to involve. In the classic detective story one remembers the settings and a few of the characters; one reads them with pleasure. The modern detective story can be equally memorable, often more so; but it lifts the mask of polite society, the veil of incomprehension, to reveal something from which one might prefer to avert one's eyes. Such books are remembered with respect for their understanding and revelation; but they rarely offer the innocent pleasure which less ambitious novels gave. These are not worlds to which the wandering imagination could return for solace, for the experience of something preferable to reality; modern detective novels display something which is worse than what we choose to see. Pessimism is the order of the day.

Victorian readers of sensation novels escaped from boredom to excitement; those of the period between the wars are supposed to have sought imagined danger from their own safety. Julian Symons was able to say in 1972 that the British/American supremacy in crime writing was based partly on the social stability of the two countries; he also thought that another depression on the scale of that of the 1930s might lead to a revival of the detective story, traditionally a comfort in hard times. His book was published in 1972, the year before the 'oil crisis' and was perhaps prophetic, for while such writers as James and Rendell were at work in the 1960s, their great popularity grew in the depressed 1970s. Yet the contemporary detective novelists do not affirm our security; they terrify us with the threats to it.

The assumption is that our society is more unstable and threatened than was that of the period between the wars and that this is reflected in fiction. Yet to one who knows the period only through history books, the thirties hardly seem a period of superior stability. The social pressures must have been even greater, when war was both remembered and awaited, when poverty meant starvation, and when middle classes feared a revolution of the kind which had occurred in other countries. After all, it is only hindsight which assures us that British tradition would survive the war. Surely those who looked ahead to gas attacks, air raids, invasion and persecution, cannot have felt safe.

Nor can one say that the lives of contemporary writers have been so different from those of women born towards the end of the nineteenth century. External war and international tensions were also prevalent in the twenties and thirties; the personal experiences of love and marriage are similar in all periods; and the social *mores* are much less different today than is generally assumed. Agatha Christie and Ngaio Marsh are accused of writing about a rural never-never land. In my experience the country village of the 1980s is hardly distinguishable from Colin Watson's 'fly-in-amber land, Mayhem Parva'. The retired officers and civil servants, the tweedy doctor, the reliable solicitor, the omnipresent vicar, as well as their gardening, public-spirited wives, all behave as their ancestors did in similar environments. They play bridge; they organise fêtes; they grumble about poverty, sit on the bench, have a drink at 'the local'; and where their mothers discussed the servants, they discuss the machines which do the servants' work.

It is not because it no longer exists that few writers now use this setting for their fiction. It must be because it is thought untypical of our society, an anachronism, the traditional personnel obsolete. Christie, Marsh, Sayers and Allingham knew better than to suppose that the world they described was dead; to their heirs it is moribund, but the seedy underworld of cities is far less familiar to most respectable English women, and when they create bedsitterland, or the claustrophobic world of the lower-middle-class suburb, it is a real feat of the imagination. That is the composite world which has replaced 'never-never land'. Women writers now set their books in towns and suburbs. In 1979 P. D. James was praised by Julian

Symons for breaking away from the English village settings of her earliest books and venturing into a more astringent world. From the collected works of contemporary crime writers, one derives an impression of seediness, loneliness and fear. The message is not that of the essential security of British life, lurching, until righted by the hero detective. It is of the everyday urgency of a society continuously under threat. The casts are usually of people who seem very ordinary on the surface. They lead lives which are, at first sight, ineffably average. The atmosphere is one of urban uniformity. The author opens closed doors on to secrets and aberrations which might undermine all our lives. The reader 'identifies' with what he almost knows, instead of moving into a world which is agreeably different from his own.

Of course, there are still traditional detective novels being published by respectable English ladies. Some have had long careers, like Gladys Mitchell, Elizabeth Ferrars and Josephine Bell. But the women, respectable in their own generation, who are regularly hailed as 'the successor to Agatha Christie' or the 'heir to Dorothy Sayers', offer the literature of revelation, not escape.

There is a generation gap in the treatment of characters too; understanding may teach us to forgive, but rarely to like. Christianna Brand, for instance, is a popular writer whose output has not been very large, but whose books have evoked much affection. She was born in 1907 and published her first detective novel in 1941. Her latest appeared in 1979, so her career spans the period from the end of the Golden Age to the present day. Her characters are amusing and attractive; her heroines, naive and sweet. The writers who began their careers in the last twenty years have colder eyes. It is inconceivable that Ruth Rendell, another of the very popular writers of today, whose first book was published in 1964, could ever use such words, or even such concepts.

Rendell typifies the attitude of those writers who feel that modern life, and those living it, are doomed or worthless. The evil often flourish, the good often suffer. This is no longer the fiction whose convention forbade the murder of a child or of a sympathetic character. We cannot start such books in the comforting certainty that our brains will be exercised but our emotions untouched, for many of them are harrowing in the extreme, only too convincing analyses of aberrant behaviour.

Christie, Allingham and Rinehart said, and by implication Sayers, Marsh and Tey agreed, that they wished to write books which would not leave readers dismayed. There are still women writers who share this aim, but they seem to work in the field, hitherto an unusual one for women, of adventure thrillers. Even now, far fewer women than men write spy stories; women are more likely to write any other kind of crime story than a thriller. This is not really surprising. The spy stories which have been most successful, from Buchan through Fleming to Le Carré, have been written by people who knew at least something of the subject in real life. On the other hand, plenty of men, and few women have written spy thrillers, or action thrillers, entirely from imagination. This must be because action for its own sake, whether violent or merely energetic, has been alien to women's experience or desires, due either to nature or nurture. The fact is that traditionally at least women have been passive not active, submissive not aggressive. This may or may not be deplorable. But it certainly tends to make women writers avoid books whose major ingredient is a succession of energetic episodes.

Thrillers have offered their readers the dubious pleasure of vicarious blood-letting. Their heroes may beat up or kill their villains without any qualms of conscience. They epitomise the attitudes of boys' schools and men's clubs, of wild places subject to rough justice. Women have been educated to avoid and to rationalise brutality; they need more intellectual justification than the assertion that might is right.

The assumption of the thriller is that there will be an unpredictable series of fights and killings, love and hate affairs. In war novels, whole battalions are written off. In modern thrillers, corpses litter the page. The individual (apart from the hero) is less than the cause.

In most women's novels, individual people are of major importance, both as victims and participants in events: threats to groups, nations or the whole world have been of less interest than threats to recognisable personalities. In detective novels, the least important person still matters. This must be one reason why women, not yet educated to waste regiments, write and read them. For few women have learnt to sacrifice private for public life, or have yet had the chance to do so. Equal opportunities may change this, too.

Nor have women writers shared the modern obsession with treachery. The lack of moral certainty in the contemporary spy story, the doubt whether we are on the right side, and whether those on our side are trustworthy, is a major feature of the spy and adventure story but those by women have different ingredients. Women thriller writers still offer a pleasant escape to readers of light fiction; they also, like the detective novelist of former years, offer a conservative, conformist standpoint.

Helen McInnes was born in Scotland, and is married to an English professor of literature; they have lived in the United States for many years. She is particularly interested in international politics, and some of her recent books have become (very right wing) propaganda, as much as the exciting tales her enormous public expects. The fashionable disillusion and suspicion of other thriller writers is abhorrent to her. 'I feel that our times involve a perpetual test of character, a test of people, a test of standards, and I think that we must maintain solid and rather high moral standards. We must have a frame of reference to decide what is right and what is wrong. To think that everything is relative, that nothing matters in the end, is an invitation to disaster.' (From an interview in *Counterpoint*.)

McInnes uses accurately and elaborately detailed European capitals as the setting for most of her books, and in them employs brave young Americans as the heroes of urgent chases.

The travelogue aspect of this kind of book is even more noticeable in the work of Mary Stewart. She is an Englishwoman, married to a professor of geology and resident in Scotland. She has had a world-wide success with her romantic mystery thrillers. Like McInnes, she adheres to the conventional, traditional standards:

Perhaps there's the thought that I don't want anyone to be the worse for having read anything I've written . . . I don't like the anti-hero. He fails, to my mind, because it is terribly hard to identify oneself with someone whose views run counter to everything one believes to be right. I think that what this age needs is exactly the opposite. We need a hero—a hero pattern—not the old type flag-waving-stiff-upper-lip hero, but some living pattern of rightness that fits our time. Something positive. (From *Counterpoint*).

Here, surely, in the romantic thriller writers, speak the heirs to the respectable English women who were so good at murder. They are heirs by a more direct line of descent than those writers who open our eyes to the horrors of real life. In the work of those who believe in heroism and villainy, right and wrong, is the appeal to that inner imagination, of which we may not be proud, which we may not be well able to defend, but which has been a human characteristic since story telling began.

Bibliography
of Non-Fiction

Note Below are listed the books which I have consulted and quoted. Of the numerous writers cited, a few have established an indispensable framework for the study of crime fiction, I have referred repeatedly in the text to their work: Jacques Barzun with W. H. Taylor, Howard Haycraft and Julian Symons.

Adams, Donald (ed), *Mystery and Detection Annual* (Donald Adams, 1973)

Altick, Richard D., *The English Common Reader* (Chicago University Press, 1957)

Amis, Kingsley, *What Became of Jane Austen (and Other Questions)* (Cape, 1970)

Anderson, Rachel, *The Purple Heart Throbs—The Sub-literature of Love* (Hodder & Stoughton, 1974)

Auden, W. H., *The Dyer's Hand* (Faber & Faber, 1948)

_____ *A Certain World* (Faber & Faber, 1970)

Barnard, Robert, *A Talent to Deceive—An Appreciation of Agatha Christie* (Collins, 1980)

Barzun and Taylor, *A Catalogue of Crime* (Harper & Row, 1971)

Barzun, Jacques, *The Energies of Art* (Harper, 1956)

Bennett, Arnold, *Books and Persons, 1926–1931* (ed Mylett, Chatto & Windus, 1974)

Bentley, E. C., *Those Days* (Constable, 1940)

Berkeley, Anthony, *The Second Shot*, Preface (Collins, 1938)

Brabazon, James, *Dorothy L. Sayers* (Gollancz, 1980)

Bradbury, Malcolm, *The Social Context of Modern English Literature*, (Blackwell, 1971)

Brittain, Vera, *Testament of Youth* (Gollancz, 1933)

Butler, William Vivian, *The Durable Desperadoes* (Macmillan, 1973)

Calder, Jenni, *Heroes, from Byron to Guevara* (Hamish Hamilton, 1977)

Cawelti, J. G., *Adventure, Mystery and Romance* (Chicago University Press, 1976)

Chandler, Raymond, 'The Simple Art of Murder' in *Atlantic Monthly* (December 1944)

_____ *Raymond Chandler Speaking* (ed Dorothy Gardner and Kathryn Sorley Walker, Hamish Hamilton, 1962)

Christie, Agatha, *Come, Tell Me How You Live* (Collins, 1946)

_____ *Autobiography* (Collins, 1977)

Cockburn, Claud, *Bestseller—The Books that Everyone Reads 1900–1939*, (Sidgwick & Jackson, 1972)

Connolly, Cyril, *Enemies of Promise* (Routledge & Kegan Paul, 1938)

_____ *The Evening Colonnade* (David Bruce & Watson, 1973)

Darwin, Francis (ed), *Life and Letters of Charles Darwin* (John Murray, 1887)

Del Buono and Eco, *The Bond Affair* (Macdonald, 1966)

Dickens, Charles, 'Those Detective Pieces' in *Complete Works* (Chapman & Hall, 1938)

Gilbert, Michael (ed), *Crime in Good Company* (Constable, 1959)

Glover, Dorothy and Greene, Graham, *Victorian Detective Fiction* (Bodley Head, 1966)

Graves, Robert and Hodge, Alan, *The Long Weekend* (Macmillan, 1941)

Greene, Graham, *Collected Essays* (Bodley Head, 1969)

Gross, John, *The Rise and Fall of the Man of Letters* (Weidenfeld & Nicolson, 1969)

Hall, Trevor H., *Dorothy L. Sayers: Nine Literary Studies* (Duckworth, 1980)

Hannay, Margaret P. (ed), *As Her Whimsey Took Her* (Kent State University, 1979)

Haycraft, Howard, *The Art of the Mystery Story* (Biblo & Tanner, 1976)

_____ *Murder For Pleasure* (Peter Davies, 1942)

Hitchman, Janet, *Such a Strange Lady* (New English Library, 1975)

Hone, Ralph E., *Dorothy L. Sayers* (Kent State University, 1979)

Keating, H. R. F., *Murder Must Appetise* (Lemon Tree Press, 1975)

_____ (ed), *Agatha Christie, First Lady of Crime* (Weidenfeld & Nicolson, 1977)

_____ (ed), *Crime Writers* (BBC Publications, 1978)

Leavis, Q. D., *Fiction and the Reading Public* (Chatto & Windus, 1932)

_____ 'The Case of Miss Dorothy Sayers' in *Scrutiny*, 63 (December 1937)

Lowndes, Marie Belloc, *I Too Have Lived in Arcadia* (Macmillan, 1941)

McCarthy, Mary, 'Highbrow Shockers' in *Nation* (8 April 1936)

MacKenzie, Compton, *Literature in My Time* (Rich & Cowan, 1933)

Mallowan, Max, *Memoirs* (Collins, 1977)

Mann, Peter H., *Books, Buyers and Borrowers* (Andre Deutsch, 1971)

Marsh, Ngaio, *Black Beech and Honeydew* (Collins, 1966)

_____ Contribution to *Mystery and Detective Annual* (1973)

Maugham, W. Somerset, *The Vagrant Mood* (Heinemann, 1952)

Murch, A. E., *The Development of the Detective Novel* (Peter Owen, 1958)

Nash, Ogden, *The Face is Familiar* (Little Brown, 1940)

Newquist, Roy, ed, *Counterpoint* (Allen & Unwin, 1965)

Orczy, Baroness Emmuska, *Links in the Chain of Life* (Hutchinson, 1947)

Orwell, George, *Decline of the English Murder, and Other Essays* (Penguin, 1965)

Ousby, Ian, *Bloodhounds of Heaven* (Harvard University Press, 1976)

Paget, Francis, *Lucretia, or The Heroine of the Nineteenth Century* (Masters, 1868)

Palmer, Jerry, *Thrillers* (Edward Arnold, 1978)

Quayle, Eric, *The Collector's Book of Detective Fiction* (Studio Vista, 1972)

Queen, Ellery, *Queen's Quorum* (Gollancz, 1953)

Ramsay, G. C., *Agatha Christie, Mistress of Mystery* (Collins, 1968)

Raverat, Gwen, *Period Piece* (Faber & Faber, 1952)

Reynolds, Barbara, 'The Origin of Lord Peter Wimsey' in the *Times Literary Supplement* (22 April 1977)

Richardson, Joanna, *Enid Starkie* (John Murray, 1973)

Rinehart, Mary Robert, *My Story* (Cassell, 1932)

_____ *The Mary Roberts Rinehart Crime Book* (Rinehart & Co, 1957)

Robyns, Gwen, *The Mystery of Agatha Christie* (1978)

Routley, Erik, *The Puritan Pleasures of the Detective Story* (Collins, 1972)

Saunders, J. W., *The Profession of English Letters* (Routledge & Kegan Paul, 1964)

Sayers, Dorothy L., Introduction to *Detection, Mystery and Horror* (Gollancz, 1928)

_____ Introduction to *Tales of Detection* (Everyman, 1936)

_____ *Unpopular Opinions* (Gollancz, 1946)

_____ Introduction to *The Divine Comedy of Dante Alighieri* (Penguin, 1949)

The D. L. Sayers Historical and Literary Society, *Talking of Dorothy L. Sayers* (Witham, 1979)

Scott, Sir Walter, *The Lives of the Novelists* (Everyman, 1959)

Scott, Sutherland *Blood in their Ink* (Stanley Paul & Co, 1953)

Showalter, Elaine, *A Literature of Their Own* (Princeton University Press, 1977)

Slung, Michele B., *Crime on her Mind* (Michael Joseph, 1976)

Steinbrunner and Penzler, *Encyclopaedia of Mystery and Detection* (Routledge & Kegan Paul, 1976)

Stevenson, R. L., and Osbourne, Lloyd, *Epilogue to The Wrecker* (Cassell, 1892)

Stewart, R. F., *And Always a Detective* (David & Charles, 1980)

Strickland, Margot, *Portrait of a Lady Novelist—the Life of Angela Thirkell* (Duckworth, 1977)

Symons, Julian, *Bloody Murder* (Faber, 1972)

Tey, Josephine, *Claverhouse* (Collins, 1937)

Trollope, Anthony, *Autobiography* (Oxford Classics, 1953)

Usborne, Richard, *Clubland Heroes* (Barrie & Jenkins, 1953)

Vidocq, E. F., *Memoirs* (1828, republished by Cassell, 1928)

Watson, Colin, *Snobbery with Violence* (Eyre & Spottiswoode, 1971)

Weiner, Dora B., and Keylor, William R. (eds), *From Parnassus, Essays in Honour of Jacques Barzun* (Harper & Row, 1976)

Wells, Carolyn, *The Technique of the Mystery Story* (Home Correspondence School, Springfield, Mass, 1913)

Wheatley, Dennis, *Drink and Ink* (Hutchinson, 1979)

Whelpton, Eric, *The Making of a European* (Johnson, 1974)

Williams, Raymond, *The Long Revolution* (Chatto & Windus, 1961)

Wilson, Edmund, *Classic and Commercials* (Farrar Straus & Co, 1950)

Winn, Dilys, *Murder Ink* (Westbridge Books, 1977)

Wortley Montagu, Lady Mary, *Letters* (ed Robert Halsband, Clarendon Press, 1965–7)

Selective Bibliography
of Fiction Quoted

Allingham, Margery, *The Beckoning Lady* (Chatto & Windus, 1955)
____ *Blackerchief Dick* (Hodder & Stoughton, 1923)
____ *Black Plumes* (Heinemann, 1940)
____ (with P. Youngman Carter) *Cargo of Eagles* (Chatto & Windus, 1968)
____ *The Case of the Late Pig* (Hodder & Stoughton, 1937)
____ *The China Governess* (Chatto & Windus, 1962)
____ *The Crime at Black Dudley* (Jarrolds, 1929)
____ *Coroner's Pidgin* (Heinemann, 1945)
____ *The Dance of the Years* (Michael Joseph, 1943)
____ *Dancers in Mourning* (Heinemann, 1937)
____ *Death of a Ghost* (Heinemann, 1934)
____ *The Fashion in Shrouds* (Heinemann, 1938)
____ *Flowers for the Judge* (Heinemann, 1936)
____ *Hide My Eyes* (Chatto & Windus, 1958)
____ *Look to the Lady* (Jarrolds, 1931)
____ *The Mind Readers* (Chatto & Windus, 1965)
____ *More Work for the Undertaker* (Heinemann, 1948)
____ *Mystery Mile* (Heinemann, 1929)
____ *The Oaken Heart* (Michael Joseph, 1941)
____ *Police at the Funeral* (Heinemann, 1931)
____ *Sweet Danger* (Heinemann, 1933)
____ *Tiger in the Smoke* (Chatto & Windus, 1952)
____ *Traitor's Purse* (Heinemann, 1941)
____ *The White Cottage Mystery* (Jarrolds, 1928)
Anonyma, *The Experiences of a Lady Detective* (London, 1861)
Austen, Jane, *Northanger Abbey* (London, 1818)
Bawden, Nina, *The Odd Flamingo* (Collins, 1980)
Bentley, E. C., *Trent's Last Case* (Nelson, 1913)
Braddon, Mrs M. E., *Dead Men's Shoes* (London, 1876)
____ *Lady Audley's Secret* (Tinsley Bros., 1862)
____ *Henry Dunbar* (Maxwell, 1864)

Brand, Christianna, *Green For Danger* (Bodley Head, 1945)

Buchan, John, *Sick Heart River* (Hodder & Stoughton, 1941)

Carter, P. Youngman, *Mr Campion's Falcon* (Chatto & Windus, 1970)

_____ *Mr Campion's Farthing* (Chatto & Windus, 1969)

Chesterton, G. K., *The Innocence of Father Brown* (Cassell, 1911)

Christie, Agatha, *Appointment with Death* (Collins, 1938)

_____ *The Body in the Library* (Collins, 1942)

_____ *Cat Among the Pigeons* (Collins, 1959)

_____ *Dead Man's Folly* (Collins, 1956)

_____ *Death Comes as the End* (Collins, 1945)

_____ *Death on the Nile* (Collins, 1937)

_____ *Lord Edgware Dies* (Collins, 1933)

_____ *Mrs McGinty's Dead* (Collins, 1952)

_____ *Murder at the Vicarage* (Collins, 1930)

_____ *Murder in Mesopotamia* (Collins, 1963)

_____ *The Murder of Roger Ackroyd* (Collins, 1926)

_____ *The Mysterious Affair at Styles* (John Lane, 1920)

_____ *The Mystery of the Blue Train* (Collins, 1928)

_____ *Partners in Crime* (Collins, 1929)

_____ *Sad Cypress* (Collins, 1940)

_____ *The Secret Adversary* (John Lane, 1922)

_____ *Towards Zero* (Collins, 1944)

Cox, A. B., *The Second Shot* (Collins, 1930)

Dickens, Charles, *Bleak House* (London, 1853)

Doyle, Conan, *A Study in Scarlet* (Ward Lock, 1887)

Fielding, Henry, *Jonathan Wild the Great* (London, 1743)

_____ *Amelia* (London, 1751)

Forester, Andrew, *The Female Detective* (Sixpenny Volume Library, 1864)

Freeman, R. Austin, *The Penrose Mystery* (Hodder & Stoughton, 1936)

Gaboriau, Emile, *L'Affaire Lerouge* (Paris, 1866)

Gaspey, Thomas, *Richmond, or Scenes from the Life of a Bow Street Runner* (London, 1827)

Green, A. K., *The Leavenworth Case* (Putnam, 1878)

_____ *The Affair Next Door* (New York, 1897)

Greene, Hugh, *The Rivals of Sherlock Holmes* (Bodley Head, 1970)

_____ *More Rivals of Sherlock Holmes* (Bodley Head, 1971)

Herbert, A. P., *Holy Deadlock* (Methuen, 1934)

Hume, Fergus, *The Mystery of the Hansom Cab* (Melbourne, 1886)

Iles, Francis, *Malice Aforethought* (Gollancz, 1931)

Innes, Michael, *Hamlet, Revenge!* (Gollancz, 1937)

James, P. D., *Shroud for a Nightingale* (Faber, 1971)

_____ *Death of an Expert Witness* (Faber, 1978)

Jesse, F. Tennyson, *Solange Stories* (Heinemann, 1931)

Lewis, Matthew Gregory, *The Monk* (London, 1795)

Lowndes, Marie Belloc, *The Lodger* (Hutchinson, 1911)

____ *The Terriford Mystery* (Hutchinson, 1913)

Marsh, Ngaio, *Artists in Crime* (Bles, 1938)

____ *Black as He's Painted* (Collins, 1974)

____ *Clutch of Constables* (Collins, 1969)

____ *Colour Scheme* (Collins, 1943)

____ *Death at the Dolphin* (Collins, 1966)

____ *Death in Ecstacy* (Bles, 1936)

____ *A Man Lay Dead* (Bles, 1934)

____ *The Nursing Home Murders* (Bles, 1936)

____ *Off With His Head* (Collins, 1957)

____ *Opening Night* (Collins, 1951)

____ *Spinsters in Jeopardy* (Collins, 1953)

____ *Surfeit of Lampreys* (Collins, 1940)

____ *Swing Brother Swing* (Collins, 1949)

Mason, A. E. W., *At The Villa Rose* (Hodder & Stoughton, 1910)

Meade, L. T., *A Maid of Mystery* (F. V. White & Co., 1904)

____ (with Robert Eustace) *The Brotherhood of the Seven Kings* (London, 1899)

Millar, Margaret, *How Like an Angel* (Gollancz, 1963)

Milne, A. A., *The Red House Mystery* (Methuen, 1922)

Mitchell, Gladys, *Speedy Death* (Michael Joseph, 1929)

Orczy, Baroness Emmuska, *Lady Molly of Scotland Yard* (Cassell, 1910)

____ *The Old Man in the Corner* (London, 1909)

Poe, Edgar Allan, *Tales of Mystery and Imagination* (New York, 1845)

Radcliffe, Mrs. Anne, *The Mysteries of Udolpho* (London, 1794)

Reach, Angus, *Clement Lorimer* (David Bogne, 1848–9)

Regester, Seeley, *The Dead Letter* (1867)

Rinehart, Mary Roberts, *The Confession* (Rinehart & Co., 1925)

____ *The Circular Staircase* (Bobbs Merrill, 1908)

____ *The Wandering Knife* (Holt, Rinehart & Winston Inc., 1943)

Russell, William, *Recollections of a Detective Police Officer* (London, 1856)

Sayers, Dorothy L., *Busman's Honeymoon* (Gollancz, 1938)

____ *Clouds of Witness* (Ernest Benn, 1926)

____ *The Documents in the Case* (Gollancz, 1930)

____ *Five Red Herrings* (Gollancz, 1931)

____ *Gaudy Night* (Gollancz, 1935)

____ *Hangman's Holiday* (Gollancz, 1932)

____ *Have His Carcase* (Gollancz, 1932)

____ *In the Teeth of the Evidence* (Gollancz, 1939)

____ *Lord Peter Views the Body* (Gollancz, 1928)

_____ *Murder Must Advertise* (Gollancz, 1933)

_____ *The Nine Tailors* (Gollancz, 1934)

_____ *Striding Folly* (New English Library, 1973)

_____ *Strong Poison* (Gollancz, 1930)

_____ *Unnatural Death* (Ernest Benn, 1927)

_____ *The Unpleasantness at the Bellona Club* (Gollancz, 1928)

_____ *Whose Body?* (Ernest Benn, 1923)

Taylor, Tom, *The Ticket of Leave Man* (London, 1863)

Tey, Josephine, *Brat Farrar* (Peter Davies, 1949)

_____ *The Daughter of Time* (Peter Davies, 1951)

_____ (as Gordon Daviot) *The Expensive Halo* (Ernest Benn, 1931)

_____ *The Franchise Affair* (Peter Davies, 1948)

_____ (as Gordon Daviot) *Kif: An Unvarnished History* (Ernest Benn, 1929)

_____ (as Gordon Daviot) *The Laughing Woman* (Gollancz, 1934)

_____ (as Gordon Daviot) *Leith Sands* (Duckworth, 1946)

_____ *To Love and Be Wise* (Peter Davies, 1950)

_____ (as Gordon Daviot) *The Man in the Queue* (Methuen, 1929)

_____ *Miss Pym Disposes* (Peter Davies, 1946)

_____ *The Privateer* (Peter Davies, 1952)

_____ (as Gordon Daviot) *Queen of Scots* (Gollancz, 1934)

_____ (as Gordon Daviot) *Richard of Bordeaux* (Gollancz, 1933)

_____ *A Shilling for Candles* (Methuen, 1936)

_____ *The Singing Sands* (Peter Davies, 1952)

_____ (as Gordon Daviot) *The Stars Bow Down* (Duckworth, 1939)

Verne, Jules, *Round The World in Eighty Days* (Paris, 1873)

Vidocq, E. F., *Memoirs* (Paris, 1828)

Walpole, Horace, *The Castle of Otranto* (London, 1764)

Warden, Florence, *The House on the Marsh* (Wm. Stevens, 1864)

Wells, Carolyn, *The Mystery of the Sycamore* (J. B. Lippincott Co., 1921)

Wentworth, Patricia, *Danger Point* (Hodder & Stoughton, 1942)

_____ *Out of The Past* (Hodder & Stoughton, 1955)

Westmacott, Mary (Agatha Christie) *Unfinished Portrait* (Collins, 1934)

_____ *Absent in the Spring* (Collins, 1944)

Wood, Mrs Henry, *East Lynne* (London, 1861)

_____ *The Master of Greylands* (London, 1873)

_____ *Danesbury House* (London, 1860)

Worboise, Emma Jane, *Thorneycroft Hall* (Christian World, 1865)

Index

Allen, Dr Hugh, 161, 164
'Alleyn, Roderick', 88-90, 110, 111, 212, 221, 223, 225, 227, 229
Allingham, Emily, 189, 190, 191, 199, 202
Allingham, Herbert, 189, 190, 191, 192, 193, 199
Allingham, Joyce, 190, 203, 209, 210
Allingham, Margery, 9, 47, 49, 51, 53, 60, 61, 71, 83, 86-9, 90, 107, 109, 137, 189-209, 219, 226, 231, 232, 240, 242
Allingham, Philip, 190, 203
Amis, Kingsley, 51, 239
Anderson, Rachel, 50
Anonyma, 27, 93
Anstey, P.T. College, 211
Archaeology, Institute of, 148-9
Arlen, Michael, 222
Armstrong Murder Case, 234
Arundel, Dennis, 180
Athenaeum, The, 55
Auden, W.H., 117
Austen, Jane, 17, 207

Bailey, H.C., 73
Balliol College, 171
Bantock, G.H., 45
Barnard, Robert, 151
Barnett, Charis, 160
Barzun, Jacques, 33, 48, 52, 53, 59, 97, 179, 221
Bawden, Nina, 236
Bell, Joseph, 69
Bell, Josephine, 241
Benn, Ernest, 166, 174, 212, 213
Bennett, Arnold, 10, 12, 30, 47
Benson's Agency, 167, 169, 174
Bentley, E.C., 37-8, 72, 85, 91, 109
'Beresford, Tommy and Tuppence', 130
Black Coffee, 148
Blackwell, Basil, 163, 164
Blackwood's Magazine, 55
Blake, Nicholas, 12, 105, 106
Bles, Geoffrey, 224

Bodkin, M. McDonnell, 93
de Boisgobey, F., 27
'Bond, James', 62, 75, 109, 118
Bowen, Elizabeth, 107
Brabazon, James, 154, 155, 181, 183, 187
Bradbury, Malcolm, 46
Braddon, M.E., 24-5, 32, 67
Brand, Christianna, 57, 136, 241
Brazil, Angela, 159
British Broadcasting Corporation (BBC), 182-3
Brittain, Vera, 126, 127, 160, 161
Browning, Elizabeth Barrett, 207
Brown's Hotel, 152
Buchan, John, 61, 82, 117, 118-19, 242
Butler, William Vivian, 81
Byrne, M. St Clair, 160, 162, 179, 181
Byron, Lord, 19, 42

Calder, Jenni, 92
Calder, Ritchie, 136
'Campion, Albert', 73, 86-9, 109, 110, 190-6, 198, 204, 208, 209
'Campion, Amanda', 105, 106, 109, 110, 137, 204
Canterbury, Archbishop of, 187
Canterbury, University of, 230
Carlyle, Thomas, 39
Carter, P. Youngman, 192, 194, 199, 200, 201, 204, 210
Cartland, Barbara, 61
Casson, Stanley, 140
Cawelti, J., 57
Chandler, Raymond, 12, 47, 48, 58, 71, 74, 75, 106, 107, 108, 143, 225
Charles II, King, 218
Charteris, Leslie, 119
Chesterton, G.K., 76, 84, 207
Christian Globe, 190
Christie, Agatha, 9, 47, 49, 50, 51, 58, 60, 77, 102, 105, 109, 121-53, 157, 208, 226, 237, 240, 242
Christie, Archibald, 127, 128, 130-8 *passim*, 148

Chubb, Margaret, 160
Claverhouse, 214
Coleridge, S.T., 39
Collins, Wilkie, 20, 23, 24, 27, 67, 108, 174, 176
Collins, William, 131, 231
Conington, J.J., 12
Connolly, Cyril, 9, 10, 56, 58
Corelli, Marie, 41
Cournos, John, 85, 168-9, 170
Cox, A.B., 73, 234
Crawford, O.G.S., 146
Crispin, Edmund, 59
Croft, Freeman Wills, 72

Daily Express, 195
Daily News, 134
Dante, 184, 185, 186, 187
Darwin, Charles, 40
Daviot, Gordon, *see* Tey, Josephine
Deighton, Len, 237
Delafield, E.M., 12, 145
Dickens, Charles, 20, 23, 41, 45, 65
Douglas, Alfred, 222
Douglas, Norman, 9
Doyle, Conan, 11, 37, 47, 69, 70
Durham, University of, 187

Eberhart, M.G., 101, 103
Edinburgh Journal, 65
Edinburgh Review, 43
Eliot, George, 21, 23, 41, 68
Eliot, T.S., 9
Elizabeth, Queen, 152
Ellis, Robert, 210
Eustace, Robert, 93
Evening Standard, 40, 142

Faulkner, John Meade, 177
Ferrars, Elizabeth, 241
Field, Inspector, 65
Fielding, Henry, 18, 62, 63
Firbank, Ronald, 10
Fisher, Charlotte, 131, 133, 134, 135, 138
'Fitton, Amanda', *see* 'Campion, Amanda'
Fleming, Alice, 193
Fleming, Anthony, 169, 171, 187
Fleming, Ian, 108, 117, 118, 242
Fleming, O.A., 170-5 *passim,* 183, 186, 187
Fleming, Mrs O.A., 171
Forester, Andrew, 27, 93
Forester, C.S., 10, 61
Freeling, Nicolas, 74
Freeman, R. Austen, 31, 71, 91, 108
French's, 201

Gaboriau, Emile, 27, 54, 68, 70

Galsworthy, John, 10
Gaskell, Elizabeth, 50, 154
Gaspey, Thomas, 65
Gielgud, John, 210, 213
Girls' Cinema, The, 195
Girton College, 122
Glasgow Herald, 212
Goddard, Superintendent, 136
Godolphin School, 159
Godwin, William, 18, 26
Gollancz, Victor, 166, 177, 180
Graeme, Bruce, 12
'Grant, Alan', 212-13, 214, 216, 217
Green, A.K., 27-30, 33, 37, 50, 94
Green, Peter, 188
Greene, Graham, 51, 53
Greene, Hugh, 70, 93
'Greyfriars School', 159

Hall, Trevor, 177
Hammett, Dashiell, 12, 58, 97
'Hawkshaw', 65
Haycraft, Howard, 9
H.M. Criminal Statistics, 43
Hearne, W.M., 191, 195
Henry VII, King, 217
Herbert, A.P., 133
Heyer, Georgette, 10, 61
Higham, David, 175
Highsmith, Patricia, 236, 237, 238
Hitchman, Janet, 85, 154, 164, 188
Holbrook, David, 46
Hollow, The, 149
Holmes, Sherlock, 30, 37, 57, 65, 69, 70, 77, 223
Holtby, Winifred, 107
Household, Geoffrey, 56
Hughes Massie Ltd, 131, 223
Hughes, Maud, 191
Hull High School, 163, 182
Huxley, Aldous, 9

Iles, Francis, 234
'Inklings, The', 184
Innes, Michael, 12, 57, 74, 78, 105, 112, 228
Inverness Academy, 211
Inverness Courier, 215
Irving, Henry, 147

Jaeger, Muriel, 160
James, Henry, 41
James, P.D., 9, 57, 74, 80, 86, 237-8, 240
Jameson, Storm, 12
Jesse, F. Tennyson, 94
John, Augustus, 197
John Bull Magazine, 200
Joyce, James, 9, 41

Kennedy, Margaret, 12
Kent, Constance, 67
Kenward, Deputy Chief Constable, 135, 136
Kipling, Rudyard, 10, 193

Lancing School, 140
Landor, W.S., 122
Lane, John, 128, 129, 130
Lathen, Emma, 151
Lawrence, D.H., 9, 41
Leavis, Q.D., 41, 42, 44, 46, 179
le Carré, John, 47, 239, 242
Lehmann, Rosamund, 107
Lewis, C.S., 185, 186
Lewis, M.G., 18, 42
Lewis, Wyndham, 9
Lindbergh, 170
Literary Review, 212
Lowndes, Marie Belloc, 36, 37
'Luke, Charles', 204-6, 208
Lynch, Lawrence, 32
Lytton, Bulwer, 39, 45

Macdonald, Philip, 73
Mackenzie, Compton, 21
Malefactors' Bloody Register, 43
Mallowan, Max, 80, 132, 140-53 *passim*
Manning, Frederick and Maria, 65
Maoris, 228-9
'Marlowe, Philip', 77, 108
'Marple, Jane', 101-3, 147, 152
Marryat, Captain, 39
Marsh, H.E., 218, 231
Marsh, Ngaio, 9, 47, 49, 50, 57, 74, 80, 88-90, 108, 109, 110, 111, 217, 218-33, 237, 240, 242
Marsh, Rose, 218, 219, 220, 224
Mary, Queen, 149
Mason, A.E.W., 51, 56, 72
Mass Observation, 147
Mathers, Helen, 32
Maugham, W.S., 10, 48, 56, 163
McCarthy, Mary, 179
McFee, William, 191, 192
McInnes, Helen, 243
McIntosh, Colin, 210, 211
McIntosh, Elizabeth, *see* Tey, Josephine
McIntosh, Jean, 210
McIntosh, Josephine, 210, 211
McIntosh, Mary, 210
Meade, L.T., 32, 93
Methuen, 212
Metropolitan Police Act, 64
Millar, Margaret, 232
Miller, Alice Duer, 203
Miller, Clara, 121-4, 131
Miller, Frederick, 122, 124
Miller, Madge, 124, 128, 131, 136, 138, 141

Miller, Monty, 124
Milne, A.A., 73
Mitchell, Gladys, 103-4, 241
Mitford, Nancy, 10, 222
Montague, M.W.M., 17
Moore, George, 9
Morgan, Henry, 216
Morrison, Arthur, 72
Mountbatten, Lord L., 131
Mousetrap, The, 125, 149
Mudie, Mr, 43

Nash, Ogden, 96
National Trust, 214
Neele, Nancy, 132, 133
New Theatre, 213
Newgate Calendar, 43
Newlands Corner, 134, 135, 137, 171
New Statesman, 47
News of the World, 171
Nicolson, Marjorie, 11
Nimrud, 150
Normanton, Helena, 94

Observer, The, 212
'Oliver, Ariadne', 129, 143
Oppenheim, E. Phillips, 51, 59, 94
Orczy, Baroness, 33-6, 37, 51, 93
Orient Express, 139
Orwell, George, 74

Paget, Francis, 20
Perse School, 191
Phillpotts, Eden, 128
Poe, Edgar Allan, 17, 26, 54, 64, 68, 70
'Poirot, Hercule', 61, 73, 76-80, 104, 109, 129, 130, 141, 147
Pope, Mildred, 162
Prichard, Matthew, 149
Prichard, Rosalind, *see* Christie, Rosalind
Priestley, J.B., 47
Purkis, C.L., 32

Radcliffe, Anne, 18, 19, 54
'Raffles', 237
Ramsay, Allan, 42
Raverat, Gwen, 91, 123, 126
Reach, Angus, 27
Reade, Charles, 20
Regent St Polytechnic, 193
Regester, Seeley, 27
Rendell, Ruth, 239, 241
Reynolds, Barbara, 72, 73, 85, 86, 187
Rhode, John, 12
Richard III, King, 216, 217
Rieu, E.V., 184
Rinehart, Mary Roberts, 13, 37, 97-101, 103, 242

Rinehart, Stanley, 98-101 *passim*
Robertson, E.A., 107
Roches, Les, 165
Roedean School, 122
Routley, Erik, 204, 207, 216, 221
Russell, William, 27, 65

St Anne's House, 184
Salter, Dr, 198, 199
Sandoe, James, 143
Sapper, 82, 119
Sargeant, J.S., 197
Saunders, J.W., 45
Sayers, Dorothy L., 9, 10, 11, 47-52, 58,
    60, 61, 71, 72, 76, 80-6, 91, 97, 102,
    105, 109, 111-13, 146, 154-88, 219,
    227, 232, 240, 242
Sayers, Helen, 155, 156, 169, 171
Sayers, Reverend Henry, 155, 157, 180
Sayers, D.L. Historical and Literary
    Society, 154, 173
Scott, Walter, 42, 54, 55
Shaw, Bernard, 10
Shaw, Reeves, 200
Shelley, Mary, 18
Shrimpton, Ivy, 169, 171
'Silver, Maud', 94-6, 101, 102
Sketch, The, 130
Slung, Michele B., 93
Smith, D. Maynard, 12
Smith, Ernest Bramah, 71, 91
Society for Pure Literature, 43, 46
Somerville College, 160, 162, 164, 178
Spectator, The, 181
Spencer, Herbert, 23
Spillane, Mickey, 12, 97
Spring, Howard, 46
Starkie, Enid, 162
Stephenson, Elizabeth, 26
Stevenson, R.L., 30
Stewart, Mary, 243-4
Strachey, Lytton, 9
Strand Magazine, The, 200
Struther, Jan, 203
Sue, Emile, 26
Sunday Express, 220
Sunday Times, 174
Symons, Julian, 53, 72, 76, 95, 179,
    216, 235, 236, 239, 240

Tatler, The, 195
Taylor, Tom, 65
Taylor, W.H., 32, 52, 97, 179
Temple Bar, 40
Tey, Josephine, 9, 13, 50, 109, 210-17
Thirkell, Angela, 12, 193
Thompson, Campbell, 142
Times, The, 64

Tolkien, J.R.R., 185
Trollope, Anthony, 21
Trollope, Fanny, 21
'Troy, Agatha', 90, 105, 106, 109, 110,
    227, 229

Uhnak, Dorothy, 54
University College Hospital, 146
Ur of the Chaldees, 139

Van Dine, S.S., 91
'Vane, Harriet', 81, 83, 86, 97, 105,
    106, 111-13, 156, 158, 166, 177, 178,
    181, 227
Verne, Jules, 67
Vidocq, 27, 54, 64, 68

Wade, Henry, 12
Wallace, Doreen, 162
Wallace, Edgar, 94, 119
Walpole, Horace, 18
Walpole, Hugh, 47
Warden, Florence, 32, 68
Watson, Colin, 57, 59, 237, 240
Watts, Madge, *see* Miller, Madge
Waugh, Evelyn, 50, 222
Wells, Carolyn, 32-3
Wells, H.G., 10
Wentworth, Patricia, 94-6, 101
West, Rebecca, 235
Westmacott, Mary, *see* Christie, Agatha
Westminster Gazette, 212
Westminster Review, 21, 212
Wheatley, Dennis, 51, 118
Wheaton College, Illinois, 154
Wheeler, Mortimer, 146
Whelpton, Eric, 85, 164, 165, 166
Whicher, Inspector, 67
Whistler, J.A. McN., 197
Wild, Jonathan, 63, 64
Wilkie, Allan, 220, 221
Williams, Charles, 184, 185
Williams, Raymond, 51
Wilson, Edmund, 39, 152, 177
'Wimsey, Peter', 65, 72, 73, 80-6, 102,
    105, 111-13, 159, 165, 167, 170,
    178-81 *passim,* 239
Wodehouse, P.G., 10, 61
Wood, Mrs Henry, 22-3, 32, 67
Woolf, Virginia, 9, 41
Woolley, Katharine, 139, 140, 141, 142
Woolley, Leonard, 139, 140, 141
Worboise, E.J., 20
Wordsworth, William, 39

Yates, Dornford, 82, 119
Yeats, W.B., 9